Critical Muslim 43

Ignorance

Critical Muslim is published quarterly by C. Hurst & Co. (Publishers) Ltd. on behalf of and in conjunction with Critical Muslim Ltd. and the Muslim Institute, London.

All editorial correspondence to Muslim Institute, Canopi, 7-14 Great Dover Street, London, SE1 4YR
E-mail: editorial@criticalmuslim.com

C. Hurst & Co (Publishers) Ltd., New Wing, Somerset House, Strand, London, WC2R 1LA

ISBN: 9781787388185 ISSN: 2048-8475

To subscribe or place an order by credit/debit card or cheque (pounds sterling only) please contact Kathleen May at the Hurst address above or e-mail kathleen@hurstpub.co.uk

Tel: 020 7255 2201

A one-year subscription, inclusive of postage (four issues), costs £50 (UK), £65 (Europe) and £75 (rest of the world), this includes full access to the *Critical Muslim* series and archive online. Digital only subscription is £3.30 per month.

Critical Muslim

Subscribe to Critical Muslim

Now in its eleventh year in print, *Critical Muslim* is also available online. Users can access the site for just £3.30 per month – or for those with a print subscription it is included as part of the package. In return, you'll get access to everything in the series (including our entire archive), and a clean, accessible reading experience for desktop computers and handheld devices — entirely free of advertising.

Full subscription

The print edition of *Critical Muslim* is published quarterly in January, April, July and October. As a subscriber to the print edition, you'll receive new issues directly to your door, as well as full access to our digital archive.

United Kingdom £50/year
Europe £65/year
Rest of the World £75/year

Digital Only

Immediate online access to *Critical Muslim*

Browse the full *Critical Muslim* archive

Cancel any time

£3.30 per month

www.criticalmuslim.io

CM43

SUMMER 2022

CONTENTS

IGNORANCE

Raphael Appignanesi, 'Schrodinger's Dilemma', relief etching, 19x23cm, 2019

ARTS AND LETTERS

REVIEWS

ET CETERA

IGNORANCE

INTRODUCTION: IGNORANT THINGS

Ziauddin Sardar

'You have to watch things'.

In her perceptive, elegant essay, 'Things are Against Us', the British novelist Lucy Ellman confesses that she is the kind of person who is losing things, dropping things, breaking things '(even bits of my own body, bones, teeth, heart)'; and generally, 'becoming a cropper over THINGS'. The problem is that things 'do not have your best interests at heart'. They have their own priorities and agenda, and, as such, there are so many 'cruel, cunning little acts of malice perpetuated upon us by THINGS'. Thing is, 'THINGS are out to get us'.

But what is a thing? Philosophers have been pondering the question, but no real answers are forthcoming. The dictionary only tells us it could be any material thing or indeed anything that becomes a thought. A friend of mine spent around fifteen years pondering the question for his doctoral thesis. Irfan Ahmad Khan (1931–2015) was an exceptionally superb human being, as well as a brilliant philosopher and scholar of Islam. A ride in his car was an education on the nature of things, and how ignorant we are of things; and a close encounter or two, as he seldom paid attention to the road when in full lecture mode, with that thing called death. The thing that bothered him the most was how ignorant contemporary Muslims are of the thing called the Qur'an. He spent the last decades of his life writing a monumental commentary on the first two chapters of the Sacred Text. '*Jan-e-mun* (my life, my darling)', he would say, 'to repair a broken thing one has to work out why it is broken, and to repair it one has to actively follow the path of replacing evil with goodness.' But how could you do that if you were knee deep in ignorance, things were always changing, you had no idea of how to change things, and worse, no understanding of goodness?

Paradoxically, the thing we are most ignorant about is a thing itself called ignorance. We know a lot about knowledge. But remarkably, we know next to nothing about ignorance. Given, as American historian of science, Robert Proctor, notes '(a) how much ignorance there is, (b) how many kinds there are, and (c) how consequential ignorance is in our lives'. Indeed, Proctor has suggested, ours is the age of ignorance. And, it's everywhere.

It is ever present in popular parlance. 'Ignorance is bliss', 'blind ignorance', 'ignorance of the law is no excuse'. Indeed, ignorance is even used as a form of argument. In medical research, for example, a medication may be considered safe even though we may be ignorant of its potential side effects; as long as there is no evidence that it is unsafe. Courts judge a person 'not guilty' when we lack evidence of guilt. 'These are judgments of practice, of course, and subject to practical conditions,' notes the American philosopher Daniel DeNicola, 'but the arguments on which they rest are appeals to ignorance, nevertheless.' Then, there are such things as fake news, deep fakes, and racist algorithms and chauvinist AI. Big data, now used for most research, incorporates as much indecent ignorance as decent information. An ocean of ignorance is proliferated by social media and the communication channels that amplify lies and disinformation, harden cognitive maps, and seem to be taking us towards some sort of violent conclusion. Certain television stations have no other function than to spew ignorance twenty-four hours a day.

The meticulously researched Channel 4 series, 'The Undeclared War' (2022), illustrates how far we have travelled and where we have reached. A television station, not far removed from Fox News or Russia Today, establishes websites for two non-existing organisations: 'Putin for Labour' and 'Take Back Control of Luton'. A young perturbed journalist confronts the mature editor, 'it's all made up. The whole thing'. No, the editor replies: 'it exists. On this page it's got ninety-six members.' The two non-existing but opposing groups soon take a real shape and confront each other on the streets leading to violent chaos. The editor explains: 'whether it is faked isn't the point. I mean everything that is reported is fake one way or another...The point is to get the people used to the idea that everything is a lie. That there is no truth. Once they accept that, well, the biggest liar wins.' Them's the rules.

On top of all this we have such things as conspiracy theories. The world is awash with them – from QAnon and Trumpism to Barack Obama birtherism, the moon landing hoax to alien abductions, the *Protocols of Zion* to myths about the Holocaust. 'The trouble with the conspiracy theory,' writes Robin Yassin-Kassab in this issue, 'is that it over-simplifies, over-generalises and over-explains. It assumes that one specific conspiracy wields the power to cancel out all others. It reduces the dazzling complexity of reality. It seeks to boil everything down to one key factor. It sees one overarching plot rather than a jumble of a trillion.' Thus, 'a child's refusal to pray can be put down, very simply, to polio drops,' which the dastardly Americans are using to sterilise innocent Muslims.

There is ignorance that actually threatens our survival – ignorance about the consequences of the behaviour of our own species, such as micro plastics throughout the planetary environment and in our bodies, the proliferation of man-made chemicals and their interaction with each other and the biota, the potential future consequences of all varieties of genetic engineering, and AI enhanced killer robots. Not to mention our ignorance of other species on the planet. We don't know, reports Colin Tudge, '*even to an order of magnitude* how many different species share this world with us. Fewer than two million have been formally described and named (which means several per day for the past 200 years). But even among the best-known and best-studied species – birds, mammals, frogs, fish, insects, flowering plants – new discoveries are still being added, probably faster than ever. So modern scientists now estimate that the true number of living species could be anywhere from five to 30 million – or 100 million-plus if we include bacteria and archaeans. Eight million is a conservative ball-park figure. So, *at best* we have observed and formally described less than a quarter.' When it comes to the creatures lives and relationships, how they create and maintain ecosystems, how known even less.

Considerable amount of ignorance in our times is deliberately manufactured. Nation states use digital technologies to enhance the ignorance of their own citizens; and engage in cyberwars with the clear aim of increasing the ignorance of societies they perceive as enemies. Whether it is Russia's misinformation war, or China's use of digital technology to maintain and control its citizens – and, in some cases, eradicate their religion and culture – or, the old-fashioned CIA 'black ops', the end goal is the same: suppress knowledge and truth and promote ignorance. Big business often suppresses genuine knowledge and fosters ignorance. Think of tobacco companies consistently denying the dangers of smoking, preventing regulations that would reduce smoking, and promoting cancer sticks as a sign of 'liberation' and what is 'cool' in advertising as well as cinema. Or oil giants who bank-rolled 'research' that deliberately caused doubts on climate science, set up lobbies that denied the impact of human action on climate change, and systematically undermined regulation to promote renewable energy sources. Much of advertising is in fact lies that hide the dark side of the product being sold.

Given that we are shrouded in what I have elsewhere called 'the smog of ignorance', why is so little attention being given to ignorance? What we know and what we don't know is a product of cultural, social, political, ideological, and institutional structures that surround us. Knowledge does not emerge from a vacuum but arises from a particular cultural milieu that determines what is important to know and what is not, what is central to its worldview and what is marginal and irrelevant, what needs to be controlled and managed and what needs to be promoted and elevated, and what needs to be made visible and what needs to be suppressed and hidden. We know a great deal about the male body, but our knowledge of female bodies is pitiful largely because biology and medicine have been hitherto dominated by men. The dominant culture often presents its knowledge as truth while attributing ignorance to other cultures thereby producing its own kind of ignorance of other cultures. That is why we know so much about Western epistemology and are so ignorant of the epistemologies of the South. Orientalism, for example, was/is constructed ignorance about Islam and Muslims designed both to relegate them to the margins and deprive them of the power of self-representation. Anthropology emerged not so much to gain knowledge about other cultures but to discover how they can be controlled and managed – made into good colonial subjects. The subaltern really does not speak in modern and postmodern scientific, political, and cultural arenas.

In *The Fire Next Time*, the brilliant American novelist and thinker James Baldwin accuses his country and fellow white countrymen (and women), of a heinous crime for which they will never be forgiven. It has taken hundreds and thousands of black lives – a thing called slavery – on an institutionalised and industrial scale. But Baldwin does not accuse them of racism. Rather, he accuses them of ignorance: 'they do not know it and do not want to know it'. Moreover, it is this ignorance that continues to perpetuate the crime in its manifestation as racism. And as Gordon Blaine Steffey shows, this ignorance is deeply embedded in 'neutral' institutions of American society and democracy, the police and zoning laws, what is taught as history, in liberal categories of reason and neutrality, and in knowledge production itself. Critical Race Theory (CRT) aims to expose this ignorance: it 'is an indispensable tool for disclosing a more truthful story about America because it unsentimentally exposes the past in our present with an eye to an America that is yet to come'. This is precisely why right-wing America wants to suppress and raise doubts about CRT.

Contemporary modes of knowledge production and practice themselves lead to ignorance. Indeed, Western epistemologies are also theories of suppressed, neglected, deliberately constructed, and other varieties of ignorance. Knowledge structures, notes Linda Martin Alcoff, American philosopher and women's studies professor, impress 'a pattern of self-forming practices' that create 'systematic ignorance'; they establish '*specific* knowing practices inculcated in a socially dominant group'. So, ignorance becomes not just absence of knowledge but an integral, substantive part of knowledge production and practice.

We can see this in philosophy and science. The prime focus of philosophers is on analysis – on the sources, structures, evidence, arguments, and justification of knowledge. The emphasis is on the delineation of knowledge from mere belief, supposition or unsupported hypothesis. Philosophers, after all, as Andrew Bennett, the British literary critic, notes, 'seek to go beyond their own exploration of ignorance, to produce "positive" or "constructive" knowledge'. Plato was not impressed by Socrates's mantra that all he knew was that he knew nothing – 'awareness of ignorance is the beginning of wisdom'; 'admitting one's ignorance is the first step to acquiring knowledge'. He banned poets from his *Republic* for their 'disease' of ignorance. Philosophy, notes Bennett, 'can be seen as a discourse, before all others, that in the end because it knows ignorance, defends against it and exposes it, thereby cutting it'. But it is like cutting the branch one is sitting on.

Modern science too banished ignorance. After all, science was a war against ignorance and superstition; and 'scientific method' was supposed to deliver Truth. Scientific progress, as Tudge says, meant 'complete understanding of life, the universe, and everything, all expressed with the neatness and finality of $E=mc^2$'. Economics too followed a similar path, suffering 'physics envy' just like life sciences. The 'dismal science', whether happy or not with that moniker, would lean into that idea that at least a 'science' had an answer for its problems, yet its attempt at knowledge creation has resulted in some of the most oppressive ignorance produced to date – that constantly befuddles our complex and interconnected world. For much of modern history, ignorance has been the unthought of knowledge production: something to suppress, escape, eradicate, be left out of sight, ignored as the outliers.

Not surprisingly, until quite recently, we did not even have a word for the study of ignorance. The word ignorance itself comes to English from the French who derived it from the Latin *ignōrāns*, or 'the want of knowledge or information'. An initial term for the theoretical study of ignorance was suggested by the Scottish rationalist philosopher James Frederick Ferrier (1808-1864). Ferrier coined the term epistemology for the theory of knowledge and suggested 'agnoiology' for the study of ignorance. But much like ignorance itself, agnoiology largely remained neglected. More recently, the term agnotology has come into vogue, introduced by Robert Proctor and Londa Schiebinger in their 2008 edited volume, *Agnotology: The Making and Unmaking of Ignorance*.

So finally, ignorance is emerging from the shadows of Western academia. It is being taken seriously in philosophy, science, and technology studies, and a host of social science disciplines. Its diverse causes are being investigated – from denial, suppression, and secrecy to neglect, myopia, and wilful manufacture. And forgetfulness - so movingly explored in this issue of *Critical Muslim* through a very personal essay by Alev Adil. The conscious, unconsciousness, and structural dimensions of ignorance are being explored. This is well illustrated by the *Routledge International Handbook of Ignorance Studies* – with a graffiti image on the cover that declares: 'Not ignorance, but ignorance of ignorance, is the death of knowledge' – edited by German sociologist and science studies scholar, Mattias Gross and British sociologist, Linsey McGoey. The *Handbook* covers a wide variety of ignorances, including literary, scientific, economic, journalistic, rational, and white ignorances, providing historical and methodological perspectives, and explores the connection between ignorance and power. It is quite a treasure trove of ignorance!

The co-editor of the *Handbook*, McGoey, is a pioneer and can be considered a doyen of ignorance studies. In her contribution to this issue of *CM*, she analyses her notion of 'strategic ignorance' defined as 'the mobilization and exploitation of the unknowns in a situation in order to command resources, deny liability in the aftermath of disaster, and to assert expert control in the face of unpredictable outcomes'.

The story of ignorance in Muslim culture is somewhat different. Knowledge in Islam, it is generally accepted, is not just knowledge for the sake of knowledge; it ought to have a purpose, and as such, its immediate object is its own ignorance. Muslims were well aware of what German theologian Nicholas Cusanus (1401–1464) called 'learned ignorance'. As Bruce Lawrence states, 'there is a long legacy of attention to ignorance, both simple and compound, in Islamic intellectual history'; and William Franke acknowledges, there are 'outstanding figures of genius who have made unmistakable the eminent role that Muslims have played in developing knowledge which, at its truest and highest, cannot but be an *unknowing* knowing'.

Lawrence takes a closer look at *Knowledge Triumphant*, the majestic 1970 book of Franz Rosenthal (1914–2003), the German-American scholar of Islam. Rosenthal shows that during the classical period, Muslim scholars produced over 500 definitions of *ilm*, the term for knowledge in Islam, many related to *jahiliyah*, the term for ignorance in Islamic parlance. In contrast to knowledge, to which the Qur'an devotes considerable space, *jahiliyah* is mentioned in the Qur'an only four times. The term is sometimes used to describe the pre-Islamic period, but, as Rosenthal points out, its true meaning is an 'ignorant person'; and such a person could also be someone who has some type of knowledge. Indeed, Iblis, the angel who rebels against God and is thrown out of heaven, is a very knowledgeable entity but determined to be wicked. In his *Book of Knowledge*, al-Ghazali (1058–1111) categorises certain kinds of knowledge

as 'blameworthy', for they could lead to wickedness even though they may
be based on evidence and rational inquiry. Ignorance, then, is seen in
Islamic history as an essential dimension of knowledge, and an integral part
of the thought of a knowledgeable individual. Or, as Lawrence puts it: 'all
human knowledge, precisely because it comes from God, is shadowed by
ignorance'. Hence, the universal command in Islam to constantly say, no
matter who you are, 'I do not know'. The Prophet emphasised this when
he said, 'it constitutes part of knowledge to say, if one has no knowledge,
Allah a'lam' – God knows best.

Ilm is often equated with other terms to draw attention to its ignorance.
One term often mentioned in conjunction with *ilm* is *marifa*, or coming to
know with experience or reflection. This is the domain of the unknowable
and the unsayable that Franke explores in the thought of the great mystics Ibn
Arabi (1165–1240) and Rumi (1207–1273). Here, our knowledge, derived
through contemplation of God, turns out to be nothing but a cosmos of
ignorance; for 'God is not degraded to identity with things; he is in no way
any *thing*. Rather, all things are nothing, except in him'. Ignorance becomes
a resource that is essential for acquiring certain kinds of knowledge; and
knowledge and ignorance are not viewed as competing perspectives at
loggerhead with each other but as two sides of the same coin.

It is interesting to note that another term used for experiential
knowledge is *tahqiq*, which literally means investigation. This investigation
begins with the attempt 'to know things by verifying and realising their
truth and reality for oneself. One cannot verify the truth and reality of
things without knowing them first hand, in one's own soul, without any
help from anyone other than God'. This is intellectual knowing: 'true self-
knowledge knows the nothingness of the self and the absoluteness of the
Other that it can know at first only as Nothing'. Intellectual knowing,
argues Franke, is 'Islamic philosophy's greatest breakthrough towards
modernity'. And there is an urgent need to leverage this Muslim tradition
'in constructing the genealogy of an alternative modernity'.

Meanwhile, current modernity has lumbered us with a host of problems,
not least of which is climate chaos. Shanon Shah looks at the manifestations
of ignorance of climate emergency in Muslim societies, and focusses on
three countries: Egypt, Malaysia, and Saudi Arabia. Shah uses two criteria
for examining the policies of each of the three states: what influence it

exercises on shaping a contemporary understanding of Islam; and does it acknowledge its own contributions and responsibility in tackling climate change, seeks forgiveness for its environmental sins (makes *tawbah*), and is ready to make amends. Egypt, it turns out has destroyed its environment, and nearly killed the great river Nile that provides water for five countries, through shear old fashioned ignorance. It represents the *jahils*, the ignorant people the Qur'an condemns as those 'who have hearts with which they do not understand, and they have eyes which they do not see, and they have ears with which they do not hear' (7:179). Malaysia displays a different kind of ignorance. It is seen as a modern state, but its influence on shaping Islamic understanding of climate change is marginal. It has the right policies and appears to be saying and doing the right things on the surface. But the underlying reality is otherwise: it is actually destroying its rainforests at a frightening pace and endangering the entire planet. It has knowledge, but scrumptiously chooses the path of ignorance. Shah describes this as *munafiq* ignorance – the ignorance of the hypocrites. Their outward appearance, the Qur'an says, is pleasing; but 'they use the oaths as cover', 'what they have been doing is truly evil'; 'they are like propped up timbre' (63:2-5). Finally, Saudi Arabia, which exercises major influence on how Islam is perceived and understood, and which has played a significant role in promoting fossil fuels and thwarting global efforts to tackle climate change, is assigned a totally different category of ignorance. Saudi Arabia is not just in denial, consciously and unconsciously, of climate change. Rather, it has set itself 'up as a Divine authority whilst defiling Allah's creation'. It is committing *shirk*, which is not just ignorance via denial, but ignorance that represents an existential threat here and now as well as in the Hereafter.

Climate change, Shah points out, is a 'wicked problem'. It has numerous contradictory variables that are changing, it is socially, culturally, and politically complex, has many varieties and dimensions of ignorance, and is therefore not particularly amenable to a single solution. Strictly speaking, wicked problems have no solutions. But climate crisis is not the only complex issue currently facing humanity. The world is full of wicked problems. Virtually all our economic, environmental, and political issues, are wicked problems, which cannot be resolved in binary true or false fashion, or have a given solution that can be discovered through trial and error. Wicked problems are a product of our interconnected, interdependent world. We are faced not just with accelerating change that is global in scope and reaches to the scale of the individual, but change also happens simultaneously in several arenas of human endeavour. The outcome is mindboggling complexity – proliferating contradictions, and frequent chaos. In other words: the nature of change is itself changing. In such postnormal times, understanding ignorance in all its multiple dimensions is an imperative to our survival, and the endurance of the planet. Wicked problems and complex issues cannot be managed and controlled. We need to navigate our way out of postnormal times to more viable futures – and ignorance is a quintessential component of the compass we need.

The emergence of agnotology and ignorance studies is thus both vital and timely. But we cannot be content with the way things are. Agnotology has been criticised, particularly from a science studies perspective, for being limited in scope, ignoring institutional and structural mechanisms that produce ignorance, and ascribing ignorance mostly to corruption in science, perpetuated by corporations, industries, private interests, and the odd bad apple. This shortcoming, it has been suggested, can be met by giving due attention to things that are not explored and studied: 'empty spaces' in all areas of research, and 'undone science' – the lack of knowledge on certain issues and problems identified by activists and concerned citizens, but neglected by mainstream research. A new discipline, dubbed 'political sociology of science', is emerging to meet this need.

But there is a bigger challenge. The study of ignorance in disciplinary silos, based on paradigms that demonstrably are increasingly irrelevant and no longer work, will not take us very far. The first ignorance we need to overcome is the ignorance of disciplines themselves as well as disciplinary boundaries. Most social science disciplines are 'zombie disciplines' – things that are dead and continue their ravenous existence nevertheless. Zombie disciplines, note Shamim Miah and Liam Mayo, 'disseminate ideas and concepts that are no longer representative of reality but continue to shape minds and imagination, education and policies, outlooks and futures'. They are products of 'modernity, diseased by neo-liberalism, unchanged and increasingly irrelevant in postnormal times'. These disciplines range from anthropology and political science to economics (held together with mindless rotting notions such as perpetual growth and the putrid plaster of illusory free markets). They also include 'development studies, cultural studies to media studies, all varieties of "area studies", certain types of history and philosophy, particular perspectives on biology, and many other "subjects" in between'.

This is the 'normal' world of academic disciplines. A graffiti slogan that appeared in a variety of languages and syntax throughout the world in response to the globe-stopping first wave of the Covid-19 pandemic, roughly reads: 'We don't want to return to normal. Because normal was the problem in the first place.' The disciplinary structures of knowledge, which is largely a product of imperialism and emerged during the colonial period, is itself based on ignorance; and hence, the major problem and challenge for initiating the study of ignorance.

At the very least, ignorance needs to be studied from multi-, inter- and trans-disciplinary perspectives. A good example is provided by Bennett who suggests that literature and philosophy should join hands with regard to ignorance to explore 'whether or not one moves beyond aporia or perplexity, beyond not knowing'. While philosophers aim at producing affirmative knowledge, literature is a discourse 'which doesn't (or doesn't always or doesn't necessarily) move (or attempt to move, or desire to move) beyond perplexity or aporia, beyond ignorance'. The inability to know is not necessarily a disadvantage; indeed, it can be turned into an advantage. The key to the flip resides within such profound simplicities.

The point is that we need to move from disciplinary enclaves to integration of knowledge. This journey begins with the acknowledgment of: (a) the limitation of disciplinary perspectives that cannot deal with complex problems and issues; and that (b) complex problems need complex approaches that can only be gained through multiple perspectives; (c) multiple perspectives need many different modes of knowing; (d) different ways of knowing cannot be supplied by a single culture but require plurality of cultures, each with its own definition, notions and concepts of knowledge and ignorance; and (e) the total abandonment of the ignorant belief that Western culture is the only culture entitled to produce knowledge, and is the only culture that has produced knowledge. However, it is not good enough simply to acknowledge that other cultures have produced knowledge and continue to do so. We need to engage with knowledge systems of non-Western cultures within their own notions and conceptual frameworks. We need to give equal attention to the epistemologies of the South, tacit knowledge of indigenous cultures, and experiential knowledge, not just of mystics, but also that found in everyday lives. This is not an exercise in arrogant assimilation, or alienating reduction, but in holistic synthesis aimed at seeking knowledge about the limits of knowing. A knowledge production system inspired by a network, as opposed to a hierarchical or pejorative system, assists the maintenance of equality towards equity. Most of all, this requires humility, appreciation, understanding, and imagination free from the colonised constraints of disciplinary structures and the obsessions and fantasies of a single dominant culture. It's time to usher in a new understanding of goodness.

At the end of her essay, Ellmann realises that there may be sound reasons why things are against us. We are, she says, 'polluting THINGS, shooting THINGS, refuting the nature of THINGS…we are always wrecking THINGS, exploiting THINGS, belittling THINGS, dislodging THINGS'. She could have added we are creating things that kill us, things that are destroying the planet, things that are altering our biology. We use things that belong to the dead-end of modernity, academic things that have passed their 'sell by' dates, and things that will not help us find a way out of our current impasse. A thing that goes under the rubric of capitalist ideology has devastated ordinary lives. The thing called Western civilisation has brought us to the brink of extinction with its hubris. Meanwhile, we keep building things that, as James Brooks says, are nothing more than a Can of Ham, and keep 'filling our time and heads' as we stare at things we call screens.

Ellmann concludes: 'we are ignorant of THINGS'. But more than that: we are just ignorant things.

KNOW THAT YOU DO NOT KNOW

Bruce B Lawrence

From Southeast Asia comes a voice of reason hard to ignore. His name is Haji Abdul Malik bin Abdul Karim Amrullah, better known as Hamka (d. 1981). He wrote, talked and worked for Muslim reform within the Archipelago. His life has been etched by a number of biographies. The most recent from Khairudin Aljunied is titled: *Hamka and Islam: Cosmopolitan Reform in the Malay World*. 'Hamka built upon the reformist legacy of making apparent the crisis of thought in Muslim minds,' observes Aljunied,

> but rather than dealing with symptoms as exhibited in the practice of *taqlid* among Southeast Asian Muslims, Hamka directed his attention to the root of the problem: 'the stagnant mind' (*akal yang beku*). By 'the stagnant mind,' he meant a type of mind that was not able to think critically, logically, or rationally to address issues pertaining to life and faith. Muslims with stagnant minds came from all walks of life, from the scholarly class to the laity. They accepted everything that had been taught to them by their teachers, and were unable to think creatively or to interrogate their inherited beliefs and traditions. Their inactive minds brought about sloppiness and unoriginality in their writings, their speeches, and their conversations. 'And when stagnancy (*pembekuan*) happens, the understanding of religion becomes rigid and the light that shines from it becomes dim.' …Hamka went further to argue that Muslims with stagnant minds can be categorised into two main groups: those characterised by simple ignorance (*jahil basit*) and those characterised by compound ignorance (*jahil murakab). Jahil basit* persons are ignorant because of their lack of experience and socialisation. This group could be enlightened through teaching and reminding, since they are usually open to knowledge, learning, and reasoning. *Jahil murakab* are ignorant yet too proud to learn anything from anyone. Hamka was convinced that members of the second group were dangerous because their lack of knowledge coupled with their arrogance would lead them astray along with others who followed their path. He wrote that the ignorance

of the second group 'may be likened to walls that would always hinder man from reaching their objectives, especially in thinking about pertinent issues'.

There is a long legacy of attention to ignorance, both simple and compound, in Islamic intellectual history. Franz Rosenthal, a noted philologist and intrepid translator, evokes 'compound ignorance' from several sources as follows:

> We often hear scholars castigate the 'compound ignorance' defined as a person's not knowing that he does not know. Human failure with regard to the possession of comprehensive knowledge was most commonly and universally acknowledged by the constant repetition of the command to admit one's ignorance, if such was the case. 'Saying, "I do not know", constitutes one half of knowledge' is both a Prophetical tradition and a saying found in Graeco-Arabic wisdom literature. The phrase most widely recommended for use was to add 'I do not know'. Aristotle was described as saying that he was so fond of using it that he used it also in cases where he possessed the required knowledge. No educational device is omitted to hallow its constant employment. A somewhat less explicit admission of doubt and ignorance is the use of the phrase *Allah a'lam,* 'God knows better (best)'. The *hadith* commands: 'It constitutes part of knowledge to say, if one has no knowledge, *Allah a'lam.*'

Rosenthal then goes on to elaborate many instances from Syriac and Greek philosophy which reflect on popular ways that not knowing, and admission of not knowing, rather than outright ignorance is itself a form, a higher form, of knowing. He cites the eleventh century Persian poet and polymath Ibn Hindu, himself fond of quoting Socrates on the dilemma of 'not knowing'. According to Ibn Hindu, Socrates said: 'I often used to dream that I was the most learned of my contemporaries. I could not find myself deserving of this description except by virtue of the fact that I often say, "I do not know", in reply to matters I am asked about.' Ibn Hindu adds another version: 'It was revealed to me that I was the most learned of men. I was surprised, because I was aware that I did not deserve this description, but revelation never lies. Thus, I deserve this description, because I know that I do not know, whereas other people do not know and do not know that they do not know'. Ibn Hindu goes on quoting an Arabic verse to the effect that 'the poor fellow does not know that he does not know.' The verse rather castigates 'compound ignorance' and does not aim at praising the philosopher's despair of achieving true knowledge.

The same despair, he notes, is echoed in a verse cited by Usamah b. Munqidh, the twelfth century Syrian poet:

> You are ignorant, and you do not know that you are ignorant.
> I wish I could see to it that you know that you do not know.

Ibn Munqidh, the twelfth century poet and diplomat, also provides a versification of the Socratic saying:

> Is it not remarkable that I am a man
> Mighty in disputation, subtle in the choice of words,
> Who dies with his soul possessing as its only knowledge
> The knowledge that he has no knowledge?

It is understandable, concludes Rosenthal, that this great Greek idea re-occurs in a passage allegedly of Persian origin that says that 'it is part of knowledge to know that you do not know'.

The seriousness of 'compounded ignorance' in Hamka and the playfulness of its invocation in Greek/Socratic and early Arabic/Muslim poetry cited by Rosenthal evokes the deeper question: how do we separate ignorance from knowledge, or what marks true knowledge in the formative, that is, the middle phase of Islamic history – extending from tenth to sixteenth centuries? To answer this query, I find it useful to troll through the evidence largely unmined and undervalued in Franz Rosenthal's *Knowledge Triumphant: The concept of knowledge in medieval Islam*. The book is an encyclopedic philological inquiry, the mark of Franz Rosenthal as a German-trained, US-based academic who mastered most of the languages of Late Antiquity and made ready reference to a dazzling array of sources.

The book begins with antiquity and ends with education. The chapter titles explore knowledge systematically, with teleological precision. After a brief Introduction, Rosenthal explores The Knowledge before

Knowledge (1), the Revelation of Knowledge (2), The Plural of Knowledge (3), and Definitions of Knowledge (4). These frame chapters are followed by four more chapters on knowledge within the annals of pre-modern Islamic scholarship: Knowledge is Islam (5 – Theology and Religious Science), Knowledge is Light (6 – Sufism), Knowledge is Thought (7 – Philosophy), and Knowledge is Society (8 – Education). In his Concluding Remark, Rosenthal contrasts the major Islamic accent on knowledge with its rival, Greco-Roman philosophy, always attached more strongly to ethics, as was China, where 'action was man's overriding concern'. Only Indian speculation 'went deeper into the abstract problem of knowledge than Muslim scholars ever did' but with 'no single dominating term' so that knowledge, per se, cannot be said to define Indian civilisation as it did premodern Muslim civilisation. The book ends with a flickering query: how did focus on one notion of what was acceptable knowledge pose limits as well as benefits for Islamic futures?

The question remains unanswered though as the initial quote from Hamka reveals: one cannot talk about Islam or the 'rational person' without reference to some of the same categories – the evidence, the arguments, the outcomes – channelled by Rosenthal in a book that, according to American Arabist, Dimitri Gutas, was his own response to Ibn Khaldun's *The Muqaddimah,* a work whose translation into English had occupied Rosenthal for decades. Published in three volumes in 1958, Rosenthal's rendition of *The Muqaddimah* had just been published in its abridged paperback edition in the year prior to his completion of *Knowledge Triumphant* in 1969. And so, Rosenthal attempts to mirror the boldness of his Maghribi precursor, to summarise all of Islamic civilisation in one concept: knowledge or *'ilm,* at once a quest and a question.

The pursuits of two scholars merge, yet it is the quest behind the question that looms large for Rosenthal. The eternal problem of translation shows itself here at its most intractable. 'Every term translated is a term distorted, no matter how much care has been spent on finding the most suitable English equivalent.' And so knowledge is at once central and ambivalent in the quest to understand the tone and temper, the scale and scope of Islamic civilisation.

One can do a word count with a string of possible meanings, which he does in Chapters 2 and 4, but more intriguing is his search for, and reference to, equivalents to the Arabic word *'ilm,* the poster child of knowledge in Islam. Noting that it does not have a large play in pre-Islamic culture, he also observes that its counterpart *jahiliyah,* cited four times in the Qur'an, does not mean 'ignorance per se' or period of ignorance but rather those who are ignorant. It is a mark of his attention to textual detail that he scans the deeper resonance of *jahiliyah* passages in the Qur'an. 'Although there is at least one clear instance in the old *hadith* where *jahiliyah* denotes an abstract quality ("you are a man in which there is *jahiliyah*"), the passages of the Qur'an seen as they are and not through the eyes of traditional interpretation do not require an abstract meaning for the term. *Jahiliyah* here might be considered a collective plural of *jahil* "ignorant (person)".' In support of the interpretation of *jahiliyah* as a collective plural, it should be noted that in all its occurrences in the Qur'an, *jahiliyah* is used next to plural forms referring to people. There is nothing to indicate in the Qur'anic passages that *jahiliyah* signifies some such concept as a definite 'period of ignorance' or a well-defined 'paganism'. All they say is that there is or was *jahiliyah,* meaning, perhaps, 'ignorant persons' who spoke and acted contrary to what Muhammad considered the right way of thinking and behaviour. Only the use of the adjective *al-ula* 'first' in 33:33 could give us pause. Intended as a numeral, *al-ula* might suggest the existence of a sharply defined first group (or period) of *jahiliyah* which was followed by a second (and, possibly, a third, etc.) one. The Qur'an interpreters have, in fact, understood *al-ula* in this manner and have tried to fix the actual dates of the first and second *jahiliyah*s in terms of the history of the Jewish-Christian prophets. However, *al-ula* may as well be understood as 'first' in the general sense of 'from early times', as is often the case in the Qur'an. This seems to be the more likely interpretation. It would define *al-jahiliyah al-ula* rather noncommittally as 'previous *jahiliyah*' (where *jahiliyah* could be 'ignorant persons'). It suggests, however, the placing of *jahiliyah* into a more remote past than is required by the context of the other three passages.

Rosenthal then proceeds to compare and contrast *ilm,* the opposite of *jahiliyah,* with its synonyms, which are not however its equivalents: *hikmah* 'wisdom', *ma'rifah* 'gnosis', *'aql* 'reason' and also *adab* 'ideal comportment'. The trickiest of all these equivalents is *ma'rifah* about which Rosenthal himself notes at the end of his introduction:

> the Arabic terms are never unequivocal. The distinctions among them — all, as a rule, very subtle in nature — were not always observed with sufficient precision, even by writers aware of the technical intricacies of the choice of terms. It was possible for the same author to adhere strictly to technical terminology in one place, and make loose use of the same term in another. The terms *'ilm* and *ma'rifah* for instance, could be used as plain synonyms. They were also differentiated enough to be used for defining each other. They could be treated as contrary and almost mutually exclusive concepts of mental activity. Or they could designate quite different and clearly defined subject matters. Various English terms can be used to translate them, but wherever this is done, the coherence created by terminology, which is strongly felt in Arabic, is severed. An additional problem in the particular case of *'ilm* and *ma'rifah* is peculiar to English which does not share with French or German the distinction between *savoir-connaitre* or *wissen-kennen* which often approximates the one that exists between the two Arabic roots. Except using the untranslated Arabic terms or adding them in strategic positions wherever deemed necessary or making some artificial and potentially misleading distinction in translation between 'knowledge' and 'cognition', 'knowledge' and 'gnosis', 'knowledge of' and 'knowledge about' or the like, as has been inconsistently attempted in the following pages, not much can be done about this situation. The realm of abstract speculation, which is the foundation of all higher civilisation, is a realm of terms, without which the human mind cannot operate. Transference from one language to another always disturbs unique thought patterns. It can lead at best to approximations. The realisation of these facts is, perhaps, the master key to the understanding of our subject.

Despite this caveat, Rosenthal embarks on a quest to answer the single query that framed much of his academic life: 'what distinguishes knowledge for Islamic civilisation?' and by extension, 'what marks ignorance as the underside, the shadow of this quest for knowledge'? Indeed, we might paraphrase the title of his book to suggest that 'knowledge (in Islam) is triumphant, precisely to the extent that knowledge – and knowledge alone – is able to triumph over ignorance'.

With so much dependent on knowledge, it becomes crucial not only to trace its genealogy but its epistemology: what does knowledge mean, and what are different key terms that connote knowledge? If *'ilm* is to 'triumph', it might also triumph all possible usurpers, and that includes *iman* or faith. Why would faith not be an alternative to ignorance, with ignorance merely the underlying condition for false faith (*kufr*) or idolatry (*shirk*)?

While the evidence of pre-Islamic poetry offers slim evidence, the Qur'an itself prioritises *'ilm* with repeated use of the term in reference to God at all levels. One may speak not merely of the revelation of knowledge but also of knowledge as revelation, and Rosenthal notes not only the statistical but pedagogical use of *'ilm* in Qur'an with special attention to 102, *Surah Al-Takathur* ('Striving for More'), where knowledge gained at death on the threshold of divine judgment is registered as *'ilm al-yaqin*, *haqq al-yaqin*, and finally *'ayn al-yaqin*, so that there is a progression, in each case from a lower to a higher level of knowledge. In this Surah, as elsewhere, there is the fraught relationship between human knowledge and divine knowledge. According to the Qur'an, God's knowledge is undeniably superior in quantity to that of human beings. 'God knows, and you do not know,' the Qur'an says frequently. But it is also somehow different in quality: God knows about secret matters, the knowledge of which escapes human beings (for instance 6:59 and also 11:31).

All human knowledge, precisely because it comes from God, is shadowed by ignorance. Thus, it is evident that human beings cannot know more than God (2:140). Even the angels know only what God has taught them (2:32). Nothing of the divine knowledge can be known except if God wills it (2:255). Much more important, however, is the obvious assumption throughout the Qur'an that human knowledge, that is, true human knowledge, is to be equated with religious insight. In this connection, it is worthy of notice that is supposed to have been possessed preferably by Biblical figures who succeeded in achieving knowledge of the true religion. Indeed, the prophets are in the possession of a knowledge coming to them from God such as ordinary human beings do not possess (7:62). But there are also numerous passages which show clearly that for Muhammad, *'ilm* 'knowledge' was to be equated with the divine revelation he himself, and his less successful predecessors among the Biblical prophets, had received. In a passage whose precise interpretation is not altogether certain, the Holy Book itself is described as 'a book which We have set out according to knowledge' (7:52). Elsewhere, it is argued that faith follows upon knowledge, and the question is asked, how could anyone knowingly not believe? (3:71). The equation of religious faith with knowledge finds its clearest indication in certain passages where the intended meaning is thrown into bold relief by the time-honoured use of parallelism, *'ilm* and *iman* appear once paired in a set phrase, which usually employs only *'ilm* (30:56).

Rosenthal then provides numerous other examples before concluding that 'all human knowledge that contains any true value and deserves to be called "knowledge" is religious knowledge' and so faith and knowledge – *iman* as *'ilm* but also *'ilm* as *iman* are – inextricable, which also means that *jahl* or ignorance is inextricable from *kufr* or unbelief. Yet these parallel antinomies raise the larger question: what does it mean to 'know God' or is it preferable to say even the most devout believer only knows about God but does not fully, in any verifiable epistemology, know God? The priority of faith over knowledge looms large for some groups, including the Ikhwan as-Safa, the ninth-and-tenth-century group of Muslim philosophers, whom Rosenthal quotes at length in Chapter 5 titled Knowledge is Islam. 'The prophets first asked their particular nations to acknowledge (*iqrâr*),' according to the Ikhwan,

> then they challenged them to believe (*tasdiq*), after clarity had been achieved (*bayân*), and then they urged them to study the true matters of knowledge (*al-ma'ârif al-haqîqîyah*). Proof of the correctness of our statement is these passages from the Quran: 'Those who *believe* in the supernatural (2:3)'. Here, God does not say, '...*know* the supernatural.' God urged the people to seek knowledge, saying: 'Consider, men of understanding,' or 'men of insight (59:2).' Then, God uttered praise, saying: 'God will lift up by degrees those of you who have come to believe and those who have been given knowledge (58:11).' And He said: 'Those who have been given knowledge and faith (30:56).' This is sufficient (proof of the existence of) a difference between knowledge and faith.

Numerous Muslim linguists have elsewhere taken up the query of what does it mean to know God 'because there is no explicit mention of man knowing God in the Qur'an'. The eleventh century Qur'anic scholar, ar-Raghib al-Isfahani, in his philological discussion of the Qur'anic vocabulary, stated that:

it could well be said that 'someone knows about *('-r-f)* God', but it would not be possible to say that 'someone knows *('-l-m)* God', because the human knowledge about *(ma'rifah)* God derives from reflection about the observable signs of His works but is not, as the term *'ilm* would imply of necessity, a perception of His essence. This kind of reasoning is hardly applicable to the language and intellectual climate of the Qur'an. Nor is it a distinction that could be said to fit the later history of the idea of man's knowledge of God in Islam in any consistent manner. *'Ilm* and *ma'rifah* came to be employed with little tangible distinction in this respect, although *ma'rifah* may appear to have been the term more commonly used. The real distinction derived from the various purposes connected with the notion of knowing God in the minds of those who spoke about it.

Rosenthal then plunges into a long discussion of various theologians but also Sufi exponents who framed 'knowing God' around various forms of *'-r-f* but especially *ma'rifah*, including the famous pseudo-*hadith*: 'he who knows about himself, knows about his Lord', though its exponents render this same *hadith* in more direct terms as 'who knows himself knows his Lord' (a frequently cited Sufi dictum). Rosenthal uses this distinction between knowledge of God *(ilm)* and knowledge about God *(ma'rifah)* to talk about the emergence of God's knowledge, with *'ilm* one of the *sifat* or attributes linked to God's knowledge, His omniscience. Though he voices scepticism about the circular nature of this exercise, he delves into what he describes as 'the mystery of intellectual creativity' which impelled Muslim scholars to develop at such length the series of Divine Names – *al-asma' ul-husna* – with ramifications and sidebars in other fields of linguistic, theological and philosophical discourse. The focus on knowing about God but not knowing Him also leads Rosenthal to discuss how the unknowing of God directly leads to Ibn 'Arabi's distinction between two *ma'rifah*s, one of *haqq* or Truth, God accessible through His names and attributes, the other of *haqiqa* or Reality, which is unattainable for humans. After exploring other approaches extensively, he concludes: 'there is no true knowledge of God for man, but human knowledge can achieve some realisation of His being'.

One is reminded of the popular dictum: 'Meditate on His attributes not on His essence', that is to say, God is unknowable in His essence but His modes or modalities of expression can be understood, and engaged, through His attributes. At the same time, one feels that ignorance of God's Reality is a domain of discomfort for Rosenthal as it is for most academics, Muslim or non-Muslim, devout or sceptical, looking at the evidence of centuries of scholarship on knowledge-ignorance. Rosenthal is on much more secure, and defensible, turf when he discusses the role of *'aql* or reason in one of the longest, most satisfying chapters: Chapter 7 'Knowledge is Thought'. It involves competing schools of thought, Mu'tazilah ('rationalist') and Ash'arite ('occasionalist'), who nonetheless agree that 'reason' or *'aql* plays a crucial role in the human quest for divine certainty. While all knowledge remains speculative, it stands in stark contrast to 'its opposites: ignorance (*jahl*), doubt (*shakk*), or guesswork (*zann*). Reason (*'aql*) involves all the necessary knowledge there is.'

For Rosenthal Sufism poses a special case for assessing the dominance of *'ilm* (knowledge) as the defining character of Muslim civilisation. He dedicates an entire chapter, Chapter 6 – Knowledge is Light to Sufism. He displays his vast erudition at every turn, looking at avenues and parallels from the Hebrew Bible, Hellenistic and Manichaean sources that precede and inform the Islamic corpus. Is God ontological being or literary metaphor, and how does one reconcile the two emphases in Sufi dicta? He examines at length the stress of as-Suhrawardi *al-maqtul*, the twelfth century founder of what became known as the Iranian school of illuminationism. Everywhere he is intent to show how key words shift in valence, over time, place and provenance. The battle between *'ilm* and *ma'rifah* is ongoing, with each vying for 'superiority' by various Sufi expositors of Light as Truth. He himself is prone to favour 'the knowledge-centered mysticism of Ibn 'Arabi', as it was exposited by Shaykh al-Akbar himself but also by Sadr-ad-din al-Qonawi, the thirteenth century Persian mystic, as in his declaration that 'knowledge is not just light, but the essence of light, pure light, the light of divine being'. At the same time, the constant distinction between outer and inner is upheld, so that 'outward knowledge is said to constitute the "form of light", while inner knowledge constituted "the idea (or source) of light".'

It is not just *'ilm* and *ma'rifah* that vie with one another for precedence but so do *yaqin* (certainty) and its opposite *shakk* (doubt). *Yaqin* indeed superseded *'ilm* in the pyramid of striving for Truth, since in its Qur'anic usage *yaqin* could, and did, encompass both Truth and Knowledge, but from a human perspective. Indeed, certainty is marked, above all, as a human striving; it has no divine counterpart, as does *ilm*, with *'alim* as one of the frequent and prized of God's Beautiful Names. And so we find this parallel: 'While the opposite of *'ilm* knowledge was *jahl* "ignorance", the opposite of *yaqin* "certainty" was *shakk* "doubt". Doubt had an emotive, feeling tone that also transferred to its opposite, *yaqin*, distancing both from the Divine Other.'

Perhaps Ibn 'Arabi provided the most suitable gradation of stages for *yaqin,* all of which he linked to the Qur'an, and reference the *Ka'bah*: there is the declaration of the *Ka'bah's* existence, but more certain is an actual visit to the *Ka'bah*, while the deepest, firmest certainty only comes from learning about the *Ka'bah's* real meaning. And there persists a fascination with Ibn 'Arabi that captivates Rosenthal and animates his chapter on Sufism, detailing how knowledge is light, and again, like the above example of the 'certain' *Ka'bah* it comes in three stages: 1) knowledge of the outer mind, reason through intellect 2) knowledge or taste of the inner self, and 3) knowledge of the (divine) secrets, the highest form of knowing. He delineates four areas of knowledge: logic, mathematics, physics and metaphysics, with the last being the highest to which the Sufi aspires. It mirrors Greek knowledge, observes Rosenthal, with one distinct difference: 'God cannot be rationally known' (that is the outer mind has not just a limit but a barrier), 'while it is understood that He can be reached through gnosis (*ma'rifah*), itself a stage of *'ilm*'. While Ibn 'Arabi praises knowledge and all the domains of knowledge, he lauds the Sufi domain as its highest station, so much so that 'each one of the stations (*manzil*) on the mystic path can claim to be an *'ilm*'.

What is absent in this scan of scholars, seekers and advocates of Sufi knowledge is the ambiguity that pervades not just between *'ilm* and *ma'rifah* as key terms but between spheres of reality marked by shadows or bridges. In short, one needs to peruse *barzakh*, a term that never comes up in Rosenthal's otherwise encompassing and insightful survey of knowledge in the formative, late Antique period of post-Axial history. It has a long history in Muslim intellectual history, including Ibn 'Arabi, but at its simplest it registers a point notable here about opposites or antinomies.

Barzakh is a Persian word found in the Qur'an in three passages (23:99-100, 25:53 & 55:19-20). At its simplest, the *barzakh* evokes the division between this life and the next, between our present life in this world and a future life beyond knowing (23:99-100), but *barzakh* is also the divide between salt and fresh water, found in some oceans and rivers (25:53; 55:19-20). *Barzakh* is a barrier, yet at the same time it is also a bridge. It is a barrier that moves beyond the dyad, either/or, that is, either mind or body. Instead *barzakh* logic confirms both/and, both mind and body, as the metaphor of engagement with knowledge/ignorance. Mindbody might be defined as: non-reductive, undiluted connection, linking two things – whether two cosmic realms or two bodies of water or two opposite reflexes – without reducing or diluting either. It is at once a concept and a method. Neither knowledge nor ignorance stand alone. Both embody, then project an arc of hope that is simultaneously barrier and bridge, gap and gift. In the language of contemporary religious discourse, 'ignorance' has become hard wired as the undesirable opposite of knowledge, yet each defines, and redefines, its other.

Central to understanding the irreducibility of knowledge/ignorance is the irreducibility of the *barzakh* relationship that coheres them. Above all, neither can be co-opted by the other: one does not, and cannot, absorb and so erase the other. At the same time, however, these two extremities cannot, and must not, be combined in some new third form that utilises them while exceeding their boundaries and setting new limits. Ignorance and knowledge cannot be triangulated to produce yet another form of disembodied abstractionism. There is no knowing ignorance, nor ignorant knowing. What makes both work is their constant interaction, so that if *barzakh* logic is to prevail in grasping ignorance and knowledge, it requires constant vigilance against the reflex back to binary logic – one over the other – and in its place, a commitment to a more restrained, patient engagement with dyadic logic, twos combined or elided, as in 'knowing what you do not know', or in the case of Hamka, excoriating 'those who don't know what they don't know'. Crucially, the logic of epistemic separation persists even in the most graphic moments of seeming convergence.

THE ENLIGHTENMENT OF IGNORANCE

Linsey McGoey

It seems obvious that knowledge is more powerful than ignorance, that facts are preferable to fallacy, and that truth is a matter of patient empirical investigation. And especially since the Enlightenment period, when scholars and theologians such as Immanuel Kant exhorted people to 'dare to know' differently (to use Kant's arresting phrase), a cleavage grew more pronounced between the realm of religion and the realm of secularism. Secularism was upheld as the space of science and reason, while religion was seen as the domain of different types of truths, those less 'rational' than scientific reason. We might not have the capacity to 'know' God fully and absolutely, the new thinking seemed to suggest, but we *can* know ourselves. There is nothing in men and women beyond human consciousness, given enough time. The spectre of complete omniscience seemed tantalisingly possible to many nineteenth-century thinkers who took up the gauntlet launched by Kant.

Early social scientists such as Auguste Comte hoped to develop a new science of society that took on board the best available evidence and applied it in the impartial service of humankind. Statesmen establishing new republics declared their commitment to a new politics of knowledge, insisting that knowledge will always triumph over ignorance. The US statesman James Madison reflected this certainty when he wrote, 'Knowledge will forever govern ignorance.'

To many eighteenth- and nineteenth-century thinkers, the attitude between knowledge and ignorance seemed obvious – one is good, the other bad – and the relationship between them appeared to be clear and linear, with ignorance gradually giving way to knowledge, like a blurred window wiped clean. Throughout the twentieth century, this impression continued. Vast subfields within the social sciences emerged advancing the study of how knowledge is obtained and diffused. The study of knowledge and knowledge attainment is a core aspect of economics, sociology, psychology and anthropology, to name simply four disciplines. For a long time, there was no parallel field or fields dedicated to the opposite: the study of ignorance and how societies and individuals often thrive from the deliberate effort not to know the consequences of their own individual or collective actions.

Recently, this has changed. First scoffed at, now widely cited, the growing field of 'ignorance studies' is changing attitudes to the relationship between ignorance and knowledge. Rather than seeing ignorance as the mere *lack* of knowledge, those of us who have pioneered this field's growth examine the ways that ignorance can be an 'active accomplishment', to cite a Handbook in this field that I co-edited and first published in 2015, with a second edition published in 2022.

What are our goals? Why is the study of ignorance important? What new insights are visible in our work?

I'll start with offering a definition of a core concept in this field: that of 'strategic ignorance'. At first glance, it seems possible to define in a fairly simple way, at the individual level. But looked at more closely, the concept also has a collective, group dimension. It's visible in different political, social and legal realms, in a way that reveals new understandings of how power is wielded in different societies.

In my research, I use different terms to refer to these two ways of understanding strategic ignorance. I refer to them as 'type 1' or 'micro-ignorance,' and 'type 2' or 'macro-ignorance'. Elaborating on what's meant by these terms clarifies how both types are visible all around us in different ways.

Type 1 ignorance largely corresponds to how 'strategic ignorance' is perceived and analysed in the field of psychology. It's seen as a type of confirmation bias at the individual level, where people deliberately avoid seeking out or accepting the reality of various facts that could disconfirm their own earlier ideological or political standpoint. This tendency is not something that is confined to either the political left or the right. People across the political spectrum do it. Examples are visible throughout history, such as when evidence of Stalin's forced suffering and starvation of Ukrainians during the Holodomor was consistently denied by left-wing intellectuals such as George Bernard Shaw. They had the evidence that could have alerted them to the scale of atrocities. They chose not to accept it.

Examples from the political right are visible from the rise of Donald Trump's popularity in the US, where opinion polls of voters suggest that many supporters would deny some of Trump's political attitudes even when he openly admitted them. For example, in October 2019, *USA Today* reported that: 'A new poll shows that only four in 10 Republicans believe President Donald Trump talked to the Ukrainian president about investigating political rival Joe Biden, even though Trump has acknowledged doing so.' The news report quoted an expert who describe the tendency as a type of 'partisan tribalism', where affinity for one's own community and their beliefs outweighs fidelity to the truth. George Orwell didn't use the jargon of type 1 or type 2 ignorance, but he was referring to this type of ignorance when he observed, 'To see what is in front of one's nose needs a constant struggle.'

Strategic ignorance at the cognitive level is clearly a problem, leading people to act ostrich-like about facts that they don't like. It's a problem that may be growing worse the more that people practice a sort of personal cognitive dissonance when it comes to ignoring the negative environmental effects of excessive personal consumption and energy use, for example. But it's not the sole way to understand ignorance. About a decade ago, I introduced a sociological definition of the phenomenon that is broader and more distinctive than cognitive ignorance at the individual level. I define strategic ignorance as the mobilisation and exploitation of the unknowns in a situation in order to command resources, deny liability in the aftermath of disaster, and to assert expert control in the face of unpredictable outcomes.

What's the difference? At the individual level, type 1 or micro-ignorance is something that is broadly shared. We all do it. Even people who insist they're more 'objective' in their reasoning may simply be naïve about their capacity to turn away from inconvenient information. But when looked at from the type 2 perspective, it's possible to see that the capacity to manufacture ignorance is *not* equally distributed. There are hierarchies of ignorance. Powerful organisations (governments, corporations, schools, media) have more capacity to engage in type 2 strategic ignorance than so-called lay individuals, shaping what is known or unknown about reality. Macro-ignorance involves the institutional capacity to foment ignorance about the past, the present and future policy options.

In short, the powerful can often be *better* at strategic ignorance than less powerful groups. Not because they're necessarily any smarter or more innately gifted at the distortion or manipulation of facts. But because of the legal and political resources and advantages powerful and wealthy people have at their disposal to propagate their own views more widely. Macro-ignorance is my term for *structural* ignorance that is often perpetuated through institutional decision-making and through patterns of educational blind-spots that are repeated across generations. For example, through the insufficient teaching of the violence of British colonialism in British classrooms, or through corporate confidentiality laws that protect big businesses and insulate them legally from the need to disclose how their profiteering harms the environment and people's health.

This argument challenges the dominant way that ignorance has been understood in the social sciences in the past. For too long, ignorance has been wrongly seen as a more widespread and pernicious problem at the *bottom* of social ladders than at the *top*. In contrast to this, I argue that powerful groups tend to have the most need for strategic ignorance, because their power often rests on obscuring evidence of how their power and enrichment stems from violence against others.

A few examples can help to illustrate what I mean. A key aspect of macro-ignorance involves the value of something that sociologists have termed 'non-decision-making power'. This entails the capacity *not* to investigate spurious or illegal behaviour in situations where people in power believe that there is little individual or institutional incentive to punish illegality.

For example, the former UK Prime Minister Tony Blair pressured his own Attorney General, Lord Goldsmith, to halt a corruption investigation into BAE Systems, a British defence company accused of bribing Saudi officials in exchange for lucrative arms deals. Although there was clear evidence of wrongdoing at BAE, Blair intervened to pressure Lord Goldsmith to drop the effort to hold BAE executives liable for their own illegality. Blair's private concern, later described in a *Guardian* investigation that unearthed secret memos to Lord Goldsmith, was that holding BAE accountable for its crimes might compromise Saudi-UK political and diplomatic relationships. As *The Guardian* reported, the documents 'show that the prime minister also personally vetoed a proposal that BAE could plead guilty to more limited corruption charges', because of his worry that admitting to even more minor charges might cause 'offence' to the Saudi royal family, even though BAE Systems is a British company. Another underlying worry was likely the fear of reducing the economic competitiveness of a significant corporate employer in the UK.

Whether Blair's actions were defensible or not from the perspective of overall national wellbeing, the result is that by avoiding a criminal charge, BAE appears more 'innocent' and blameless than the company really was. Blair's authority as prime minister to thwart a judicial proceeding from going ahead helped to shield the company from wider public scrutiny and disapproval. By circumventing any legal confirmation of wrongdoing, Blair helped to fuel wide public ignorance about BAE's actions, thus generating a wider 'unknown' about just how corrupt a major UK arms dealer actually was. In this case, Blair's questionable actions were eventually leaked to the media. But more often, the decision not to hold companies accountable is not exposed in a scandalous manner. That's the great asset of strategic ignorance – it's a strategy that is most successful when it works.

Another important point to make about strategic ignorance is that some forms of unknowing and truth-telling are more advantaged and privileged than others, in that they depend on different legal protections when it comes to, say, worker's rights.

Quips like Orwell's above, while making good points about our shared tendency to have trouble 'seeing' what's in front of us, tell only half the story. Sure, seeing uncomfortable truths *can* be hard. But it's not always *equally* hard. For example, for staff who work inside corporate or civil service organisations, it can often be dangerous to be a whistle-blower. Even when one's motive is to protect the public from harm, if a person tries to disclose information that higher-ups have commercial or political reasons for not revealing, it can lead to personal and even familial backlash. In many different spheres of life, speaking out about injustice or institutional wrongdoing can often be threatening to one's own job security, so people are compelled, typically for social or economic reasons, not to dissent openly. Speaking out about worker exploitation can often quite literally cost someone their livelihood.

Given that people can face differing consequences for speaking truth to power, it's important to examine the political economy of ignorance, analysing in granular detail which groups have the authority to dismiss or to penalise the experiences of other, more subordinated groups, maintaining a shield of ignorance around institutional wrongdoing.

In my work on the politics of ignorance, I have drawn on recent insights from philosophy, and particularly the scholarship of the Jamaican-American philosopher Charles Mills, who developed the concept of 'white ignorance', something that can be defined in part as collective unknowing within Anglo-American populations about the scale of the violence and suffering inflicted on colonised and neo-colonised groups.

For example, both knowingly and unwittingly, education systems can propagate carefully constructed mythologies that efface a dominant group's history of violence in order to make that history more tolerable to descendants. Much of what we know about history reflects not 'knowledge', but rather a type of 'curated ignorance', as sociologist Paul Gilroy describes it – a sort of non-knowledge that reflects an elite group's imperative to know 'what not to know' in different eras.

As work by scholars such as Gilroy and Mills shows, when a minority group or individual tries to challenge a dominant group's claims of blamelessness or moral worthiness, they are often penalised for trying to do so. Mills gives the example of an African American woman who voiced her experiences under Jim Crow racial segregation laws: 'My problems started when I began to comment on what I saw ... I insisted on being accurate. But the world I was born into didn't want that. Indeed, its very survival depended on not knowing, not seeing – and certainly, not saying anything at all about what it was really like.'

New York Times journalists Susan Chira and Catrin Einhorn found a similar phenomenon when they investigated sexual harassment and discrimination endured by blue-collar workers at Ford plants in the United States. One woman who they interviewed spoke plainly about the problem, explaining that 'when you speak up, you're like mud in the plant'.

I found the same problem when I interviewed whistle-blowers working inside organisations such as the Food and Drug Administration (FDA) in the United States. Those who were more vocal about calling out flawed drug approval processes often face the most censure and penalty by their managers. In leading business schools (I know personally from having worked previously at the Saïd Business School at Oxford University), students are regularly taught that 'good' managers seek more information about how their own management is problematic or harmful to subordinate groups. But this is something of a fairytale. In practice, knowing what not to know is an asset, and 'successful' managers typically thrive from curtailing the ability of lower-rung groups to speak out.

Another way that 'strategic ignorance' can be a tool of the powerful is when it comes to the discounting of the advantages conferred through personal inheritances and other family or cultural advantages. This type of discounting is especially widespread in so-called meritocratic societies that appear to value and reward individual effort more so than inherited advantages. As social science data shows, during interviews, wealthy individuals often tend to 'forget' or discount the way that various structural advantages – old boys' networks, inheritance, family connections – helped them to earn a higher foothold in society than other people. *Guardian* columnist Nesrine Malik offered examples of this 'forgetting' or denialism in a perceptive article about the narratives of Tory highfliers Liz Truss and Rishi Sunak regarding their family backgrounds. As she pointed out, their efforts to make themselves seem less economically privileged than they actually are is a type of 'class discounting – a way for people to establish that their status, whatever it was, was earned and not bequeathed'.

The special goals and tactics of different forms of denial, forgetting and non-acknowledgement of harm encompassed by terms like 'macro ignorance' and 'white ignorance' can shift over time. The capacity of a group's ability to ignore inconvenient information is not necessarily finite. Eventually, their denial is often exposed for the denialism that it is. But new inconvenient 'unknowns' typically emerge in the place of exposed ones. A core aspect of the power of strategic ignorance is the capacity for a dominant group to misperceive and uphold their own worldviews as neutral or universal knowledge, rather than self-serving ideologies. Strategic ignorance, in short, involves the capacity to dismiss some people's knowledge as 'subjective' or merely experiential, while treating other people's knowledge as more authoritative or objective than it deserves to be seen.

The post-2016 era has sometimes been described as a 'post-truth' period. I disagree with this. What is different today is not necessarily that we have entered a uniquely 'post-truth' era, but rather that we have become more *alert* to powerful groups' capacity to shape a historical narrative. And that is making different groups angry, leading to deepening mistrust in Western governmental authorities who in many ways don't deserve to be seen as the paragons of 'rationality' or 'liberalism' or 'facticity' that they elect themselves to be. People want *more* truth about how the world is governed, not less.

Of course, it has long been a truism that 'history is told by victors', and that partial truths emerge as a result. But the advantage of 'ignorance studies' is to show how ingrained this practice is throughout all of the social sciences, not simply within dominant historical narratives, but within sociology, economics and psychology as well.

Scholars in this growing field have sought to dispel one of the lasting binaries bequeathed from the original Enlightenment period: the (false) belief that the secular social sciences alone are the realm of fact and 'hard' truth, while the realms of religion or spiritualism are, on the other hand, a space of mysticism or perceived irrationality. In reality, the arenas of so-called secular fact-making have long been riven by partial truths and biased understandings of what counts as truth and facts. What is changing today is that we have become more alert to our own ignorance.

ILM, IGNORANCE AND CLIMATE CHANGE

Shanon Shah

In his contribution to the anthology *Progressive Muslims*, the perceptive Ebrahim Moosa suggests that we need to ask some 'uncomfortable questions' about Islam. 'If we do not, then the responsibility of learning and faith has gone unanswered.' Moosa's essay, entitled 'The debts and burdens of critical Islam', begins by outlining the recurring struggle for contemporary reformist Muslims – how to combine respect for traditionalist interpretations of Islam with modernist ambitions to bring about a longed-for revival of Islam. The risks, according to him, are that modernists and traditionalists might fall into two common traps. The first, 'textual fundamentalism', results in the quest for picayune doctrinal precedents to justify 'proper' Islamic responses to contemporary problems. The second, the strategy of 'purposive interpretations', runs the danger of emptying Islam's sacred texts of historical context in the zeal to craft novel solutions to modern problems, distorting their content in the process.

How might we take up Moosa's call for Muslims to ask 'uncomfortable questions' about Islam as a 'responsibility of learning and faith'? How might Muslims respond to knowledge that challenges or contradicts dominant understandings of Islam? At first glance, this concern might appear moot, given the primacy that Islamic thought has always given to *ilm* – a term that synthesises what English speakers would understand as knowledge, wisdom, ethics, and action. Does *ilm* not already integrate the need for Muslims to ask 'uncomfortable questions' as a religious obligation?

In reality, these noble ideals of *ilm* are not always borne out in practice. Many Muslims have found injurious ways of betraying the ideals of *ilm* – not merely through passive ignorance, but by perpetuating systemic denial about some of the core issues confronting Muslim societies. Ignorance is, of course, a phenomenon that is present in all populations and societies, not just Muslim contexts. But each community has its own collective habits of thinking that produce specific modes of ignorance. Inspired by Moosa, I'd like to pursue some uncomfortable questions about the relationship between *ilm* and ignorance from a Muslim perspective by focusing on one big challenge facing humanity – the crisis of climate change. *Ilm* needs to be reimagined and reimagined *ilm* can help us cope with the climate crisis. But contemporary understandings of *ilm* are deeply intertwined with ignorance and must be liberated.

The motifs around *ilm* have been discussed by many past and present Muslim thinkers. But what possibilities do these conceptions of *ilm* open for tackling ignorance?

The ummah and ilm

When discussing *ilm*, modern Muslim writers usually start by establishing its centrality as a concept within Islam. *Ilm* is often imagined as the glue that binds Muslims to their environment, infusing Islam with dynamism and life. There is also usually a reminder of how Muslims are enjoined to seek knowledge 'from the cradle to the grave', and that the Qur'an, in a rare exception to its egalitarian ethos (in Q39:9), identifies *ilm* as a marker of privilege. Indeed, hundreds of Qur'anic verses refer explicitly to knowledge and wisdom, and adjacent terms or concepts such as observation, reason, reflection, and the study of natural and social phenomena.

At the same time, Muslim thinkers have been careful to point out that *ilm* does not merely mean 'knowledge'. There is often a reminder that *ilm* is not and should not be confined only to religious knowledge, but encompasses scientific, modern and secular knowledge. Neither is it a mere abstraction – as a concept, *ilm* embraces theory, action, education, and what can be understood as the scientific method. Translating *ilm* as 'knowledge' is also regarded as reductive, if we compartmentalise knowledge as 'religious' or 'secular'. Instead, *ilm* encompasses the religious and the secular and it connects epistemology and ethics.

Yet, for writers such as Ziauddin Sardar, the 'true significance' of *ilm* is now neglected and lacks deep appreciation in Muslim societies, largely as a result of European colonialism and continuing Western domination. The centrality of *ilm* in the way many Muslims have conceptualised Islam's historical glory – and contemporary failings – has even led some commentators to regard it as what sets Islam apart from its Abrahamic older sibling, Christianity. As the Islamic Studies scholar Kate Zebiri has observed, notwithstanding their internal variety and diversity, Christian answers to the 'big questions' largely follow the 'nexus of sin-redemption-salvation (or living in a state of grace), while the corresponding Muslim nexus is ignorance-guidance-success (in this world and the next)'. We can see this even in the ways that many Muslims mark the advent of Islam by referring to the pre-Islamic era as the *Jahiliyyah* – the Age of Ignorance. This is not the only way to conceptualise '*jahiliyyah*', as Bruce Lawrence also explains in his contribution to this volume of *Critical Muslim*.

Juxtaposing the concept of *ilm* against an analysis of ignorance raises the question of how conventional Islamic thinkers traditionally dealt with our lack of knowledge, or the limits in our pursuit of knowledge. Even the Qur'an constantly reminds humanity that our knowledge in all spheres and disciplines is limited. In Islamic thought, therefore, different classifications of knowledge were developed. Among these, the most relevant demarcation to highlight here is that between knowledge of the seen (*ilm al-shahadah*) and knowledge of the unseen (*ilm al-ghaib*). Humans are only able to know what they can see, and are unable to know the unseen. The unseen can be subdivided into the absolute (*ghaib mutlaq*) or the relative (*ghaib nisbi*). Humans can never acquire knowledge of *ghaib mutlaq* except via revelation.

The concept of revelation, however, contains built-in mechanisms for humans to overcome their lack of knowledge – the Qur'an repeatedly reminds its community of listeners that natural phenomena and the cosmos are also *ayat* or signs of revelation. Therefore, it is possible for humans to acquire knowledge by observation (*ilm tajribi*), transmission (*ilm naqli*), or analysis and understanding (*ilm aqli*). In fact, traditional Muslim thinkers recognised *ilm al-yaqin* – which is based on the need for empirical evidence – as an important source of knowledge.

On this basis, conventional Islamic thought recognised the validity and interdependence of different sources of knowledge – revelation, inference, intellect, and empirical observation. These sources also provided intersecting safeguards against errors and distortions. For example, divine revelation (*wahy*) is received by the soul, while empirical observations are apprehended by the physical senses of sight, sound, touch, taste and smell. The intellect (*aql*) is needed to understand *wahy* and make inferences based on empirical observations. At the same time, *wahy* protects *aql* from making mistakes and provides it with information about the unseen. Guidance for achieving this harmonious balance is expressed and preserved through the Divine Law (*shariah*). In fact, in his exegesis of the Light Verse (Q25:35), the Persian polymath Ibn Sina (d. 1037) made the case that God has provided us with the building-blocks of knowledge, *and* a system for integrating that knowledge into our existing knowledge-store as well as its potential deployment in the world.

There is a dark side, however, to this seemingly fool-proof system. This can be seen in recurring Islamic portrayals of Iblis – the personal name of the Devil in Islam – as one of Allah's most knowledgeable subjects. There appears to be a warning here about the ethical imperatives of *ilm* – knowledge that is acted upon in evil, or that is not acted upon, is the source of abomination. This potential dark side of knowledge-acquisition and knowledge-bearing also recurs in other contemporary and traditional Islamic idealisations about *ilm*. Muslim thinkers often insisted, for example, that *adab* (decorum or etiquette) must be a precondition in the pursuit of knowledge, and a legitimate authority must delineate the acceptable boundaries of knowledge.

Thus, conventional Islamic narratives about *'ilm* also incorporate analytical insights about ignorance, including bad intent in the pursuit and application of knowledge. How does this conventional Islamic framework compare with other ways of addressing ignorance and the strategies to overcome them?

Varieties of ignorance

The study of ignorance is now emerging as an exciting new discipline. Not surprisingly, there are numerous definitions, categories and approaches to tackling ignorance. Ziauddin Sardar, for example, argues that ignorance is not merely the lack of knowledge, and that defining ignorance in relation to knowledge is inadequate, as far as existing taxonomies go. According to Sardar, unlike other contemporary conceptual frameworks, postnormal times (PNT) theory deals with ignorance per se. Rather than define it negatively as non-knowledge or an absence of knowledge, Sardar maintains that PNT theorists associate ignorance with 'increasing uncertainty and with complexity, contradictions and chaos – the 3Cs of postnormal times'. In this scheme, the levels of ignorance can be classified as 'Plain, Vincible, and Invincible'.

Plain ignorance describes the absence of knowledge but also covers 'common prejudices like anti-Semitism and Islamophobia, deliberate manufacture of falsehood and lies, denial of established truth and scientific research, and their weaponisation'. *Vincible ignorance* consists of three components – firstly, the knowledge that there are things we do not know (for example, how consciousness works or why dreaming is important); secondly, 'constructed misrepresentation based on knowledge', which can include epistemological biases such as Orientalism or Eurocentrism, and; thirdly, ignorance that can only be dispelled via knowledge that is acquired in the future, e.g., the impacts of genetic engineering on society. Vincible ignorance can be overcome, over time, with serious, conscious effort and the unfolding of the future. *Invincible ignorance* is basically what we do not know we do not know – unknown unknowns which are a product of our 'Unthought'. It cannot be tackled with existing, conventional tools of our worldviews. According to PNT theory, ignorance is increasingly moving from the periphery to the centre of knowledge production due to factors such as the emergence of big data and Artificial Intelligence.

My focus is on what Sardar refers to as 'plain ignorance', specifically its manifestations within Muslim contexts – especially the more wilful and entrenched varieties – and whether dominant conceptions of *ilm* can be a sufficient corrective. I admit that this is risky because these so-called concerns about Islam are bread-and-butter issues for Islamophobic ideologues, especially in the West. Many Muslim readers will know the drill. Why don't we challenge Islamist terrorism more robustly? Why don't we challenge Muslim governments that persecute or oppress certain religious minorities? How could our scholars, or *ulama*, possibly defend the continued denial of equal rights to Muslim women? How do we Muslims explain the existence of hostility or violence towards lesbian, gay, bisexual, or transgender Muslims within their families and communities?

Often in the West, these questions are vexatious and recurring attempts at Muslim-baiting and Islam-bashing. And no, I'm not manifesting my own ignorance or making excuses by pointing out the ideological agenda that often lurks behind these questions. These recurring motifs exemplify what Ziauddin Sardar and Merryl Wyn Davies refer to as the 'distorted imagination' of 'how the West has envisioned the Other', including Muslims and Islam.

Yet, just because these questions are tropes in Islamophobic rhetoric, it does not mean they do not present genuine concerns for Muslims. In fact, they are now being asked by increasing numbers of Muslims with reformist tendencies, often at the risk of censure by Muslim authorities and majority opinion in Muslim contexts. Islamophobia is a given — analogous to the invisible but pervasive presence of atmospheric pollutants — but the question remains: how and why does this censure exist *within* many Muslim contexts? This is not just about 'plain' ignorance — it is also about the construction and pervasiveness of wilful ignorance.

According to the philosopher Daniel DeNicola, despite claims that we live in a 'knowledge society' or in an 'Information Age', there are still varieties of ignorance that cause concern. There is, for example, 'public ignorance' — 'widespread, reprehensible ignorance of matters that are significant for our lives together', including 'political ignorance'. Harmful forms of ignorance flourish in situations where they become an 'ideological stance' and are systematically produced in a 'culture' of ignorance.

Yet what does the very term 'ignorance' refer to? DeNicola begins with three criteria — first, that ignorance has 'intentionality' (i.e., 'to be ignorant is to be ignorant *of something*'), second, that it is important to identify the perspective of the person who claims to have knowledge and the person who is labelled ignorant and, third, claims of ignorance are also affected by a temporal reference, e.g., recognising one's ignorance in hindsight. Thus, to study ignorance effectively, it is always important to ask '*who* is ignorant of *what* and *when*'.

Of direct relevance to us is DeNicola's typology of 'intentional' ignorance. This is not simply ignorance of what we do not yet know or what we can never know, but of 'what we or others have *determined* we are not to know'. In other words, while my preoccupation with 'wilful ignorance' in this essay is valid, this is only a subset of the 'intentional ignorance' specified by DeNicola. He lists five types of intentional ignorance – 'rational ignorance, strategic ignorance, wilful ignorance, secrecy, and forbidden knowledge'. According to DeNicola, a 'person is commonly called wilfully ignorant about a matter when he persistently ignores the topic despite its likely salience and even resists learning about it or assimilating facts that bear on it'.

There is some overlap between DeNicola's definition of 'wilful ignorance' and the sociological study of denial. Denial is a paradoxical cognitive and emotional state – it requires the denier to claim ignorance about something that is already known, or should be known, about the world or about the denier's own self. The sociologist Stanley Cohen offers a formal definition of denial worth quoting in full:

> A statement about the world or the self (or about your knowledge of the world or your self) which is neither literally true nor a lie intended to deceive others but allows for the strange possibility of simultaneously knowing and not knowing. The existence of what is denied must be 'somehow' known, and statements expressing this denial must be 'somehow' believed in.

This definition complements DeNicola's category of 'intentional' ignorance, and adds the caveat that our psychological makeup – individual and collective – can complicate the concept of 'intention'. Yet it does not ignore the political dimensions of ignorance either. Cohen gives the example of the majority of ordinary citizens who know that their government is abusing an ethnic minority. Do these citizens deliberately avert their eyes from reality by no longer reading or watching news on the subject? Do they simply not perceive that anything is actually wrong because all of this is simply part of their 'taken-for-granted' view of the world? Do they see what is happening but refuse to believe it because it is just too difficult to take it all in? Are they indifferent? Or are they aware of the reality but trust that those in power 'know better'? Are they bothered, disturbed or even outraged but refuse to speak out, because of a fear of standing out, powerlessness, self-protection, or the inability to see a solution? Some of these questions and the responses to them are not about denial – several are about apathy or submissiveness.

Cohen's typology of ignorance basically aligns with DeNicola's parameters for studying ignorance. In other words, we must pay attention to: the content being denied (the 'what'); how this denial is organised at different levels by different social agents (the 'who'); and, whether what is being denied is a contemporary or historical event (the 'when'). Perhaps an extra dimension Cohen introduces is the element of 'space and place', or the role of relationships within specific social contexts in fostering denial. Synthesising these insights from Cohen and DeNicola, the parameters for studying ignorance might usefully be expressed as: 'who is ignorant of what and when – and where'.

For Cohen, the antidote to denial is 'acknowledgement' – but not merely the performance of superficial recognition of past wrongs when this about-face stops being costly. Rather, the true acknowledgement by 'ordinary people' of 'the suffering of others' – and the effort to 'find the right channel of action or to improvise their own' – is what really matters. These are effectively stories of true conversion or repentance, akin to the Islamic concept of tawbah. Yet this version of acknowledgement or tawbah rarely happens in a vacuum, and is never merely about an arbitrary, individual change of heart. Two factors are key in determining whether tawbah can take place and be translated into action – personal experience and political power (or the lack of it).

According to the sociologist Patricia Hill Collins, personal experience is a key ingredient in the construction of knowledge – and, by extension, ignorance. What we come to recognise as 'legitimate' knowledge has to go through 'knowledge validation processes'. These processes are constrained by two criteria – first, the experts who evaluate particular knowledge claims bring with them 'a host of sedimented experiences that reflect their group location' and, second, each expert's credibility is defined by the 'larger population in which it is situated and from which it draws its basic, taken-for-granted knowledge'. These intertwining criteria often result in authoritative knowledge claims that exclude, dismiss or suppress competing claims to knowledge – for example, by an ethnic majority towards ethnic minorities, or by men towards women. In these situations, seemingly objective debates about knowledge can mask deep-set ignorance or denial that is the product of unequal social relations.

Taking the example of African American women, whose social and political analysis was often dismissed or ignored by men (white and black) and white women, Collins argues that 'lived experiences' are crucial 'to assess more abstract knowledge claims'. The lens of lived experience allows us to see that despite being subjected to multiple axes of oppression, African-American women were producing – and continue to produce – social theory for their own self-preservation and collective empowerment. But recognising the intellectual work done by Black women requires us to look beyond conventionally recognised forums of academic knowledge, and, for example, to locate Black feminist thought in works of fiction and Blues music. It also forces us to contend with the centrality of diverse *experiences* of oppression in the development of Black feminism. These experiences of Black feminist thinkers encourage us to inquire about whole sections of Muslim societies that have been excluded or marginalised from historical and contemporary productions of *ilm*.

This reflection on the people whose experiences are marginalised in the production of *ilm* brings us to the theme of power. In critical pedagogy, specifically, the concept of power helps us to focus on the individual and collective processes required to recognise and analyse oppression as part of a broader movement to achieve social justice. The Brazilian philosopher Paulo Freire produced the concept of *conscientizacao*, which contains echoes of the more holistic interpretations of *ilm* discussed earlier. Freire describes *conscientizacao* as a two-fold process – first, learning 'to perceive social, political and economic contradictions', and second, taking action 'against the oppressive elements of reality'. People who are oppressed must see their situation not as a 'closed world from which there is no exit, but as a limiting situation they can transform'.

Freire distinguishes between 'educational projects', that should be co-developed between educators and oppressed peoples as a method of social organising, and 'systematic education', which can only be changed through political power. Educational projects have to dissolve the teacher-student dichotomy. Teachers are not merely cognitive providers for students who, in turn, are not merely docile receptacles of knowledge. Teachers and students together must become 'critical co-investigators' –

teachers present students with material for the students' consideration, and they enter into dialogue as they refine their positions based on each other's shared considerations. Teachers and students thus become partners in developing 'their power to perceive critically *the way they exist* in the world *with which* and *in which* they find themselves', and 'come to see the world not as a static reality, but as a reality in process, in transformation'.

Freire's critical pedagogy forces us to revisit the noble ideals of *ilm* and ask to what extent *ilm*, in reality, is a product of power – to liberate or to oppress certain individuals or segments of society. Do 'legitimate authorities' in Islam acknowledge and invite oppressed or marginalised people – including those who are critical of the Muslim status quo – to become 'critical co-investigators' in the formulation of *ilm*?

The ummah *and the crisis of climate change*

The critical role of personal experience and power relations in the formation of *ilm*, on one hand, and in the maintenance of ignorance and denial, on the other hand, can usefully be explored by reflecting on the growing crisis of climate change. According to the climate activist and researcher George Marshall – and PNT theory – climate change is a 'wicked problem'. It is 'exceptionally *multivalent*', meaning that it has global coverage, with complex, intersecting causes and effects. Climate change is also '*uncanny*, creating a discomfort and unease that we seek to resolve by framing it in ways that give it a familiar shape and form'. In other words, the crisis of climate change is so complex, daunting and scary that it forces many people into positions of intentional ignorance or outright denial.

Climate change is moreover a social justice issue because the majority of people who are disproportionately affected – poorer communities largely in the Global South and some in the Global North – were never responsible for the problem in the first place. Addressing the climate crisis will require current generations – especially those living in rich, advanced economies – to make significant material sacrifices to avert danger for future generations. Even though climate change is framed as a 'global' issue, in reality, some communities or countries are much more vulnerable than others, especially those that were impoverished or damaged by colonial exploitation and domination. Many of these countries are situated in the Global South, and many have large populations of Muslims within their borders. At the same time, some Muslim governments, such as Saudi Arabia, are key blockers of international climate negotiations. The crisis of climate change is therefore a formidable issue that is relevant for our analysis of *ilm* and ignorance.

To sharpen this focus, I'd like to revisit my adaptation of DeNicola's specifications for the study of ignorance – '*who* is ignorant of *what* and *when* and *where*'. We have now specified the 'what' – the causes and impacts of climate change. 'When' has also been answered – now, the present, and the future. 'Who' needs a bit more precision – since the dimension of power is integral to the construction of ignorance or knowledge, I've decided to focus on Muslim-led nation-states. But which Muslim states? This connects with the 'where' part of the question – climate change is a global crisis, but it has specific drivers and implications in different geographical locations. The choice of which states to analyse is therefore also a geopolitical consideration and requires the development of basic, usable criteria.

Two effective criteria could help us to choose some illustrative examples. First, to what extent does a particular Muslim state exercise dominant influence or control over our understandings of Islam? Second, to what extent does this Muslim state acknowledge its own contributions and responsibility in tackling climate change – or, to what extent is a Muslim state willing to make *tawbah* about its own sins in perpetrating environmental injustice? The combination of these two variables produces four 'ideal types' of Muslim states that can be studied, as follows.

First – a state which demonstrates true *tawbah* on the climate crisis *and* commands universal respect from the *ummah* regarding its application of Islamic teachings. This would be our Islamic equivalent of the Holy Grail. Sadly, such a utopian state does not exist.

Second – a Muslim state that is relatively minor in terms of its actual power to influence global Islam, yet seems to demonstrate *tawbah* in regard to climate change. Such a state does exist, on paper at least – Malaysia, often seen as the *ummah*'s underdog. But underneath the sheen of its ethical and green Islamic projects, we will explore whether Malaysia really is as committed as it seems in tackling environmental injustice.

Third, there are several more states which lack influence in regards to their take on Islamic teachings *and* which seem not to be handling the climate crisis particularly well, even on paper. These states can be regarded as the *ummah*'s wake-up call – we will look at Egypt, as it provides a clear illustration of the problem even as it is set to host the major UN climate talks, COP27, in November 2022. Egypt's position in relation to its influence on global Islam needs some explaining – whilst it is home to the much-respected Al Azhar University and historical dynamism in relation to Muslim thought leadership, Egypt is technically a secular state that has declined in its ability to exert Islamic influence globally.

Finally, regarding a state that consistently blocks efforts to address climate change whilst enjoying disproportionate influence on the global politics of Islam, we have a candidate *par excellence* – the Kingdom of Saudi Arabia.

The prototypes represented by Egypt, Malaysia and Saudi Arabia map neatly onto three Qur'anic concepts which can be interpreted as categories of ignorance or denial. *Jahiliyyah* (5:50) is basically a description of plain and overt ignorance – the example of Egypt's historical response to climate change will illustrate this. But how might we describe a country like Malaysia – a 'moderate', 'model' yet marginal Muslim state that seems to be saying and doing all the right things on the global stage whilst suppressing social and environmental justice movements at home? The Qur'anic term *munafiq* (Chapter 63), or hypocrite, fits. Finally, the Qur'anic term for the act of setting oneself up as a Divine authority whilst defiling Allah's creation – *shirk* (associating partners with Allah), for example 7:148-150 and 71:23 – ironically and controversially applies to Saudi Arabia in regard to climate change. The monarchy styles itself as the guardian of Islam's two holiest mosques in Makkah and Madinah and yet, as the world's biggest oil exporter, is one of the stubbornest wreckers of international treaties on social justice and the environment.

Egypt

The Nile Delta is one of three 'mega-deltas' in the world – alongside the Ganges-Brahmaputra in Bangladesh and the Mekong in Vietnam – that is extremely vulnerable to sea-level rise. Egypt is one of the countries that is most exposed to catastrophic sea-level rise – the impacts are already acutely felt. Yet the vulnerability of the Nile Delta population is not merely due to geographical or topographical bad luck – it is also socially produced, via the mismanagement and corruption of the Egyptian state. While the regime of Hosni Mubarak (who governed from 1981 to 2011), for example, was vaunted by Egypt's Western sponsors as a neoliberal success story, the countryside became increasingly militarised and mass unemployment skyrocketed alongside demand for housing.

The social crises unleashed by Mubarak's neoliberal policies eventually led the regime to initiate a national scheme for settling and developing 'reclaimed lands' in 1987, known as the Mubarak Project. This was a grand plan to reclaim marginal, mostly desert land through irrigation, fertilisation, cultivation and human settlement as a means of providing housing to unemployed youth. In the 1990s, they were joined by evicted land tenants. According to the scholar-activist in the field of human ecology, Andreas Malm, and his co-researcher, the Iranian activist Shora Esmailian, the Project was emblematic of the recurring motifs of the Mubarak era – 'unemployment, dispossession of farmers, agribusiness expansion, and dependency on international institutions'.

What the Mubarak regime was ignorant of, however, was that the foundations of the Nile Delta were already undermined by the Aswan dams – the Low Dam built by the British in 1902 and the High Dam by Gamal Abdel Nasser in the 1960s. The northern sector of the Delta is actually sinking as a result. This sinking, coupled with global warming, has produced a slow but steady sea level rise and salinisation of the soil – in theory, people can settle in the 'reclaimed lands' but they are unable to grow anything in the salty, sinking ground. To overcome crop failure, farmers have had to resort to pouring sand on the land to raise it artificially above the salty water table, and they have to do it more and more frequently. But sand rarely comes for free – there is now a black market for it. This unprecedented procurement of sand, in turn, depletes the naturally occurring sand dunes and destroys their ability to form barriers against floods and storms.

In short, at the very time when vulnerable people need the most protection from the ravages of the climate emergency, the Mubarak Project has actually worsened their suffering and dispossession. The

Project therefore exemplifies *jahiliyyah* – through the experiences of a Muslim-led state that actively sowed the seeds of climate breakdown amongst its population through its own ignorance.

Malaysia

At the 2015 United Nations Conference on Climate Change in Paris (COP21), Malaysia made a commitment to reduce its carbon emissions per unit of GDP by 45 per cent, from 2005 levels, by the year 2030. The Malaysian government, via the Malaysian Green Technology Corporation (GreenTech Malaysia), launched an ambitious Low Carbon Cities Framework. This laudable commitment was preceded by Malaysia's launching of a green sukuk, or Islamic bond, in 2017, which can be used to fund environmentally sustainable projects, such as facilities for renewable energy generation. The Assistant Governor of the Central Bank of Malaysia said the country is 'at the forefront of green sukuk' – the 'preferred mode of investment for those that prefer investments with a positive environmental impact'. Even Wall Street luminaries are behind the idea that green sukuk will be vital for achieving the goals of the historic Paris Agreement that was reached at COP21.

The devil is in the details. Malaysia has made all the right noises and launched all the right frameworks and financial policies to demonstrate its leadership in global climate action. Yet the story at home is starkly different. Throughout the 1980s and 1990s, the Malaysian government also instituted neoliberal policies that degraded the environment and violated human rights, including development projects involving land grabs for dam construction, timber logging, highway construction, mega shopping complexes, and high-rise luxury apartments. Many of these projects also involved dispossessing Orang Asli and Orang Asal (indigenous peoples) of their land and livelihoods through deforestation.

Malaysian authorities are experts in ignoring or downplaying public opposition regarding the state's environmental policies. For example, despite widespread protests from local communities – not just the usual suspects amongst hardcore environmentalists – the government approved the construction of a rare earth refinery plan by the Australian company Lynas Corporation in 2012 in the state of Pahang. Rare earth metals are used in products such as smart-phones, flat-screen television sets, hybrid cars and computers, and produce radioactive waste. Yet the state-controlled Malaysian media was awash with headlines declaring the safety of the Lynas plant, and its legal triumph as a 'victory' for ordinary Malaysians against the pesky protesters who were portrayed as aping neo-colonial Western environmentalists. These sycophantic media reports were made worse by the political regime's suppression of freedom of information and expression, for example, through the Official Secrets Act.

The Lynas case remains one of several environmental scandals that the Malaysian government has been embroiled in, notwithstanding its sweet-sounding announcements about the Paris Agreement. To this day, deforestation continues at an alarming rate, further dispossessing indigenous peoples. This is significant because, while the majority of the world's carbon emissions are caused by the burning of fossil fuels, the remainder are largely the result of deforestation and the burning of vegetation. Meanwhile, Malaysia continues to experience an increasing frequency and intensity of deadly landslides and flooding, most recently in late 2021 and early 2022, largely as a result of rampant deforestation and environmental damage. Malaysia thus fits into the category of climate-change *munafiq* – for flaunting its commitment to 'green' Islamic finance whilst continuing its rampage against the environment and vulnerable populations.

Saudi Arabia

At COP21, the historic UN conference on climate change in Paris, 2015, Saudi Arabia tried its best keep the 1.5°C limit on global warming out of the agreement. According to the Climate Action Network – which comprises over 1,300 environmental civil society organisations in over 130 countries – the Saudis tried 'to torpedo three years of hard science, commissioned by governments, that clearly [showed] 2 degrees warming is too much for vulnerable communities around the world'. The Network therefore awarded the Kingdom their Fossil of the Day Award, alongside Norway and the US. Saudi Arabia also ranked at the bottom of the Climate Change Performance Index that year, which measured 'actual per capital emissions, emission trends, the use of renewable energy, energy intensity in the economy, and an overall assessment of climate policies'. It was joined by other countries well-known for their rogue positions at international climate conferences, including Australia.

The gallery of climate villains is not mainly represented by Muslim states. But it does force Muslims, especially, to ask how we got here, especially if a noble concept like *ilm* is supposedly such an integral part of our spiritual and ethical bloodstream. Significantly, this was not a one-off with Saudi Arabia – it has won multiple Fossil Awards from the Climate Action Network, including at the 2009 Copenhagen summit. Saudi Arabia is also no stranger to controversies on issues of social justice. From its killing of journalists and political dissidents, exploitation of migrant workers, and persecution of Shi'a Muslims, dissenting Muslims and women, to its direct and indirect involvement in numerous wars in the Middle East and beyond, the Saudis are a case study *par excellence* in the relationship between *ilm* and ignorance. But developing this analysis requires more extensive discussion on the Kingdom's history of energy policies.

On a pragmatic level, it is perfectly understandable why Saudi Arabia is reluctant to support global efforts to combat the climate crisis – addressing the crisis will require a dramatic shift in the Kingdom's energy production and consumption, with immediate economic consequences. And the Saudis are hardly unique. For decades, oil companies and the lobbyists and politicians aligned to them have also tried to make people doubt the human-induced causes of climate change, especially the burning of fossil fuels.

The significant production of oil in Saudi Arabia and other Arab countries started in earnest in the 1930s, leading to the breakneck pace of their development in the ensuing decades. In the latter half of the twentieth century, Saudi Arabia became the world's most important energy producer. Through its domination of the Organisation of Petroleum Exporting Countries (OPEC), it called the shots on global exports of petroleum and oil prices. In the 1970s, OPEC commanded more than sixty per cent of global oil production. The growth of non-OPEC production from countries such as Russia, currently the world's second-largest oil producer, has diminished OPEC's influence somewhat in the twenty-first century.

Still, Saudi Arabia's influence is set to continue, since it possesses the world's largest proven oil reserves. For decades now, Riyadh's petrodollars have secured it the political and military backing from the US and significant influence in politics in the Middle East. The Saudis even sell oil to the US at a discount, in what amounts to a subsidy. When the Soviets invaded Afghanistan in 1979, President Jimmy Carter declared that the US would go to war, if necessary, to defend the Gulf monarchies. The Saudis returned the favour by initiating and sponsoring armed Islamic resistance to the Soviet occupation. A decade later, the Carter Doctrine came into force when President George H. W. Bush rolled back Saddam Hussein's invasion of Kuwait.

The Saudis and the other Gulf oil monarchies did not only become the 'strategic heartland of America's security'. In addition to powering the US's suburban commuter belts, Saudi oil fuelled massive post-war economic booms in West Germany and Japan. At the same time, oil helped the Gulf monarchies to lift their populations out of poverty. Huge subsidies on energy formed key components of national development plans that provided jobs, education, healthcare, and housing to subjects who became wealthy and complacent. In return, these subjects gave their loyalty to their oil-drenched monarchy. This is partly why, as many other parts of the world are becoming more energy efficient, Saudi Arabia consumes ten times more oil than the global average per unit of Gross Domestic Product. This has produced disastrous climate change impacts even *within* the Kingdom's own borders, including record-breaking temperatures of over 50°C in the burning summers of 2016 and 2017. Still, carbon emissions from the Gulf continue to increase, currently at five percent per year since 1990 compared to the global average of two percent.

Like its smaller Gulf siblings, Saudi Arabia is now caught between a rock and a hard place. It belongs to a region that is one of the most climate-stressed in the world and in need of drastic greenhouse gas mitigation. If it does nothing, the Arabian Peninsula might be completely uninhabitable by the end of *this* century. At the same time, oil exports are its economic lifeline and the main reason for its protection by the US. Ignoring the climate crisis will lead to an existential threat, but addressing the crisis by reducing fossil fuel production and consumption could trigger catastrophic economic and security crises.

Given this background, it becomes pertinent to ask if Saudi Arabia's image has been affected at all amongst the global population of Muslims. A 2013 survey by the Pew Research Centre showed that the Kingdom of Saudi Arabia still enjoyed largely favourable views from Muslims outside the Middle East. For example, 95 percent of those surveyed in Pakistan viewed Saudi Arabia favourably, while six-in-ten or more in Indonesia, Senegal and Malaysia shared this sentiment. This proportion, however, dipped significantly within the Middle East, especially in Lebanon and Palestine. In Turkey, more than half of those surveyed held unfavourable views of the Saudis, with only 26 percent holding favourable views. Within the region, only respondents from Jordan and Egypt held overwhelmingly positive views of the Kingdom, at 88 percent and 78 percent respectively.

The Kingdom still holds a lot of spiritual authority for Muslims the world over, especially through its role as the Custodian of the Two Holy Shrines – Al-Haram Mosque in Makkah and the Prophet's Mosque in Medina. This effect can be glimpsed from the research conducted by Daniel Nilsson DeHanas at King's College London with young British Bangladeshis in Tower Hamlets, comparing their experiences of 'roots visits' to Bangladesh with the Islamic pilgrimage to Makkah. A couple of impressions of Saudi Arabia are worth reproducing in full, the first from a young man and the second from a young woman:

> [In Mecca] there is no difference between man and woman, there's no differ-ence between poor and rich – they're a minister or they're just a labourer driving a rickshaw or taxi driver. Everyone's equal from the ground. Everyone.

> Everyone [in Mecca was] a community, there was no difference in anyone, I didn't feel any different to the person standing next to me, even though they were a different colour to me, a different gender, I didn't feel any different, whereas here [in Britain], the person next to me is totally different to me, there everyone just feels united, cos we're all there for the same purpose.

In short, the majority of DeHanas's respondents from London's East End idealised Makkah and Medina as places where 'Islam is egalitarian and unadulterated', with many 'blissfully unaware of the low standing that Bangladeshis have in the Saudi status hierarchy'. The few respondents who did contest the Kingdom's moral image kept this separate from their positive experiences of pilgrimage.

In a nutshell, these responses – idealisation and mild criticism – also characterise some scholarly responses to Saudi Arabia's position on the climate crisis. On the side of mild criticism, the scholar of environmental policy Saleem H. Ali acknowledges Islam's 'inertial' position on climate change compared to its Abrahamic siblings. At the same time, Ali sees signs of hope in the 'environmental leadership' emerging in the Arabian Peninsula, including support for the 2015 Islamic Declaration of Climate Change. The fact that the Declaration was supported by bodies such as the Organisation of Islamic Conference and the Saudi-based International Islamic Fiqh Academy despite clause 3.4 – which calls for divestment from fossil fuels – indicated that the Gulf monarchies were being 'prudent'. But even this constructive criticism reads like censure compared to the philosopher Norman K. Swazo's strong defence of Saudi Arabia's stance at the 2009 Copenhagen summit. The Kingdom, Swazo argues, opposed the talks due to its desire for a 'win-win strategy' based on Islamic ideals, including a quest for 'compensatory justice' and 'distributive justice'.

Are these responses justified? Are criticisms of Saudi Arabia's energy and climate policies too harsh? To answer these questions requires another piece of the puzzle – the power that the Kingdom derives from its oil revenues to control the global discourse on Islam.

With regards to the religious establishment, the oil boom produced one significant impact, referred to by Bruce Lawrence as the 'Saudi juggernaut'. In 1984, the King Fahd Complex for Printing the Holy Qur'an was established in Medina under the Ministry of Islamic Affairs. It produces ten million copies of the Qur'an each year, including translations, to be distributed within and beyond the Kingdom's borders. The Complex not only produces but also monitors access to the Qur'an and the study of it.

The Saudi-endorsed English translation of the Qur'an, by Muhammad Taqiuddin al-Hilali and Muhammad Muhsin Khan, has been described by a Muslim reviewer as reading 'more like a supremacist Muslim, anti-Semitic, anti-Christian polemic than a rendition of Islamic scripture'. For example, the opening sura or chapter of the Qur'an, Al-Fatihah, contains verses which are widely rendered by numerous Muslim translators as follows: 'Guide us to the straight path, the path of those whom You have favoured, not of those who have incurred Your wrath, nor of those who have gone astray.' In the Khan-Hilali translation, this becomes: 'Guide us to the Straight Way, the way of those on whom You have bestowed Your Grace, not (the way) of those who have earned Your anger (such as the Jews), nor of those who went astray (such as the Christians).'

This juggernaut has not been confined to distributing copies and translations of the Qur'an. The oil boom also resulted in a flourishing of opaque, often untraceable Saudi funding for Muslim missionary efforts overseas. The London-based Saudi Arabian anthropologist Madawi Al-Rasheed suggests that the increase in the number of mosques in Britain – 'between three- and fourfold after 1974' – was a direct outcome of the Kingdom's oil boom. In the 1980s, when the Saudis were supporting resistance against the Soviets in Afghanistan, the British government gave clearance for preachers to enter and enlist young British Muslim recruits for military jihad.

It would be a mistake, however, to ignore the backlash from Muslims towards Saudi Arabia within and outside the Kingdom. It would also be lazy to label the Kingdom as a Wahhabi 'theocracy', as some commentators do. Rather, it is important to remember the symbiotic relationship between the Wahhabi religious establishment and the Saudi monarchy as two separate institutions. As Al-Rasheed puts it, 'from its early eighteenth-century history, it [Wahhabiyya] developed religious interpretations to legitimise political power which led to deep grounding in authoritarianism, and even despotism, within Islam'. The Saudi state is therefore not a Wahhabi state per se. Rather, as Al-Rasheed stresses, Saudi policies are determined by 'a coterie of individuals who do not have Wahhabiyya as their reference paradigm, but who use it as a convenient device to cloak their personal political activities'.

Besides, Wahhabism in Saudi Arabia is increasingly fragmented between the pragmatic, state-supporting 'official' components and the revolutionary, sometimes extremely violent, jihadist strands that oppose the Saudi regime. What is often rendered invisible by this dynamic is the emergence of Saudi reformers – including religiously trained leaders –

who are questioning interpretations of Islam that demonise non-Muslims, Muslim minorities, and the state-appointed moral police.

In other words, the production of wilful ignorance is built into the DNA of the Saudi Kingdom's religious and monarchical systems. Some pious and believing Muslims *within* the Kingdom see through this façade and, at great risk, are trying to recover more just and egalitarian expressions of Islam. But they are up against a formidable enemy – the Kingdom has the power and resources to continue projecting itself as the true guardian of global Islam. And this vision of Islam involves thoroughly denying any culpability or responsibility for the climate emergency. The Kingdom of Saudi Arabia thus fits the typology for *shirk* – associating partners with Allah – by designating itself as *the* arbiter of Islam even as it aids and abets the wanton destruction of Allah's creation and the repression of truth-tellers within its borders.

The examples of Egypt, Malaysia and Saudi Arabia in relation to *ilm* and the climate crisis paint a bleak and brutal picture. They illustrate the role of state power in constructing wilful ignorance, including the repression and victimisation of the populations that are most vulnerable to the impacts of climate change as a result of social injustice. But my point is that it is entirely possible to rebalance this picture by examining another approach to *ilm* – a tradition of knowing through the heart or conscience that pierces the core of Islamic legal scholarship.

A hadith has it that a companion once approached the Prophet with a question about sin and righteousness. The Prophet prodded the companion's chest three times, saying 'ask your heart, ask yourself' each time. The Prophet then said, 'Righteousness is that which the heart feels at ease with and the soul is content with and sin is that which troubles the heart and causes doubts in the chest, even if people pass fatwa (of permissibility) for you and give you verdicts.' This 'fatwa of the heart' can sound arbitrary – but only if it is divorced from the concept of acknowledgement, or *tawbah*, explored above. There are many touching and inspiring examples of people seeking a fatwa of the heart in relation to issues of social and environmental injustice. Perhaps the most relevant example for my analysis is the UK-based network for Islamic ecology and permaculture – Wisdom in Nature (WiN).

Wisdom in Nature

WiN began its life in 2004 under a different name – the London Islamic Network for the Environment (LINE). According to its founder Muzammal Hussain, LINE emerged out of his slow realisation in the 1990s that there were very few Muslims who explicitly wanted to focus on environmental justice in the UK. The few who did exist felt isolated and, in Hussain's observation, the phrase 'I thought I was the only one' almost became a mantra in those small circles. Through patient and persistent engagement through e-mail lists and in-person gatherings, Hussain eventually founded LINE.

LINE initially held open monthly forums in central London that reflected on a range of themes, 'from Qur'anic reflections to "Green Economics"; from peace activism to biofuels; from forum theatre to modern social movements; from Palestine to food and farming', and more. Soon, those involved in LINE realised that their concerns could not be placed into a neat box labelled 'the environment'. Their concerns were holistic and interconnected, spanning human rights, economic justice, societal equality, spirituality and, of course, environmental flourishing – often explored through conscious group work. And although the group's ethos was firmly derived from Islamic principles, they intended their reach and sources of learning to be universal. This is why, in 2009, LINE became WiN. The core team of WiN representatives and helpers – consisting of Hussain, Shumaisa Khan, and Valentina Maccario, whose day-to-day work with WiN is entirely voluntary – produce newsletters, web resources and online gatherings for anyone with an interest in the connections between spirituality, ecology and social justice.

Some of the discussions at WiN would be familiar to anyone who is exposed to the work of other Islamic environmental outfits in the UK, such as the Birmingham-based Islamic Foundation for Ecology and Environmental Science (IFEES). Groups such as IFEES rightfully remind Muslims that Islam contains a rich treasury of systems and institutions that can be revived in the service of environmental conservation. Examples include *hima* (a multiple-use conservation area that can be established and administered by state authorities or local communities), *harem* (a sacred area which is designated to exclude human use) and *waqf* (a financial trust or any other asset that is set aside as an endowment for social and spiritual benefits, including education, health, culture, animal sanctuaries, and the environment).

The application of this Islamic outlook and this list of historical examples is not new. Writing in 1985, Ziauddin Sardar already identified the precedents of *hima*, *harem*, and *waqf* as core principles in Islamic environmental ethics, and added an architectural dimension in the concept of the 'Islamic city' as a means of preserving ecological balance in urban environments. These examples are currently being established and promoted by the Gulf monarchies, including Saudi Arabia. These efforts are salutary, but given the fossil fuel behemoth that is Saudi Arabia, vaunting them as viable Islamic solutions to climate breakdown is the equivalent of using buckets of water to douse a forest fire.

In my experience as a relative newcomer to their events and resources – and, for the purposes of transparency, a regular monthly donor now – WiN takes these concepts and others like them and goes deeper. For example, one online workshop I attended involved a collective reflection and discussion on the Qur'anic concept of *fasaad* – 'corruption' or 'mischief' – to develop a political analysis of environmental and social injustice. Another online workshop discussed the learnings of the WiN core team from the Zapatistas – a revolutionary indigenous movement based in southern Mexico. The Zapatistas work with villages to subvert the dominant neo-liberal paradigm and have developed multiple autonomous, self-governing communities. According to WiN, this is a social movement based on 'deep purpose-driven base building, intensive skilling-up, and disciplined grassroot organising'. Participants at this workshop spent a couple of hours reflecting upon the aspects of the Zapatista struggle that resonated with our core spiritual beliefs and motivations. Attending these workshops, reading WiN newsletters, and regularly visiting their website, I feel that WiN – although small and humble – offers an alternative model of *ilm* for the *ummah*, and an antidote to ignorance.

I began with Ebrahim Moosa's call for Muslims to ask 'uncomfortable questions' as part of our 'responsibility of learning and faith'; and the dichotomy he identifies between Islamic modernists and traditionalists: modernists seek to rethink the whole system of Islam whilst traditionalists insist on finding solid precedents in the Islamic past. On balance, conceptions of *ilm* still uphold the traditionalist paradigm at the expense of finding concrete solutions to new problems.

Moosa illustrates this phenomenon by outlining an 'effective psychological trick' that can be played on Muslim audiences to win a debate on any crucial issue – just tell them that 'some past authority', such as Tabari, Abu Hanifa, or al-Shafi'i, 'held such an enlightening position on matter X, so why do you lesser mortals not adopt it'. Sadly, this also seems to describe the conventional state of *ilm* about something as existentially threatening as the climate crisis. How else can we characterise the paradox of upholding historical concepts such as *hima*, *harem* and *waqf* as Islamic environmental solutions even whilst many Muslim governments are responsible for environmental degradation and social injustice within their own borders? Perhaps if some Grand Mufti somewhere finds a *hadith* (prophetic Tradition) or a tenth century legal tract that tells us it was religiously obligatory to oppose Caliph Y for extracting and burning petroleum, we might get there.

This might sound like a caricature, but Moosa makes a similar point about 'text fundamentalism' – something both Islamic traditionalists and modernists have been guilty of. In part, this sort of orientation towards Islam's sacred sources 'perpetuates the fiction that the text actually provides the norms, and we merely "discover" the norms'. Moosa argues, to the contrary, that we *make* the norms 'in conversation with the revelatory text'. For this reason, early Muslim jurists often gave verdicts that seemingly contradicted the explicit sense of the revealed text because they prioritised the requirements of their own immediate social contexts. They did not do this willy-nilly, but employed sophisticated hermeneutical strategies. Thus, despite the Qur'anic text allowing for 'disobedient' wives to be chastised, some classical jurists argued that causing injury to the wife by beating was grounds for divorce. Another example – Abu Hanifa held no objections to non-Muslims entering the holy city of Makkah, despite an explicit Qur'anic injunction that deems 'polytheists' to be unclean and thus forbidden from entering the sacred mosque.

This legacy of flexible and context-sensitive religious interpretation is a gift for our continuing commitment to pursue and apply *ilm* holistically. Yet there is a further stumbling block – the need, according to traditional Islamic thought, for *ilm* to be vouchsafed by a 'legitimate authority'. This concept of 'authority' has, over the centuries, been narrowed to become synonymous with traditionally trained, invariably male, religious scholars. Perhaps it is time to rethink what it means to be recognised as a 'legitimate authority' in Islamic terms. This does not mean calling for the abolition of *ulama* or mullahs. But it does force us to ask who the real authorities are regarding the climate crisis, especially when the vast majority of Muslim religious and political leaders seem to have abdicated intellectual and ethical responsibility. Do we rely on so-called 'authorities' who pronounce on the matter in the abstract? Or do we need to listen to actual victims who suffer the disproportionate impacts of climate breakdown – indigenous peoples, women, children, older people, exploited workers, refugees, and people with disabilities?

The examples of Egypt, Malaysia and Saudi Arabia show that *ilm* and ignorance are products of systemic power, but the example of WiN shows that the power of resistance is also kindled by our conscience. There is no excuse to remain ignorant about victims of abuses perpetrated by Muslim-led or non-Muslim governments, businesses and other vested interests. This means that *ilm* must necessarily be a co-investigation and a co-creation between traditional Islamic authorities and other knowledge specialists, including marginalised and oppressed peoples. And it must always involve a frank and humbling search for a fatwa of the heart. Sounds like a basic and simple answer, but consider the obstacles. Moosa lists the fairly established modern Muslim thinkers who were 'harassed', had their 'lives turned into a misery', ultimately 'resulting in their marginalisation or exile' for their troubles, including Nasr Hamid Abu Zayd, Muhammad Iqbal and Fazlur Rahman. And remember, these were all *men*. Imagine the struggles awaiting women or Muslims from minority or underprivileged backgrounds.

To conclude, *ilm* is a concept that does provide us with the tools to address the most vexing problems of our times. At the same time, some of these tools have been prised out of our hands – often forcibly – and this is what has fostered systemic ignorance in vast segments of the *ummah*. This is what has resulted in contemporary manifestations of *jahiliyyah*, *munafiq* and *shirk* about the climate crisis in the actions of many Muslim governments. Recovering these tools will require Herculean effort, humility, and trust in Allah by making *tawbah* (acknowledgement or repentance) and always applying a fatwa of the heart. It will also require courage. The climate crisis demonstrates that the costs of not having the courage to uphold the ideals of *ilm* are too great. If *ilm* is indeed a central Islamic tenet, then anything short of a comprehensive approach to social and environmental justice would be a dereliction of our moral and religious duty. Without a reimagined *ilm*, Muslim societies simply cannot meet the existential challenges presented by climate change.

MUSLIM TRADITIONS OF LEARNED IGNORANCE

William Franke

In my work on apophatic mysticism and philosophies of the unsayable, I have often encountered outstanding figures of genius who have made unmistakable the eminent role that Muslims have played in developing knowledge which, at its truest and highest, cannot but be an *unknowing* knowing. These voices and visionaries from medieval Muslim tradition are among the finest and subtlest witnesses illuminating our human predicament in which knowledge that can claim genuine universality can only be cast in the mode of learned ignorance. However, the wisdom of unknowing is one that needs to be approached cross-culturally because only the limits of any and every culture can open the dimension of the universal as transcending all cultures and their historically relative terms. Muslim culture, in this regard truly cognate with its Jewish and Christian sister cultures, has made strong claims to universality throughout its history. These claims have also been based on the sense of a transcendent divinity as source of all truth and value and as approachable for humans only by negative ways and means. In this essay, I explore these themes by looking at the mystical philosophy of Ibn al-Arabi, ineffability in the poetry of Rumi, and self-reflection in Arab medieval thinkers I compare them with similar notions in Western mystical traditions.

Ibn al-Arabi and Mystic Philosophy

Called the 'supreme master' or 'greatest shaikh' (*al-Shaikh al-akbar*), Ibn al-Arabi (1165–1240) is widely recognised as representing the peak of speculation in the mystic current of Islamic tradition known as 'Sufism.' He was born in Murcia in Andalusia into the midst of the great age of Muslim influence over the southern Iberian Peninsula from the eighth through the fifteenth century. However, with the rising power of the Almohads, generally suspicious of Sufis, he migrated from Spain to North Africa and thence to the Near East, summoned to Mecca in a vision and eventually settling in Damascus. Alongside the voluminous *Meccan Revelations* (*al-Futuhat al-Makkiyah*), the *Bezels of Wisdom* (*Fusus al-Hikam*) counts as his major work from among about 400 extant treatises that can be genuinely attributed to him.

Like Sufis before him and especially like al-Ghazali (1058–111), Ibn al-Arabi's principal emphasis is on the oneness of truth and the unity of being (*wahdat al-wujud*). Wisdom is to wake up to one's own identity with Reality (*al-Haqq*: the Real, the True), with Being-Perception. Outside this Oneness, all is illusion. Whatever is, to the extent that it is, cannot but be really just this oneness. Even the illusion of separateness belongs intrinsically to Reality's consciousness of itself.

Everything that exists, or is at all, manifests the one divine Reality. Thus: 'He may be defined by every definition.' Of course, such definitions state not the divine essence—which cannot be said—but only its Names or modes. The Real, as absolutely unmanifest and incapable of becoming manifest, is absolutely different from all its Names. Yet all that they really *are* is nothing different from it. Reality is One, and all that is is from and of Him (*hu*), is in fact identical with Him as to its being or reality. Although 'strictly speaking no predication is possible' with regard to it, the Absolute is nevertheless qualified as absolute being or essence or existence – as 'existence viewed in its unconditional simplicity.'

Ibn al-Arabi is working from the mainstream metaphysical tradition flowing from Plotinus and his Neoplatonic heirs. He resembles most closely Parmenides in affirming that Being alone is one and that all else is appearance. Yet Ibn al-'Arabi also places an emphasis on the immanence of this metaphysical principle to the world of appearance. Any doctrine of pure transcendence of divine Reality he condemns as a misrepresentation. The Cosmos is the manifestation of divine Reality, in effect, the divine Name. Even as the Unmanifest, this divine Reality is apprehended in relation not to abstract thought of transcendence but rather in the manifest forms of the Cosmos.

This valorisation of the sensible world as mystical revelation is crystallised, for example, in Ibn al-Arabi's *The Interpreter of Desires*, poems inspired by the feminine charms of an enrapturing virgin of Mecca. Ibn al-Arabi took pains to exonerate himself of charges of sensual concupiscence by writing voluminous commentaries on the mystical meanings of these poems. The parallel to Dante's relation to Beatrice is not inapt: both cases suggest how metaphysical vision, when given a mystical emphasis, can twist back round towards vigorous affirmation of the senses. This legacy from Dante develops in Christian epic and prophetic poetry through Torquato Tasso (1544–1595) and John Milton (1608–1674) to William Blake (1757–1827) and Walt Whitman (1819–1892). But just such a reappraisal of sense experience in its revelatory capacity appeared much earlier in Ibn al-Arabi.

One of his masterpieces of apophatic rhetoric of negation and tautology is the *Treatise on Unity*. God is nothing that can be said or seen or known or formulated in any way. He is totally unique and incomparable and like only himself. The self must annihilate itself and know itself as nothing in order to approach the experience of God. But then it can experience God in everything. In fact, only God exists. Nothing and no one else is anything except in identity with God, and this can be realised only in the realisation of one's own utter nullity. Ibn al-Arabi takes the Islamic confession that there is no God but God in a strong sense to mean that there is no other being whatsoever besides God: nothing exists except God. This would be outright pantheism, except that the approach is from God to world rather than the other way around. God is not degraded to identity with things; he is in no way any thing. Rather, all things are nothing, except in him.

As in Christian and other mysticisms, the individual (rational) soul attains perfection and unity by its own annihilation (*fana*). In Islamic philosophy, al-Ghazali had described this stage as annihilation or extinction in unity. He is the fundamental precursor for Ibn al-Arabi, as well as for philosophical writers such as Ibn Tufayl and Ibn Rushd. Ibn Tufayl's philosophical tale *Hayy Ibn Yaqzan* is rich in apophatic passages concerning mystical experience of 'a world indescribable without misrepresentation'. He pays acute attention to specifically linguistic limits and failure: 'the ambition to put this into words is reaching for the impossible – like wanting to taste colours, expecting black as such to taste either sweet or sour.' Ibn al-Arabi turns the negative theology of Ibn Tufayl and Ibn Rushd, with whom he had direct contact, in a deliberately mystical direction and produces thereby perhaps the most deeply felt speculative reflection of Sufi mysticism on the ineffability of the divine.

The apophatic themes that subtend the whole of Sufi culture emerge with particular force and clarity from the 'bezel' or 'ring-setting' that interprets the figure of Noah in the Qur'an. Unqualified affirmation of either transcendence or immanence with respect to God is flawed. Noah's affirmation, merely of transcendence, limits the deity over the world. Only the dialectic between these two alternatives, their cancelling each other out, enacts the meaning event in which apophasis essentially consists. Neither transcendence nor immanence can be affirmed without the other. By such dialectic, Ibn al-Arabi critiques a polytheistic, as well as a strictly unitarian conception of God. Of course, uncompromising emphasis on the identity of all-in-one courts charges of pantheism. And Sufism, especially in the radical form it takes on in Ibn al-Arabi's arduous speculations, was oftentimes under suspicion from the religious authorities for infractions against the monotheistic premises of Muslim doctrine. The conflict with rigid doctrinal orthodoxy was inevitable, since for Sufis knowledge is personal rather than objective. Indeed, they acknowledge no division of subject and object. Essential to Sufism is the endeavour to re-live the Qur'anic revelation at a more interior level in ecstasy of spirit by a personal appropriation of religious truth.

The theory of the divine Names is developed in many of the twenty-seven chapters of *The Bezels of Wisdom*, but particularly in the chapters interpreting the Words of the prophets Enoch, Shu'aib, and Joseph. Ibn Arabi writes that every Name 'implies the [divine] Essence' and indeed '*is* the one Named,' yet never as Himself but rather always as other and as 'representing some particular aspect.' The divine Names 'require our existence,' but the Essence itself is completely independent of the divine Names. That the divine Names are contingent on our existence implies that God Himself is Nameless. All that can be said or made manifest belongs to the sphere of revelation of the Names of God and is infinitely removed from His Reality as such.

Rumi and Mystic Poetry

Jalal al-Din Rumi's (1207–1273) name, from 'Rum', 'Rome' in Persian, probably indicates that he came from the western, formerly Roman half of

Anatolia, that is, Byzantium (the Eastern Roman Empire). He was well-established as a learned Islamic teacher and preacher (a *mullah*), when, at the age of 37, his encounter with the wandering dervish, Shams of Tabriz, transformed him into an ecstatic mystical poet. Rumi's creative and personal life remained closely bound up with that of Shams. The poems were composed and executed as a chant accompaniment to sacred dancing by dervishes. This resulted in Rumi's founding of the Mevlevi order of the 'Whirling Dervishes'.

Rumi pursues in verse the Sufi vision that is brought to its philosophical and theological zenith by Ibn al-Arabi, whom he could possibly have met directly in Konya, Anatolia, where he lived and is buried. His poems, collected in the *Mathnawi* (rhyming or 'spiritual' couplets) and *Divani Shamsi Tabriz*, consisting in quatrains (*rubaiyat*) and odes (*ghazals*), in turn were enormously influential upon subsequent Sufism. Speaking out of the experience of ecstatic love and enlightenment, their constant deferral to experience beyond the reach of words makes them eminently merit the epithet 'mystical'. A. J. Arberry, the noted British scholar of Arabic literature and translator of the Qur'an, offers the view that 'in Rumi we encounter one of the world's greatest poets. In profundity of thought, inventiveness of image, and triumphant mastery of language, he stands out as the supreme genius of Islamic mysticism'. Such views have been current ever since Hegel in his *Encyclopedia of the Philosophical Sciences (1817)* accorded Rumi unique distinction, celebrating him as mystic poet.

Rumi's poems embody and articulate, furthermore, a theory of language according to which all our words bespeak our emptiness. Like the reed cut from the reed bed, we can only express our nostalgia for the source from which we are cut off. Our words are but resonances of this absence that is a silence at our centre. Our emptiness, like the reed's hollowness, is the enabling condition for allowing this silence to resonate:

> Listen to the story told by the reed,
> of being separated.

> 'Since I was cut from the reedbed,
> I have made this crying sound.

> Anyone apart from someone he loves
> understands what I say.

Anyone pulled from a source
longs to go back.

At any gathering I am there,
mingling in the laughing and grieving,

a friend to each, but few
will hear the secrets hidden

within the notes. No ears for that.
Body flowing out of spirit,

spirit up from body: no concealing
that mixing. But it's not given us

to see the soul. The reed flute
is fire, not wind. Be that empty.'

Hear the love fire tangled
in the reed notes, as bewilderment

melts into wine. The reed is a friend
to all who want the fabric torn

and drawn away. The reed is hurt
and salve combining. Intimacy

and longing for intimacy, one
song. A disastrous surrender

and a fine love, together. The one
who secretly hears this is senseless.

A tongue has one customer, the ear.
A sugarcane flute has such effect

because it was able to make sugar
in the reedbed. The sound it makes

is for everyone. Days full of wanting,
let them go by without worrying

that they do. Stay where you are
inside such a pure, hollow note.

Every thirst gets satisfied except
that of these fish, the mystics,

who swim a vast ocean of grace
still somehow longing for it!

No one lives in that without
being nourished every day.

But if someone doesn't want to hear
the song of the reed flute,

it's best to cut conversation
short, say good-bye, and leave.

'The Reed Flute's Song' in *Mathnawi*

Coleman Barks, who also translates the verses quoted above, points out that Persian poems typically end with a reference to the poet as a sort of signature. Rumi concluded five hundred of his odes with the soubriquet *khamush*, 'the Silent'. Barks explains, 'Rumi is less interested in language, more attuned to the sources of it. He keeps asking Husam, "Who's making this music?" He sometimes gives the wording over to the invisible flute player: "let that musician finish this poem"'. For it is not the words as such that count, but what they indicate as beyond saying—the source from which they resound. Rumi says as much in his avowal that,

This is how it always is
when I finish a poem.

A great silence overcomes me,
and I wonder why I ever thought
to use language.

from 'A Thirsty Fish,' Barks' translation

Rumi conceives meaning as an infinite sea that verbal form merely glides across. Speech is but a 'veil for the soul.' His paradoxically verbal soundings of the divine ineffability also retrace poetically the aporias enshrined in the traditional theological problematic of the Divine Names:

Sometimes I call Him wine, sometimes cup,
Sometimes refined gold and sometimes silver ore,
Sometimes grain, sometimes a snare, sometimes a quarry.

Why all this? Because I cannot [or will not] express his name!

The theme of the infinite and ungraspable as present everywhere in everything encountered in experience is pervasive throughout Rumi's work. I pick by way of illustration a couple of poems that bring this apophatic dimension into the foreground more or less explicitly yet still as ensconced inextricably in Rumi's metaphorical language. In Barks's translation:

Praise to the emptiness that blanks out existence. Existence:
This place made from our love for that emptiness!

Yet somehow comes emptiness,
this existence goes.

Praise to that happening, over and over!
For years I pulled my own existence out of emptiness.

Then one swoop, one swing of the arm,
that work is over.

Free of who I was, free of presence, free of dangerous fear, hope,
free of mountainous wanting.
The here-and-now mountain is a tiny piece of a piece of straw
blown off into emptiness.

These words I'm saying so much begin to lose meaning:
Existence, emptiness, mountain, straw:

Words and what they try to say swept
out the window, down the slant of the roof.

> 'The World which is Made of our Love for Emptiness'
> from Divani Shamsi Tabriz

The liberating surrender to emptiness at the far end of language is a powerful motive for para-liturgical praise. Our experience and love of emptiness displaces and realises the more traditional experience and love of God in mystic traditions. This experience of mystic contemplation or

'Quietness' is reached through a series of metaphorical equivalences enacted in one's own being:

> Inside this new love, die.
>
> Your way begins on the other side.
>
> Become the sky.
>
> Take an axe to the prison wall.
>
> Escape.
>
> Walk out like someone suddenly born into color.
>
> Do it now.
>
> You are covered with thick cloud.
>
> Slide out the side. Die,
>
> and be quiet. Quietness is the surest sign
>
> that you have died.
>
> Your old life was a frantic running
>
> from silence.
>
>
> The speechless full moon
>
> comes out now.

'Quietness' from Divani Shamsi Tabriz

Rumi is partially contemporary with Dante (1265–1321), and both are great mystical poets tapping resources of poetic language for expressing things that otherwise cannot be said. Both are explorers of this vast territory in strikingly original ways. Dante brings in another element besides pure poetics of the ineffable and besides purely mystical contemplation such as is found in Rumi. Dante's learned ignorance is based on a Scholastic tradition of philosophical reflection in a critical vein that also has its parallels and, in important respects, predecessors and premises, in Muslim intellectual tradition following in the wake of Aristotle and Greek philosophy. I therefore invoke Dante as counterpart to Rumi in order to transition back toward a more conceptual and philosophical approach to apophatic ignorance.

For Aristotle, at the root of Scholasticism, God is thought thinking itself, and indeed this model of self-reflection remains foundational for knowledge of the highest, metaphysical sort. Yet this high knowing needs to be conjugated with the apophatic or with unknowing knowing. Conversely, negative or apophatic awareness is always bound up with affirmative knowledge. The hinge between the two is the difficult juncture that we need to struggle to contemplate. This juncture can be found operating especially in self-reflection. Knowledge of self is fundamentally a knowledge of one's ignorance – in Socratic wisdom at the source of Greek philosophical thinking. This thinking is developed by Neoplatonist philosophers and forms the common heritage and shared foundation on which philosophy in the monotheistic religious traditions all build. Muslim philosophers have a crucial role in transmitting this knowledge/ignorance of self through the Middle Ages to modernity.

Self-Reflection as Reflection of Transcendence

'Reflection' and 'self-reflection' are modern philosophical terms, but they reconfigure age-old mental activities that were long familiar under other names. 'Speculation' in the Middle Ages was a kind of poetic knowing through analogy with created, physical beings mirroring the metaphysical realm and serving as vehicles for the ascent to God. This is the path followed famously by Bonaventure (1221–1274), the Italian Catholic Franciscan bishop, in *Itinerarium mentis in Deum*. Such mirror vision transpires 'through clouds of corporeal likenesses' and is appropriate for us as finite, sensuous creatures. 'Contemplation', in contrast, was purely intellectual. For the Scottish mystic Richard of St Victor (d. 1173), speculation took place 'when we perceive through a mirror, but *contemplatio* when we see the truth in its purity without any covering and veil of shadow'. The latter mode is like angelic vision. Any such rigid segregation, however, breaks down in Dante, who uses these terms sometimes interchangeably, elaborating on the 'speculativa vita' of the angels under the rubric of the 'contemplative life' as the 'more excellent and divine'.

Yet another crucial strand of medieval tradition emphasised the idea of self-reflection as entailing integrally a reflection of theological transcendence. Islamic thinkers (and Jewish ones, eminently Maimonides, writing also in Arabic) in the centuries directly preceding Dante had developed this notion in precise philosophical and subtly theological terms. Dante's deep debt to this Arabic-Aristotelian philosophy is well known. It becomes explicit especially in his *Convivio*, for example, in the idea of intellectual perfection—*la felicità mentale*—as the epitome of happiness and the goal of human life. Following cues from Aristotle's *Nichomachean Ethics*, the perfection of the intellect by the philosopher counted as blessedness itself and even approached divinisation.

Islamic philosophers, furthermore, translating this into the terms of their revealed religion, viewed prophecy as a matter of intellectual perfection. Ibn Sina (980–1037) placed the prophet at the top of the ladder of knowledge as possessing the highest degree of receptivity to intelligible forms. For ibn Sina, intellection presupposes a conversion of the soul to its Source. This movement is akin to that of the 'separate intellects' or angels who intellectually intuit themselves only in turning to their Source. Intellection requires a conversion of the soul back to its Origin, for only by this conversion does the soul grasp itself. The soul must know itself in and through its Cause or Ground.

Ibn Sina holds, moreover, that the intellect knows interiorly rather than exteriorly: it does not receive intelligibles from an external source but rather reflects them by reflecting on itself and becoming transparent to itself after the prophetic motto: 'Whoever knows himself knows his Lord.' This reflection is a mirror relation that presupposes the simultaneous presence of the soul and the intelligible form that it reflects. If the soul turns away from the intelligible form, the image vanishes - just as a mirror requires the presence in front of it of whatever it reflects. Nevertheless, the initiative for this relation comes ultimately from the intelligible world, which reflects itself in the mirror of human intellect. Self-reflection is most fundamentally the activity of separate (divine) substances that use human intellects as their instruments for self-reflection.

Ibn Rushd advanced the thesis of the unity of intellect (which figures among the propositions condemned in 1277), according to which man is no longer the agent in thinking but is potentially a participant through an exceptional effort of 'separate intellect' in the thinking of intellect itself and as such. 'Intellect thinking itself' was the original and true form of all thinking. Humans, in their limited manner, only take part in it. Human thinking was thus essentially a mirroring of the thinking transpiring in the universal intellect that Ibn Rushd found in the 'separate intellect' of Aristotle's *De Anima*. Ibn Rushd's most truly 'great commentary' in this regard is that on Book Λ of the *Metaphysics*, where Aristotle focuses on thought thinking (or mirroring) itself as the most pleasurable of activities. Only intellect that is always in act, unlike ours, can fully enjoy the pleasure of thinking, and it is at its most intense in *thinking of thinking itself*.

Man's becoming, like the angels, a mirror of divinity was fundamental to the mystical itinerary to God of Islamic thinkers in the Sufi tradition. Al-Ghazali builds on Ibn Sina's theories in order to exalt the religious, revealed, inspired aspect of knowledge in this perspective in which knowing has to pass through and derive from the unity of divinity, which, however, cannot be properly conceived by finite minds. There is thus always an element of *un*knowing that is built in at the foundations of any knowing exercised by human beings. This predicament of un/knowing is expressed in the Islamic tradition by the mirror analogy, with its structure of triangulation through a transcendent term. Speculation thereby renders possible a kind of union of created with increate being – such as is realised especially in the ecstatic state famously by the Persian mystics Mansour Al-Hallaj (858–922) and Bayazid Al-Bistami (804–874). However, the mirror analogy enfolds a reminder that revealed knowledge furnishes a *likeness* and does not exhaust the reality of God, who remains the Unknowable.

Al-Ghazali, as mystical philosopher, champions a knowledge by illumination that simply falls from God into the soul. Still, he is careful to avoid conflating image and reality. Rational knowledge of divinity remains distinct from simple mirror reflection: discursive knowing of causes is not the same as immediate reception of truth as a whole. But which is superior? There is here a deep-seated tension between philosophical and mystical ways of knowing. Is the perfect mirror purely passive, or does the created intellect contribute to the object known by becoming that object itself?

This mystic knowing of nothing, moreover, opens a space for the operation of the imagination. Imaginative construction is necessary in order to make an image of what is properly speaking invisible. Al-Farabi (870–950) developed a theory of symbolic expression based on ontological analogy that presupposes a participative relationship between being and beings beyond all that finite definitions can contain. Words working analogically on the mind prefigure transcendent realities. This bridging prophetically to the transcendent through the imagination was modeled by Ibn Arabi in relation to Al Khadir, his protecting angel. An immediate heavenly connection frees the imagination, as intellectual, to be a truly poetic and productive imagination rather than remaining strictly bound by the senses, as in Aristotle. This conception of imagination in Ibn Arabi owes much also to the Persian theosophist and martyr Sohrawardi (1155–91) with his 'interworld' of images and archetypes.

Direct knowledge of reality in its absoluteness (*haqq*) – as opposed to knowledge that one takes ready-made and formulated from others, without repeating and verifying it in one's own experience – is one of the essential aspects of the knowledge through self-reflection that Dante develops in his poetic odyssey by appropriating insights of Islamic philosophy. This heritage is a mighty challenge for the age of information bites that dominates the economy of knowledge in our electronic age. A strong line of continuity connects Dante with Islamic intellectual wisdom in its potential for mounting a fundamental critique of modernity. We need to leverage this Muslim tradition, as it peaks in Ibn Rushd, indirectly through Dante in constructing the genealogy of an alternative modernity. The derivation from Arabic and especially Sufi philosophy proves to be highly revealing in its inauguration of modern forms of self-reflexivity.

SENSING JINN

Alireza Doostdar

One late night in August 2008 I was enjoying dinner at the home of a college friend in Tehran when I received a worried phone call from my research assistant. Mehdi was breathless and wanted to know if I was ok. A few hours earlier that same day, the two of us had interviewed a fortune-teller and prayer-writer (*do'anevis*) in a cafe on the Western fringe of the city. Mehdi had been both disturbed and fascinated by the encounter, especially after the young woman performed a surprisingly accurate tarot reading for him and subsequently calmed his nerves through a kind of hypnosis. In hushed and anxious tones, Mehdi now explained to me over the phone that when he had returned home, he had met up with a university friend to talk about the day's events. The two young men were in the heat of conversation when, suddenly, a tall glass door on a bookcase nearby shattered to pieces. The glass cracked down the middle and fell to the floor in three explosions of fragments and noise. Amazingly, Mehdi told me, there were no shards left in the bookcase itself, and the bolts that had formerly secured the glass door slid out cleanly without damaging the wood. It was as though someone or something had punched the glass from inside.

This made absolutely no sense. Could it be, Mehdi asked himself, that some ominous presence had followed him home from the meeting with the fortune teller? Perhaps one of the jinn that she claimed to control had broken the glass? 'I have a very bad feeling about her,' Mehdi told me. He suggested that I should immediately pay some alms and slaughter a rooster to ward off any harm from my family.

I was excited by Mehdi's phone call, thinking it would make for excellent material for my research. But I also felt frightened, as though my sense of the familiarity of the world had been disturbed, some part of the world itself receding into darkness. I stood at the threshold of my host's bedroom, staring through the window curtains into the night outside. For a moment, it occurred to me that the curtains would move at the behest of an unhuman presence. I felt a chill run down my spine. Immediately I took two thousand tomans from one of my back pockets and slipped the cash into another pocket to pay later to someone in need.

What I experienced that night was a moment of anxious energy transfer, a chilling power rippling between the fortune teller, Mehdi, the glass bookcase, the curtains in my friend's dark bedroom, and my spine. It is a moment that will also resonate for anyone familiar with the anthropology of the uncanny, or in Andrew Apter's telling, the 'ethnographic X-files'. Starting at least with EE Evans-Pritchard's classic account of witchcraft among the Azande, anthropologists have presented moments like this as gateways into how the seemingly unreal can make itself felt through powerful impressions in the world of matter, including on the body of the ethnographer.

Among contemporary Muslims, experiences like the one I shared with Mehdi tend to be interpreted in one of two ways. On one side is the explanation that Mehdi hinted at, even if haltingly and with hesitation: The glass may have been smashed by a jinn. These are invisible, intelligent beings whose intentions and actions are opaque to us, and yet whose doings sometimes intersect with the world of humans in ways that tend to produce anxiety, discomfort, and terror. Jinn are said to displace or steal valuables, cause nightmares, and sometimes possess their victims and drive them to madness. But on rare occasions they may initiate friendly contact with humans and even offer their service. This interpretation of jinn-as-intelligent-cause-of-the-smashed-glass finds support in numerous Qur'anic references to these beings, as well as a vast body of Islamic literature and oral lore on their attributes, their history, and even instructions on how they might be tamed and manipulated for human ends.

The alternative explanation is diametrically opposed to the first: the shattering of the glass door at that particular moment was a coincidence with a mundane physical cause, even if that cause may not be immediately apparent to us. (Perhaps the glass fractured under the pressure of expansion in the summer heat? Or maybe the bookcase's bolts had gradually come loose and finally gave way?) Any talk of jinn, in this account, is ignorant superstitious babble, a throwback to an enchanted age before the rise of scientific explanation and the expulsion of spirits from intelligent minds.

Anthropologists who have tried to make sense of jinn or the many other spiritual entities that populate people's worlds have usually opted to bracket the question of the reality of these beings to focus on their social and psychic significance instead. For these scholars, it matters little whether jinn or ancestor spirits or ghosts or demons or dybbuks really exist (as far as the anthropologist is concerned, they probably don't). What is important is that they are 'socially' real. This means that people's stories about, relations with, and supposed experiences of these entities have real effects on how they live their lives and relate to one another. Moreover, jinn and other invisible beings sometimes offer a language, an idiom, for grappling with dimensions of psychic existence that would be otherwise hard to grasp. For example, we can think of those desires, passions, and griefs that drive people to feel beside themselves, as though they were subject to a mysterious force exceeding their comprehension or control. The anthropologist's task is to describe the social and psychic meanings of these invisible entities and contextualise them within a wider field of politics, religion, economics, and so on.

Its advantages notwithstanding, one difficulty with this approach is that even as anthropologists adopt the agnostic posture of bracketing the question of the reality of spiritual beings like jinn, they cannot avoid a covert suggestion that those people who talk about jinn are in some way ignorant. That is, these people are supposedly unable to see that the true power of jinn does not lie in the realm of the supernatural but in the social world of humans and all the impressive ways in which they create and reshape their world through the marvellous power of language and imagination. In a way, this explanatory attitude shares some of the same modernist presuppositions as that of Muslims who deny the existence of jinn and claim that belief in these beings is an archaic survival from a time when people were ignorant of the invisible contagion of bacteria and the vulnerable chemistry of the brain. The difference between them lies in their choice of what to pick out as the reality behind the illusion: biological fact, social fact, or psychic fact.

Since the early 2000s, some anthropologists have criticised this analytic tendency toward 'social reduction' among their colleagues and urged a different approach, one that takes seriously the 'agency of spirits' and other uncanny forces. They call their orientation 'ontological', by which they mean that we should treat spirits as real entities with real lives and real significance, just as our interlocutors do. But to do that, they say, we need to ask what kind of reality can accommodate spiritual entities. The anthropological task, in this view, is not to drag the other into the orbit of our preconceived ideas, but to take his or her difference (or a term preferred by the ontologists: alterity) seriously enough that it can transform our secular, scientific concepts, and perhaps even change the way we live.

But the ontological approach also runs into difficulties when we try to apply it to something like my experience with the shattering of the glass. While the ontologists can argue that their explanations more closely reflect the perspectives of some of their interlocutors (although, we might ask how they can accommodate situations where not everyone holds the same understanding of spirits, as is the case with Muslims and jinn), they tend to miss the fact that occult ontology—the status of occult things like jinn—is plagued by all kinds of ambiguities and confusions, and not just for the anthropologist. It is true that Mehdi, for example, immediately thought of the agency of jinn when responding to the shock of the broken glass, but he also hesitated and worried that he might be mistaken. We have little hope of redescribing reality in terms offered by our interlocutors when those interlocutors themselves are confused about the reality in question. If the social reductionists have inadvertently allied themselves with those Muslims who write off straightforward references to jinn as ignorant, the ontologists have put themselves in the same camp as Muslims whose straightforward descriptions of jinn are fraught with uncertainty and contradiction. I should stress that this uncertainty is not a modern problem per se. Premodern Muslims were by no means in unanimous agreement on the existence of jinn.

In what follows, I will explore an approach to jinn that is different from both the ontological and the social alternatives, or if you prefer the parallel opposition among Muslims: the jinn believers and the jinn skeptics. As we will see, my point is not only to offer a new way to think about jinn, but a bit more ambitiously, to suggest how thinking about jinn can aid us in coming to grips with those dimensions of the world that may be fundamentally unknowable or beyond the reach of our conceptual understanding.

My starting point is the moment of shock and confusion—the utter bewilderment that Mehdi felt when the glass was broken, and that he subsequently transmitted to me. This was no mere incomprehension, the kind one might feel when encountering a complex machine whose working we cannot understand. Nor was it wonder and amazement, as one might experience when confronted with a work of extraordinary art or craftsmanship, or in the bewildering majesty of nature, as in a magnificent waterfall or canyon. The breaking of the glass was dumbfounding in a way that shaded into dread and terror. It made Mehdi stutter and sent a chill down my spine. To understand jinn, I think that we need to begin with this moment of dread, an experience that is characteristic of jinn accounts more broadly. The feeling, as I will show, points to a kind of ignorance very different from what self-satisfied modernists or elites denigrate as superstition. It is a failure of conceptual knowledge that may point up the limits of human understanding itself, or perhaps even the limit of the human. That is, we might be able to think of this ignorance paradoxically as a kind of unknowability that is inseparable from our humanity and from living in this world.

The feeling of bewilderment that shades into terror matches closely some of the experiences that Sigmund Freud described over a century ago as uncanny or 'unheimlich' (sometimes translated as 'unhomely'). For Freud, the distinguishing feature of the uncanny, as opposed to other things terrifying or perplexing, was its temporal structure, its conjuring up of something that lay in the past. The uncanny, as he put it, is 'that class of the frightening which leads back to what is known of old and long familiar'. He divided these familiar things into two categories: the first and more persistent is infantile complexes like the fear of castration. The second consists of 'primitive' animistic beliefs like the idea that the world is populated by spirits, or the notion of the 'omnipotence of thought' which holds that we can affect the world simply by thinking. Freud argued that as children became adults, and as 'primitives' left their childhood to mature into civilisations, these old ideas, fears, and attachments were either suppressed or surmounted. But they never entirely disappeared. There would be moments when an experience or encounter, often very simple, would suddenly revive these familiar old impressions. The 'repressed' would thus return with a terrifying force as an uncanny feeling.

In the case of the shattering bookcase, Freud might have said that Mehdi and I had been frightened because an old and childish idea, that we could simply move things with our own thoughts, or that we could harm someone or obliterate something by directing our attention to it, suddenly returned to us in the face of an apparently inexplicable event. Add to this the concept we had both been raised with, of jinn as invisible beings that act capriciously in our material world. As we grew into adulthood and trained as social scientists, we had gradually suppressed or abandoned these ideas. This was easy because neither of us had many uncanny experiences that forced us to confront the question of the reality of jinn or of the material efficacy of thought. It also helped that we lived in a world saturated with scientific explanations and a persistent valorisation of rationality and the denigration of superstition. Even our theological attitudes had gone through a process of rational education in the Islamic Republic of Iran, where notions like the material reality or efficacy of jinn tend to be downplayed, if not entirely denied. But vestiges of our old attitudes remained buried deep in our unconscious and they returned with a vengeance when that glass door suddenly broke.

I find this Freudian analysis of the uncanniness of the shattering glass broadly persuasive. But it seems to me that there is another explanation, a more prior one, that Freud ignored but that would fit well within his overall framework: the role of the old and suppressed feeling of surprise with which we first encounter the world. Could it be that something about the world we inhabit will always elude our apprehension, and yet we have covered over this incomprehensible dimension? I say this is an 'old' feeling because it might have its roots in how infants and children experience the world as perpetually surprising. Sometimes these surprises lead to feelings of wonder and delight. At other times they produce fear. Over time, as we grow up and learn to explain and interpret our experiences in rational terms offered to us by society, this wondrous quality is diminished. But as convincing as our learned explanations might seem, they remain tentative. They offer a sense of comfort that allows us to move through life as if the world, for the most part, makes sense. Our childish sensibility for the unknowable dimension of the world is suppressed. Perhaps it's this unknowable world that returns with a vengeance in a moment like the shattering of the glass.

For the German theologian Rudolf Otto, there was an object that exceeded all attempts at rational apprehension whose qualities came close to what I'm describing here as the unknowable world. Otto associated this object with an irreducible feeling that he called 'the numinous'— irreducible in the sense that it belonged to a class of its own and could not be grouped with any other emotion (say, fear of animals or delight in artistic beauty). In theistic religions, the numinous had its primary referent in the ultimate transcendent being called God. But it could also be found in non-theistic religions, even among those so-called 'primitive' humans whose primeval feelings, Otto claimed, stood at the origin of religion itself.

Among these people, the numinous was felt in its crudest form as what he called 'daemonic dread'. Referring to forces that are neither good nor evil, neither divine nor earthly, daemonic dread was directed to the *mysterium tremendum*, something that inspired terrifying and overpowering awe, as well as a kind of astonished stupor that could only be stirred by that which was 'wholly other', an object lying outside the realm of the ordinary, the familiar, and even the intelligible. To the stupor and the awe, Otto also added fascination, a feeling of being captivated by and drawn to the numen, even as one shuddered in its presence.

Otto seemed to think of the jinn as paradigmatic objects of daemonic dread. 'The most authentic form of the "daemon,"' he wrote, 'may be seen in those strange deities of ancient Arabia… felt as deities of mighty efficacy, who are the objects of very living veneration'. What impressed him about the jinn was that they were neither 'nature deities' nor evolved out of 'souls' (human or otherwise), which meant that they contained in crude form the sui generis quality of the numinous as something wholly other. But he ignored a more important quality of the jinn: that they are notoriously capricious despite their supposed intelligence, a quality that makes it impossible to understand or predict their behaviour. This incomprehensibility also means that the jinn cannot easily be integrated into a rational conception of divine purpose. The jinn are marked by purposelessness and 'dysteleology', a term Otto used to characterise certain animals as described in the Hebrew Bible. These animals, he wrote (and he might well have added the same of jinn), 'express in masterly fashion the downright stupendousness, the wellnigh daemonic and wholly incomprehensible character of the eternal creative power; how, incalculable and "wholly other", it mocks at all conceiving.'

While Otto's framework is helpful in pointing us toward the radically incomprehensible as a hint for understanding the jinn, he commits the error of subsuming all things 'numinous' under the master sign of 'God'. This move is, of course, central to his argument that there is something irreducible about the religious feeling, and that this feeling has its ultimate and most perfect expression in the awe, veneration, and love of God. But in making this argument, he ignores the possibility that something about the world itself might be unknowable, and that, moreover, the feeling that this worldly numinous 'object' might inspire need not be of the same kind as the divine.

The philosopher Cora Diamond has offered a way to think about the incomprehensibility of the world in terms of what she calls 'the difficulty of reality'. One experiences this difficulty, she says, at certain mundane moments when one hits a wall in one's thinking and feels it come 'unhinged'. Her concern is not necessarily the sorts of experiences that Freud would have called uncanny or that Otto would have called numinous, even though to my mind there is a family resemblance. The feeling of the difficulty of reality, Diamond says, could be occasioned by something as simple as looking at a photograph or interacting with an animal. Her examples include things like our astonishment at how someone so alive in a photograph could be so completely dead. Or bewilderment at how we can kill and eat a being as marvellous as an animal. Or further, in an encounter with animals:

> ... a sense of astonishment and incomprehension that there should be beings so like us, so unlike us, so astonishingly capable of being companions of ours and so unfathomably distant... how powerfully strange it is that they and we should share as much as we do, and yet also not share; that they should be capable of incomparable beauty and delicacy and terrible ferocity; that some among them should be so mindbogglingly weird or repulsive in their forms or in their lives.

What we experience in these moments of astonishment, Diamond says, is the failure of our concepts to encompass reality, to apprehend that which we are trying to reach. If we try to think the difficulty of reality, she continues, it 'shoulders us out of life, is deadly chilling'. As the corporeal language suggests, Diamond thinks of this experience as deeply embodied.

To sit with and appreciate the difficulty of reality is to attempt to inhabit a body in a certain way, to pay attention to its movements, temperatures, and resonances. Above all, what Diamond helpfully articulates is that there may be something about mundane reality—and not just, as Otto would have it, the transcendent—that is constitutively beyond conceptual grasp.

Perhaps 'jinn' is one name for some such embodied encounters with a reality that unhinges our thought.

The idea of a worldly numinous 'something' that presents difficulties for human knowledge is clearly recognised in Islamic thought. In the Qur'an, we encounter the idea of *ghayb*, a word variously translated as hidden, unseen, invisible, or (in Muhammad Asad's translation) 'things that are beyond the reach of human perception'. The word often comes up in the context of declaring God's total and absolute knowledge of all things, and the opacity or hiddenness of much of this for humans. In 72:26, for example, we read of God's exclusive knowledge of the unseen: 'He is the knower of the unseen (*al-ghayb*), disclosing none of it (*ghaybihi* – lit., "his unseen") to anyone.' *Al-ghayb* includes many things, including God himself (67:12 – 'Indeed, those in awe of their Lord unseen will have forgiveness and a mighty reward'), the angels, the mysteries revealed to divine messengers, and the hour of the Last Day. But it also includes the future, aspects of the past, the secrets people guard in their breasts, the furtive communications between conspirators, and much else besides. Crucially, the unseen need not be immaterial or divine. From 49:18: 'Surely God knows the unseen of the heavens and earth. And God is All-Seeing of what you do.' That is, the earth, and not just the heavens, contains things unseen. Or consider 6:59: 'With Him are the keys of the unseen—no one knows them except Him. And He knows what is in the land and sea. Not even a leaf falls without His knowledge, nor a grain in the darkness of the earth, or anything—green or dry—but is written in a perfect Record.' The world is teeming with things that humans do not know and perhaps cannot comprehend.

To my knowledge, the Qur'an never refers to the jinn as categorically belonging to *al-ghayb*. Indeed, the jinn are sometimes subject to some of the same epistemic exclusions in relation to the unseen as humans, as for example in 34:14 which mocks the jinn for having failed to discern the death of their master Solomon: 'When we decreed [Solomon's] death, nothing indicated to [Solomon's jinn servants] that he was dead except the termites eating away his staff. So when he collapsed, the jinn realised that if they had known the unseen, they would not have remained in humiliating servitude.' But the invisibility of the jinn to human eyes is of little dispute in Muslim thought more broadly. This invisibility is often said to be incorporated into the name of their race, related as it is to the Arabic verb *janna*, meaning 'to conceal', 'to veil', 'to hide', or to 'descend into darkness'. Some Muslims explain that the jinn's invisibility has to do with their essence, having been created—as the Qur'an puts it—from a 'smokeless fire' (*marij min nar*, 55:15). Using more contemporary parlance, some Iranians will point out that the jinn are energetic beings devoid of matter. Energy may interact with matter and leave traces upon it, but we cannot perceive it except through its effects—shattered glass, bruised bodies, missing valuables, and so on.

But this is not exactly right. There are plenty of reports of people having seen jinn 'in the flesh'. The most colourful Qur'anic examples are the aforementioned jinn whom Solomon enslaved, forcing them to build, dive, and do his bidding. The well-known Shi'i hadith compendium *Al-Kafi* recounts several instances in which one or more jinn visit an Imam either to render service or to ask a religious question, the nature of which is not revealed. In these traditions, the narrator, a companion of the Imam, usually mistakes the jinn for either a human (for example: turbaned black men resembling men from the Sudan), an animal (like: a large serpent), or something more ambiguous (in one hadith, gaunt beautiful figures resembling yellow locusts). After asking the Imam about these wondrous beings, the companions learn of their true nature as jinn.

Even more numerous reports of jinn sightings exist outside the hadith collection. I will only mention one of the most well-known among Iranians, a story that has been repeated so frequently that it has taken on the quality of a trope. This is the report of a jinn lurking in a public bath around dawn. The story usually goes that the witness is surprised to see another man in the bathhouse. He initiates a conversation but then notices that his interlocutor's feet are hooves. At this point the terrified witness runs away, realising that he has been in the presence of a jinn.

So the jinn are invisible to humans, but not always. Several folk explanations are offered to explain the exceptions. On some accounts, the jinn can take on visible form through a kind of compression (this is based on the idea that the jinn are not so much energetic beings as composed of a very fine substance). On other accounts, the jinn may only become visible in dreams or by inducing hallucinations. Still others will deny jinn sightings altogether, attributing them to error or delusion. For these latter, whose approach parallels those who deny the existence of jinn wholesale, the hadith I mentioned are untrustworthy or need to be understood in some manner other than their apparent sense.

We might approach the exceptions to the jinn's invisibility in a different way. If we think of invisibility as hiddenness from human understanding, then the seeming exceptions show that the jinn are hidden even in their hiddenness. That is to say, the jinn are so hidden from human understanding that we cannot even say with any certainty that they are invisible. The hiddenness of the jinn would thus be much more than sensory inaccessibility: it approaches Otto's conception of the numinous as something wholly other and beyond human understanding. Not just perceptual invisibility, but radical unknowability.

Another way to understand the difficulty of saying anything about jinn is to consider their speech. Anthropologists who encounter jinn 'in the field' almost always receive jinn speech in the form of reported utterance—a story by speakers other than jinn—such that what the jinn do or say can seldom be disentangled from the words and acts of humans. But even in those instances when the jinn seem to speak more directly, their speech is still mediated by humans or is in danger of being mistaken as such. This is the case in possessed speech, for example, a kind of ventriloquism in which the jinn are said to speak through the vocal apparatus of a human. We also have whispers or insinuations like the Qur'anic *waswas al-khannas* that one might perceive as arriving from somewhere outside one's own mind. The problem with these modalities of jinn speech, of course, is that they are instances of *jinn-struck-ness (junun)*, or in other words, madness. So the anthropologist who wants to discern the speech of jinn must first sift its words from the ravings or pretensions of a human host. Again, the jinn is not necessarily concealed from the senses. It is radically unknowable.

There is a story in Muhammad Hamadani Tusi's twelfth century *Wonders of Creation* (*'Aja'ib al-Makhluqat*) that captures some of the problems with thinking of jinn as knowable beings. The apocryphal story recounts a dispute between two ninth-century Mu'tazili theologians. He writes:

Nazzam the theologian was in debate with Abu al-Hudhayl over jinn. Nazzam says that jinn exist. Abu al-Hudhayl says jinn do not exist. Their enmity ran long. The caliph of the time made peace between them and said: demons cannot be shown by proof, but must be firmly believed in by virtue of the Qur'an. So Abu al-Hudhayl had a well from which he drew water. Nazzam concealed himself in that well. When Abu al-Hudhayl threw a pail into the well, Nazzam held it with his hand. Abu al-Hudhayl pulled. Nazzam made a horrible cry and said: why do you insult demons and spirits? Abu al-Hudhayl sealed the well with a stone and informed the caliph that Nazzam has hidden in the well and pretends to be a demon and threatens me. The caliph sent someone to bring him out, and, slapping him, took him to the caliph. The caliph says: What is unseen, if someone wants to make visible and treat with proofs, he will fail... [these things] are of the ear, not of reason. And he who seeks to prove them will become humiliated like you did.

Now the claim that the jinn are radically unknowable beings still presumes that we know them to be *beings*, which is another way of saying that they are not quite radically unknowable. Many Muslims will agree with the caliph in Hamadani's story that jinn in fact are beings if only because they are mentioned in the Qur'an. The problem, for the Iranians I worked with at least, was that it was seldom clear whether the jinn mentioned in the Qur'an were beings who continued to interact with humans today. That is, for them, while the caliph might well be right, neither Nazzam's conviction nor Abu al-Hudhayl's scepticism can be justified.

Let me return to the example of Mehdi and the shattered glass. When Mehdi speculated that a jinn might have punched the glass from inside the bookcase, he was not making a casual comment on some unremarkable empirical observation. 'Jinn' was a word he uttered to bridge the gap between his feeling that things generally seemed to make sense most of the time, and the uncanny if momentary withdrawal of his world from any kind of sense—indeed, the retreat into darkness of the most intimate space of his home, a space that had suddenly become something other than itself, unhomely or uncanny.

When Mehdi voiced a suspicion that 'jinn' were responsible for the shattered glass, he was stating the possibility that the Qur'an had described something that now intruded on his experience. But this voicing ran counter to other moments when he doubted that such beings existed at all. Before the jinn acquired any positive descriptions, then, their name was the eruption of a disquiet that things were not quite as Mehdi had assumed. Perhaps at its most stripped-down level, 'jinn' was the expression of an encounter with a difficulty of reality that chilled Mehdi (and me) to the bone.

My suggestion is that we think of jinn not as unknowable beings but as a name for unknowability itself, or in other words, the terrifying encounter with a world that has withdrawn from sense. In this way, jinn are not so much presences as absences, even though they are joined to corporeal impressions like the sight of an exploding bookcase or the chill that runs down a spine. Jinn are the name that some people give to those occasions when the world slinks away from familiar sense. The genius of this name for the world's 'slinking away' is that it does not immediately try to plug absence with positive content, but instead calls it out as the darkness that it is.

Of course, people do often try to plug the gap with sense. They read books about jinn, recite prayers, wear protective amulets, pay alms, and even consult exorcists. Through these practices, people attempt to domesticate the jinn into something knowable or controllable. They transform unknowability, reducing it to a menace to be warded off through prayer, an accomplice in a social drama to be resolved, a disturbance of the soul to be treated, or a moral debt to be settled. Notice though that these resolutions do not so much suture the world back into sense as reorient attention away from the darkness and toward the light of a life made manageable. Such attempts at sense-making are not dissimilar to Diamond's account of 'philosophical deflection', the tendency to move away from appreciating a difficulty of reality and instead to zoom in on an apparently adjacent philosophical or moral problem. When anthropologists reduce jinn to a social or psychic fact, or when they conscript spirits into an ontological thought experiment, they are similarly engaged in deflection.

What, then, if we were to keep our attention focused on that moment when the world withdraws from sense? Can we dwell further on the exploding glass or the tingling spine without rushing to anthropomorphise unknowability? In his reflections on the world's uncanny power to defeat human attempts to understand or control it, Eugene Thacker suggests that we need something other than anthropology or science or philosophy to come to grips with what he calls 'the world without us', that is, the world when it slinks away into darkness. His alternative is horror, and he articulates its usefulness by turning to resources as varied as medieval Christian demonology, twentieth century weird fiction, dark mysticism, and black metal music. If I am right, ethnographic encounters with jinn can help us hone our sensibility for horror still further by amplifying its stupefying sensuousness: how the withdrawal of the world from sense can reverberate in the body, how it can multiply its absence in the flesh and in the darkest corners of the mind.

WHO'S AFRAID OF THE CRT?

Gordon Blaine Steffey

The town of Wytheville in rural southwest Virginia looks like the mythic American 'Main Street' studding the discourse of American political actors and media during campaign season. It was named in honour of a 'founding father' with no tie to the place. Its proximity to mineral resources and rail made Wytheville strategically significant during the American Civil War. Its heyday now long past, Wytheville faces an unbalanced geography of opportunity as American workers migrate to urban areas with higher job density, wage and compensation growth, and prospects for prosperity. Average yearly incomes are significantly below the national average and almost 23% of its eight thousand odd residents live in poverty, defined as individuals living on the dollar equivalent of £29 daily or a family of four on £58. With 88% of residents identifying as 'white alone' in the naive yet striking language of the US Census Bureau, Wytheville is as demographically diverse as it has been in memory.

Wytheville was also the site of one of the last of eighty-six documented lynchings in the Commonwealth of Virginia. Between 1877 and 1950 there were more than 4,400 extra-legal mob murders in the US intended to reinforce white supremacy by terrorising black folks. The term lynching originated in the Revolutionary period when Charles Lynch of Bedford County, Virginia, a justice and militia colonel, meted out extrajudicial punishment to suspected Loyalists in central Virginia (I write from the city founded by his brother John, the unhappily named Lynchburg). 'Lynch law' is far more often associated with the terroristic entertainments of the Jim Crow South, which occasionally drew the censure of state officials, often involved the complicity of law enforcement, and never resulted in accountability for participants and spectators. The 2021 short documentary *Lynching Postcards: 'Token of a Great Day'* tells the grim history of graphic postcards sold as souvenirs of these events. Bob Dylan's *Desolation Row*

(1965) opens with the lyric 'they're selling postcards of the hanging,' a reference to the 1920 lynching of three black men in Dylan's hometown of Duluth, Minnesota (a world away from Wytheville in the righteous North).

In June 1919, Private Raymond Arthur Byrd of H Company, 807th Pioneer Infantry, returned from France to his home outside Wytheville. He eventually found employment as a farmhand with white landowner Grover Grubb, who in summer 1926 denounced Byrd to police for raping his unmarried adult daughter. That daughter gave birth to a child allegedly fathered by Byrd. When investigators determined that a rape charge could not be sustained, Grubb pressured his twelve-year old daughter to report Byrd for fondling her against her will. Byrd was arrested on 7 August 1926 and confined to the ramshackle Wythe County Jail under a single guard until 15 August, when a mob of twenty-five or more masked men (some of them Klan) knocked at the jail door and the single guard delivered Byrd into their hands. Byrd was beaten, shot, and dragged behind an automobile for some of the nine miles to a wood near St Paul's Lutheran Church where he was hanged from an oak tree. The lacklustre efforts of law enforcement to prevent this white terror were matched by their failure to prosecute anyone successfully for the crime. These failures were hallmarks of the lynching era. In the end, an all-white grand jury indicted one man for Byrd's murder; that man was acquitted of the charge by an all-white jury after a 10-minute deliberation. No photographs or postcards of the lynching have come to light, but a bit of rope used to bind Byrd and saved as a memento now sits in the National Museum of African American History and Culture in Washington, D.C.

Apart from a local historian and a handful of others who were instrumental in having the injustice done to Byrd recognised on a state historical marker in 2020, most folks in Wythe County *still* do not want to talk about it. Many Americans (perhaps most) dodge difficult conversations about lynching and its multiple legacies, from the Great Migration, which saw more than 5 million black folks move from the rural south to the urban north, to mass incarceration (38.3% of the imprisoned are black though blacks constitute 13.4% of the US population). Only four years ago The National Memorial for Peace and Justice (known colloquially as the National Lynching Memorial) opened on a six-acre site overlooking Montgomery, Alabama. Promotional media describe the site as 'sacred space for truth-telling and reflection about racial terror in America and its legacy'. From its roof hang eight hundred weathered steel columns in evocation of the 'strange fruit' so hauntingly memorialised by Billie Holiday. Columns are inscribed with the names of American counties and the names (where known) of persons lynched there. The columns have duplicates waiting to be claimed by counties ready to confront their history of racial terror, which entails (at a minimum) erecting the monument in a meaningful public venue as a trigger to critical remembrance and conversation. Wythe county has yet to claim its monument.

The old jail is now green space. An installation of life-size, illuminated letters spell L-O-V-E. Commemorated on its individual letters are 'aspects of Wytheville's history that have made an impact on the community.' The impact of rail and baseball are commemorated, but the life and lynching of Byrd is not. Information about his murder has been consigned to the previously mentioned historical marker, the design and placement of which require would-be readers to stand close by. The roughly 107 x 102 cm sign holds 16 lines of text, 162 black words raised against a silvered aluminium background. Headed by 'The Lynching of Raymond Byrd,' the narrative beneath wends its way to a pacific conclusion, observing that the savagery done to Raymond inspired a pressure campaign culminating two years later in the passage of Virginia's anti-lynching law. That law was modelled on a 1918 federal bill sponsored by white Missouri congressperson, Republican Leonidas Dyer, with critical backing of the black advocacy group, the NAACP. The federal bill passed a 1922 House vote by a margin of 231-119 before falling to extortionate Southern Democrats in the Senate who threatened a legislative shutdown to gain Republican submission. On 29 March 2022 (a century and scores of failed attempts later), President Joe Biden signed into law the Emmett Till Antilynching Act, which, by amending the federal Hate Crimes Act, makes lynching a federal hate crime and increases the penalty range for the commission of such crime or conspiracy to commit. Despite the earlier success of Virginia's anti-lynching law, no white person was ever convicted under that legislation for crimes against black folks.

In July 2021, Republican candidate for Governor Glenn Youngkin was on the stump in Wytheville. His speech there made no mention of Raymond Byrd but evoked a horror of a different order. He told supporters: 'We actually have this critical race theory moved into all of our schools in Virginia.' In Virginia? Virginia, where sat the capital of the Confederate States of America and home to Confederate generals 'Stonewall' Jackson and Robert E. Lee, whose image has been a site of contention in the 'cold' civil war now afoot in the US? In Virginia where Lee-Jackson Day was a state holiday until 2020? Youngkin's framing of the penetration of critical race theory (CRT) into state curricula as *fait accompli* was always a country mile from credible. The Youngkin camp cited as evidence a handful of memoranda and seminars that belonged to larger educational equity initiatives. By way of example, the Youngkin camp pointed a finger at the Virginia Department of Education's now defunct web page headed 'Anti-racism in Education', which quoted approvingly from *How to be an Antiracist* by Ibram X. Kendi, who (along with Nikole Hannah-Jones of the 1619 Project) is to CRT detractors a high-profile agent of this 'false prophecy'. They also took amiss a 2020 memo written to parents from a school principal in furtherance of 'a culture of inclusion that supports students of all backgrounds'. Attached to this memo was an article from an educational consultant who brazenly suggests that 'teachers can allow students to apply critical lenses, such as critical race theory and Marxist theory, to the reading of news articles to allow students to think more deeply about who is being most affected and why'. In the aftermath of Youngkin's claim, several city and county school systems in Virginia went on record to disavow CRT and to disentangle it from other diversity, inclusion, and equity initiatives. The non-profit project Politifact, which rates the accuracy of claims by politicos on its 'Truth-O-Meter', reckoned Youngkin's claim to be 'false' (between 'mostly false' and 'pants on fire') and underlined CRT's absence from state-wide Standards of Learning, finding 'no evidence that critical race theory is being taught in each of the state's 1,825 public schools'.

Undeterred by facts, Youngkin recycled the claim throughout his campaign, telling a Fox News audience on 5 August 2021: 'Critical Race Theory has moved into our school system and we have to remove it'. From February 2021 Fox News escalated its slow trickle of attention to CRT to a full-bore flood; Media Matters reported that CRT received more than 1900 mentions on Fox News in the subsequent 3.5 months. Ignorance about what CRT is and fears about what it might be were a motherlode to be mined in titillation of the base and service to Republicans seeking national and state office. At the polls more than 80% of Wythe County voters preferred Youngkin to former governor, Clinton crony, and weathered politico Terry McAuliffe, who struck many as a Yankee carpetbagger (the 'Macker' was reared in Syracuse, New York). The Republican National Committee, the Youngkin campaign, and conservative media repeatedly tethered CRT to the former governor (who unsuccessfully tried to tie 'Glenn Trumpkin' to the former president). For his part, the Macker dismissed mounting coverage of and concern about CRT as a racist 'dog whistle' and ran on economic rebound post-COVID. When asked to define CRT at a debate with Youngkin in early October, Macker refused, saying: 'Doesn't matter. It's not taught here in Virginia.' Macker was oversimplifying, but it left Youngkin's view of CRT unchallenged: 'I don't think we should bucket children into certain sectors as oppressors.' This was yet another case of a Democrat declining to contend toe-to-toe on non-economic issues of voter concern and succumbing to the labour-liberal legacy of economic reductionism.

One week out from the 2 November 2020 election, education displaced the economy in polling as the number one issue for Virginia voters, and Youngkin edged McAuliffe by two percentage points. CRT played a prominent role in muddy debates about the degree of oversight parents should have in school curricula. Founded in the thick of the governor's race, the Virginia-based organisation Parents Defending Education (PDE) claims to be 'working to reclaim our schools' from what it terms the 'woke industrial complex', a network of activists and consultants pushing an 'ideologically driven curriculum ... [that] divides our children into "oppressor" and "oppressed" groups' based on 'race, ethnicity, religion, sexual orientation and gender'. The PDE website makes clear that the mechanism of division in education is 'the controversial ideology called critical race theory'. Among its initiatives to 'reclaim' schools, PDE files complaints with the US Department of Education's Office for Civil Rights against schools and districts that acknowledge systemic racism at work in schools – the strategy is to punish these schools and intimidate others with federal investigations and penalties pursuant to the violation of federal laws (specifically, Title VI of the 1964 Civil Rights Act, which prohibits race discrimination in programs that receive federal funds). Confront the past at the risk of federal investigation!

Youngkin was not the first Republican to exploit race anxiety and ignorance about CRT for political gains. Two days before his term of office ended, President Trump's 1776 Commission submitted its report, a fitting culmination to his presidency but not much more than nationalist propaganda riddled with error, distortion, and cynical political manipulation. Tasked to 'enable a rising generation to understand the history and principles of the founding of the United States in 1776', what Trump termed 'patriotic education', the Commission oozes through a review of those principles before bemoaning identity politics or the 'regime of formal inequality' that 'in the name of 'social justice', demands equal results and explicitly sorts citizens into 'protected classes' based on race and other demographic categories'. It bloats to a merciful conclusion by presenting readers with a 'clear' choice between 'the truths of the Declaration' or 'false theories' paving the way to tyranny. The target in view here was the 1619 Project, a plurally authored initiative published by *The New York Times Magazine* in commemoration of the 400th anniversary of slavery in America. The 1619 Project examines multiple enduring legacies of slavery, from the brutalities of capitalism to high sugar diets. In her framing essay 'The Idea of America', Nikole Hannah-Jones notes that 'the United States is a nation founded on both an ideal and a lie. Our Declaration ... proclaims that "all men are created equal" and "endowed by their Creator with certain unalienable rights." But the white men who drafted those words did not believe them to be true for the hundreds of thousands of black people in their midst.' Hannah-Jones observes that the idealism, resistance, and energies of black Americans helped the US to grow into its ideals and that they are as much founding fathers as those whose images typically gild our national monuments and collective memory. Some legislation and proposed legislation banning CRT specifically prohibits the use of 'divisive' materials from the 1619 Project.

As former President Donald Trump leaned into race-baiting in the home stretch of the 2020 election, he issued executive order 13950 'to combat offensive and anti-American race and sex stereotyping and scapegoating'. The order targeted a 'malign ideology' dividing Americans against one another. It cites several initiatives reflective of this malign ideology at work in federal and federal contractor workspaces before turning to the prohibition of the 'divisive concepts' at its core. Among the latter 13950 counts the view that 'the United States is fundamentally racist or sexist' and that 'an individual by virtue of his or her race or sex, is inherently racist, sexist, or oppressive, whether consciously or unconsciously'. These are cynical distortions of the evidence-based phenomena of structural and institutional racism and implicit bias. 13950 threatened to devastate federal diversity training and federally funded research on these topics until a US District Court issued a nationwide preliminary injunction banning enforcement of significant sections of 13950 and President Biden revoked 13950 by executive order on his inauguration day. Biden's order acknowledged that 'entrenched disparities in our laws and public policies, and in our public and private institutions, have often denied ... equal opportunity to individuals and communities'.

Integral to 13950 was its rejection of the 'divisive concept' that 'meritocracy or traits such as a hard work ethic are racist or sexist'. The view implicit here is that the US is a meritocracy, that the proverbial playing field is level, and that no matter her social position an individual's behaviours and choices determine her material outcomes here. A companion view is that racism is a function of individual and sometimes social attitudes and behaviours of which we may repent in pursuit of our more perfect union. In the 1980s, legal scholars working in the US argued that some of the differential outcomes we see in the social order between white and black folks follow from inequities embedded in institutions and policy. Take the example of redlining. The Home Owners Loan Corporation (HOLC), established in 1933 under the Roosevelt administration's New Deal, aimed to reduce home foreclosures during the Great Depression by refinancing mortgages. As part of its work HOLC generated 'city survey' maps, grading and colour-coding metropolitan areas around the country based on their perceived mortgage-lending risk. Neighbourhoods were graded from A or 'Best' (low risk) to D and 'Hazardous' (high risk); D graded security zones were lined and shaded in red, thus 'redlining'. Predictably, D zones were black neighbourhoods. These maps, used by other agencies like the Federal Housing Administration (FHA) and the Veterans Administration, helped to answer the question: where is it safe to insure mortgages?

Diverse complaints of discriminatory practices against black applicants at HOLC prompted sociologist Ira Reid to observe that New Deal agencies 'might just as well be administered by the Ku Klux Klan'. One of the provisions of the 1938 *Underwriting Manual* of the Federal Housing Administration – a New Deal agency with the mandate to remedy housing scarcity by increasing (and segregating) housing stock – advised that 'if a neighbourhood is to retain stability, it is necessary that properties shall continue to be occupied by the same social and racial classes'. To that end the FHA recommended that deeds include restrictive covenants of this sort: 'prohibition of the occupancy of properties except by the race for which they are intended'. Federal housing policy shored up and aggravated racial segregation in metropolitan areas. It established and reinforced metropolitan 'ghettos', defined by historian and policy expert Richard Rothstein as homogeneous neighbourhoods from which there are serious barriers to exit. It promoted investment in white neighbourhoods and perpetuated a myth correlating black residence with low and declining property values.

From 1924 to 1950 the Code of Ethics of the National Associates of Real Estate Boards (NAREB) stipulated 'a Realtor should never be instrumental in introducing into a neighbourhood a character of property or occupancy, members of any race of nationality, or any individuals whose presence will clearly be detrimental to property values in that neighbourhood'. In many ways New Deal agencies federalized longstanding discrimination practices in the real estate industry. In *Corrigan v. Buckley* (1926), the US Supreme Court unanimously found no constitutional impediments to property owners using restrictive covenants to control the racial makeup of their neighbourhoods. A property deed recorded on 6 May 1947 here in Lynchburg, Virginia, is an example of such a covenant: 'No lot is to be sold, leased, or disposed of to any person of African descent.' In a majority opinion in *Shelley v. Kraemer* (1948) the Supreme Court ruled that racially restrictive covenants violate the Equal Protection Clause of the 14th amendment, which prohibited states from denying 'any person within its jurisdiction the equal protection of the laws'. In the wake of *Shelley v. Kraemer,* the NAREB amended its Code of Ethics, striking the language between 'property' and 'whose' *without abandoning the practice.* Thus the 1963 passage of the Rumford Fair Housing Act in California found it necessary to affirm that 'the practice of discrimination because of race, colour, religion, national origin, or ancestry in housing accommodations is declared to be against public policy'. Incredibly, the following year Californians passed Proposition 14, which guaranteed property owners 'absolute discretion' to sell, lease, and rent to anyone they wished, effectively repealing Rumford. Two years later in 1966 the California Supreme Court ruled Proposition 14 invalid under the Equal Protection Clause, a ruling affirmed by the US Supreme Court in *Reitman v Mulkey* (1967). This ebb and flow was ostensibly terminated by Title VIII (known as the Fair Housing Act) of the 1968 Civil Rights Act, which prohibits racial discrimination in the sale, rental, and financing of dwellings and other housing-related transactions. I say ostensibly because the homes that black folks could have afforded in prior decades with FHA or VA mortgages were no longer within reach.

I say ostensibly also because in a 5-4 decision in *Milliken v Bradley* (1974) the Supreme Court ruled that school desegregation (required by 1954's landmark *Brown v Board of Education*) did not entail 'any particular racial balance in each school, grade or classroom', effectively smashing a planned desegregation of schools and busing in Detroit and its suburbs. While the majority opinion found 'no claim' that school districts were drafted with racist segregating intent, the majority failed to consider seriously that such intent had already been accomplished via housing policy. Because around 45% of school funding comes from local wealth (property taxes!) educational inequities have flowered between central city and suburban (the destination of 'white flight') school systems. In the runup to the 2020 election Trump predicted that the election of Biden and Harris would occasion an 'invasion' that would 'destroy suburbia'. When asked to explain what he meant, Trump whistled along to the tune fixed so long ago by New Deal housing agencies: 'Thirty-percent plus are minorities living in suburbia and when they go in and they want to change zoning so that you have lots of problems where they want to build low-income housing, you want something where people can aspire to be there, not something where it gets hurt badly.' He finished his explanation by referring contextually to *white* suburbanites who 'fought all their lives to be there and then all of a sudden, they have something happen that changes their life and changes what they fought for, for so many years'. Trump terminated the Obama-era Affirmatively Furthering Fair Housing rule, which required jurisdictions resourced by the US Department of Housing and Urban Development to provide a fair housing assessment reflective of 'meaningful actions' to 'foster the diversity and strength of communities by overcoming historic patterns of segregation, reducing racial or ethnic concentrations of poverty, and responding to identified disproportionate housing needs consistent with the policies and protections of the Fair Housing Act [Title VIII of the 1968 Civil Rights Act].'

In *Meredith v Jefferson County Board of Education* (2007), the Court reaffirmed that racial balancing of demographics in public schools was unconstitutional under the 14th amendment, with Chief Justice Roberts opining that 'the way to stop discrimination on the basis of race is to stop discriminating on the basis of race.' In June 2022, federally backed home mortgage giants Fannie Mae and Freddie Mac reported that while 72% of whites are homeowners, only 42% of black folks own a home (in 1970 those numbers were 66% and … 42%). Announcing new initiatives to close the gap, Fannie Mae's Executive VP and Chief Administrative Officer wrote that the 'racist legacy' of redlining is 'one of the root causes of economic disparity in our country'. He added that 'to pretend that our history does not affect our country's present and future – is not only wrong, it's also economically destructive'. Indeed, as a result of this dire history of reduced credit access, disinvestment, and the like, black folks were excluded from a momentous wealth building nexus (home equity) that allowed whites to transfer wealth generationally and to use that wealth to capitalise on opportunities for better employment and better wages. Black folks who were able to afford homes were contained in central city communities where home values succumbed to the self-fulfilling illogic of HOLC and FHA maps. This helps to explain why the triennial 2019 Survey of Consumer Finances (generated by the US Treasury and the Federal Reserve) reports that the median and mean wealth of Black families in the US is less than 15% that of white families. Rothstein argues that this is 'almost entirely attributable to federal housing policy implemented through the 20th century.'

This *is* Critical Race Theory. It is seeking to understand differential social outcomes through analysis of the way in which racism and racial power have been and are ingrained in institutions and policies, which are typically interdependent and mutually reinforcing at federal, state, and local levels. Housing, education, and employment, for example, have not been and are not siloed phenomena. Institutions and policies have not been and are not 'colourblind,' thus the racial caste system that persists here. That I have been invited to write on our CRT panic for an overseas audience is evidence of how successful conservative propaganda has been. It is much easier to attribute racism to bad actors who appear as anomalies in the master myth of unimpeded progress than to confront the work required to reform or replace systems and institutions that replicate racial boundaries and racial inequities. Anti-CRT activist Christopher Rufo disclosed the strategy behind anti-CRT activism in his 15 March 2021 tweet: 'We have successfully frozen their brand—'critical race theory'—into the public conversation and are steadily driving up negative perceptions. We will eventually turn it toxic, as we put all of the various cultural insanities under that brand category.' Basketing every race reform initiative in employment and education as CRT, from workplace diversity and equity training to the 1619 Project to a 2014 picture book for kids on the ills of 'separate but equal', has muddied the waters. For centuries conservatives have distorted liberal ideas and language to undermine needed progressive reforms. Ignorant, erroneous, but easily digestible soundbites about CRT from right-wing politicians stoke resentments they hope to see pay off in the polls and elections in 2022. Florida governor Ron DeSantis defines CRT as 'basically teaching our kids to hate our country and to hate each other based on race' and Texas senator Ted Cruz observes that CRT 'is every bit as racist as the Klansmen in white sheets'. In the immediate wake of 24 May 2022 mass shooting at Robb Elementary School in Uvalde, Texas, a Fox News host (in a desperate effort to shift the focus from gun policy) offered this zero-sum analysis: 'We're spending all this money hiring critical race theory consultants. How about hiring some school therapists instead?'

Youngkin's victory in Virginia (which Biden carried by ten points in 2020) suggests an education roadmap that Republicans may traverse in other states to achieve congressional gains, though the sorry state of inflation and the economy obviate the need to rely on it exclusively. That roadmap is a cynical incitement of alienated white middle- and working-class Americans anxious about shifting demographics and the change that portends. To date around thirty-five states have signed into law or proposed legislation targeting the teaching of CRT in name or under euphemisms: sixteen states (including Virginia) prohibit or restrict teaching about race in state agencies or school rooms, and nineteen states are entertaining legislation to do the same. On the day of his inauguration, Youngkin issued Executive Order Number One 'to end the use of inherently divisive concepts, including Critical Race Theory' in Kindergarten through 12th grade public education. To be clear, CRT was never *there*, but in the aftermath of the 2020 murder of George Floyd and the historic protests provoked by it many educators began to think about how to incorporate racial justice issues into their teaching.

Americans ought indeed to regard civil rights heavyweights and activists as founding fathers and mothers alongside Adams, Jefferson, and Madison. In their wake the vile markers of American apartheid - signs reading 'Whites Only' and 'Coloured' that segregated space and access to it - vanished even as the racial power embedded in uncounted social practices became more difficult to perceive. Race-neutral language and pretensions to 'colour-blindness' slowed racial-justice reform because on the surface, in the absence of lynching postcards and twangy rednecks letting fly with slurs, progress was afoot. Yet to insist on colour-blindness or deliberate inattention to race is simply to make invisible the differential outcomes of policies. It is ahistorical, wilful blindness. Redlining looks like sensible risk-averse financing unless one asks questions like who lives behind these red lines? How did they come to live there? Why don't they move?

CRT developed in opposition to the concealments of the colour-blind ideal and as a response to now subtler forms of racial power. In the words of CRT practitioner Gary Peller: 'rather than seeing "racism" as an irrational deviation from rationality, we began to explore how liberal categories of reason and neutrality themselves might bear the marks of history and struggle, including racial and other forms of social power.' Racial power was therefore to be discerned in 'knowledge' production and in the 'neutral' institutions of American society and democracy. Peller gives the example of thinking about police reform in terms of the difficult history between the police and black communities rather than in terms of the 'neutral enforcement of rules'. I have sketched what a CRT approach to the wealth gap between white and black folks might look like, namely, analysis of an historical and enduring discrimination in key mechanisms for wealth building. Racism and racial power are no longer self-evident and the most elusive poison is whiteness. To build on the achievements of our founding fathers and mothers in the civil rights movement, we required cannier tools to detect, expose, and contest subtler forms of racial power enshrined in our policies and institutions. Ugly truths are no less true for all that. We have yet to find the words to speak and listen to one another about some of our ugliest truths like lynching (though the National Memorial moves us closer to readiness), much less the twisted skein that ties the 1926 lynching of Raymond Byrd in Wythe County, Virginia to the 2020 lynching of Ahmaud Arbery in Glynn County, Georgia. Critical Race Theory is an indispensable tool for disclosing a more truthful story about America because it unsentimentally exposes the past in our present with an eye to an America that is yet to come.

THE PARAMETERS OF SCIENCE

Colin Tudge

Ignorance in its literal sense simply means absence of knowledge, as in the Latin, legal term 'ignoramus' – meaning 'we do not know'. But 'ignorance' also means pig-headedness – albeit I hope with apologies to pigs: crass, uncouth, but also – most important – wilful denial of what ought to be obvious.

The two meanings are quite different. We are all of us ignoramuses in the neutral, legal sense because, quite simply, complete and certain knowledge is beyond us, and always must be. All our nuggets of supposed knowledge are partial: we know, or think we know, only what it has occurred to us to look at – and we are able to look what we choose to look at only with our imperfect senses, and seek to understand only with our imperfect brains. Indeed, as Immanuel Kant pointed out in the eighteenth century, we can never know the world as it really is. Absolute insight is not within the gift of mere mortals. When we do feel certain of anything we can never be certain that our certainty is justified. So ignorance in the 'neutral' sense -- the state of not knowing – is not itself reprehensible. It is just the way things are. It goes with being human, or indeed with being mortal. We just have to accept our unknowingness, and make the best of it. Wisdom, said Socrates (according to Plato), is knowing that you know nothing. Confucius apparently said roughly the same thing.

Indeed, to deny our innate ignorance and to claim knowledge that we do not have – and, worse, to act upon it! – is to be guilty of *hubris*, which to the Ancient Greeks was the greatest folly and sin of all; a prime theme of Greek tragedy, exemplified best of all perhaps by King Creon in Sophocles' *Antigone*. On the other hand, and in sharpest contrast, wilful denial of what should be undeniable – and, worse, refusal even to consider whatever is inconvenient – is bigotry. Hubris and bigotry both are vile; the twin pillars of unwisdom. But alas they seem largely to define the modern world.

Hubris and bigotry, often in grim tandem, can be seen at work in all areas of thought and all politics. Alas, they are very evident too in science - physics, biology, and the underlying philosophy of science, although science, above all, should be free of both. Fortunately, though, as science grows in maturity it seems in some respects at least to be learning the essential virtue of humility – and this, I suggest, is one of the few reasons for hope in the modern world. It should be making us, and particularly our leaders and policy-makers, less gung-ho.

Isaac Newton, one of the greatest scientists of all time, was not on the surface a modest man yet he famously declared after a lifetime spent widening the horizons of physics and maths: 'To myself I am only a child playing on the beach, while vast oceans of truth lie undiscovered before me.' In sharpest contrast, in the 1890s, two centuries or so after Newton, one of America's greatest physicists, Albert Michelson – who together with Edward Morley established the speed of light – suggested in a speech at the University of Chicago, that in physics it seemed probable that 'most of the grand underlying principles have been firmly established and that further advances are to be sought chiefly in the rigorous application of these principles to all the phenomena which come under our notice'.

Yet hard on the heels of that vaunting and risky proclamation came Einstein's special theory of relativity and Max Planck's discovery of the quantum which between them have turned all physics on its head and have left us, nearly 130 years after Michelson, with far deeper insights but also with deeper mysteries than had ever been dreamt of even in the wildest flights of theology or of art.

But I watch physics only from the distance. I have been much more involved in biology for many decades and have seen the same kinds of shifts unfolding before my eyes.

Biology re-born

When I was at university in the early 1960s biologists still suffered from 'physics envy': the belief that soon the life sciences would be 'reduced' to chemistry and that chemistry would be subsumed by physics and then by the abstractions of maths. This, it was widely assumed, was what scientific progress ought to mean: complete understanding of life, the universe, and everything, all expressed with the neatness and finality of E=mc2. In particular the biology that I learnt as an undergraduate was dominated by molecular biology on the one hand and the science of behaviourism on the other – and between them they seemed to have the life sciences sewn up, just as Michelson apparently supposed that physics had been sewn up.

Molecular biology ruled. It seemed to be the key to understanding. Thus in the 1850s Charles Darwin in particular established that living creatures *evolve*: that none of us first appeared on Earth in our present forms, but all evolved from primitive ancestors. Then in the 1860s in Brno in what is now the Czech Republic, Gregor Mendel showed that heredity in plants – and presumably in all living creatures – was mediated by discrete 'hereditary factors', contained in the parental gametes and combined in the offspring. In the early twentieth century Mendel's 'factors' were re-named 'genes' and so was born the modern science of genetics. At first the digital nature of genes seemed incompatible with Darwin's concept of gradual change over time but in the early twentieth century a loose collective of avant-garde biologists in Britain and the US put Darwin's and Mendel's ideas together to create what Julian Huxley in the 1940s called 'the modern synthesis'.

By the 1940s too it was becoming clear that genes are made of DNA – an otherwise obscure organic acid discovered in the nuclei of cells in 1869 by the much-overlooked Swiss biochemist Friedrich Miescher. Eight decades later, in 1953, Francis Crick and James Watson in Cambridge, building on data from Rosalind Franklin in London, described the 3D structure of the DNA molecule – the famous 'double helix'; and from that structure they were able to infer in outline how DNA actually *works*. In a nutshell, as Crick put the matter, 'DNA makes RNA makes protein'; and proteins, in the form of enzymes, control most of the metabolism of the cell.

So it was that by the early 1960s it seemed to many biologists, and certainly to suggestible undergraduates like me, that we now knew in principle how life works. Darwinian evolution plus Mendelian genetics plus the mechanisms of DNA gave us what might have been called 'the ultra-modern synthesis' – although as far as I know nobody ever did coin that expression. The essence of biology could be summed up in a paragraph. There was nothing left to do but dot the i's and cross the t's, just as Michelson suggested was true of physics.

The ideas of behaviourism completed the picture. For it seemed at least in some circles that all psychology – learning, memory, thought, and even, absurdly, *language* – could in effect be explained in terms of reflexes, shaped by what the American psychologist B F Skinner called 'instrumental learning': rewarding behaviour that was deemed acceptable, and punishing what was not (although, encouragingly, reward seemed to influence behaviour more effectively than punishment). In the seventeenth and eighteenth centuries in the ultra-rational years of the European Enlightenment various philosophers and scientists suggested that living creatures, including human beings, could fruitfully be conceived simply as mechanisms, elaborate versions of the clockwork mannequins that were then popular. By the mid-twentieth century it seems that this conceit was being vindicated.

Yet one hangover from earliest, pre-Enlightenment times persisted. Thus *Genesis* (1:27) tells us that 'man' (human beings) was made 'in the image of God' – with the implication that other life forms weren't, so that there's a clear gap between us and the rest. So although it was considered reasonable to suppose that human brains, like animal brains, were really just elaborate circuitry, it was not considered reasonable to suppose that animals actually *feel* the emotions that we do: happiness, elation; depression; angst; puzzlement; love. Behaviourists worked on the assumption that animals really are just machines, which merely look as if they experienced human-like emotions. To suppose that animals do feel any emotions beyond hunger, lust, and fear was to be guilty of *anthropomorphism,* which in my university days was the great no-no. Mother seals, it was supposed, felt no sorrow when their pups were clubbed to death with baseball bats before their eyes. They just looked as if they did. What looked like mourning was just a running-down of hormones.

Now, though – mercifully, I reckon – all the hard-nosed certainties of mid-twentieth century biology are being questioned, just as has happened in physics; and – again as in physics – whole new vistas are opening up that earlier generations of scientists never dreamed of. Here are just a few:

1.   First – mercifully – though it is still useful of course to explore the mechanisms of brain function and to apply its lessons, behaviourism as a whole, and the virtually religious dread of anthropomorphism,

has largely died a death. Notably, in the 1960s and onwards, Jane Goodall's studies of chimpanzees in Tanganyika (now Tanzania) showed that the immensely complex behaviour and social life of the chimps could *not* usefully be explained in terms of reflexes -- any more than the peregrinations of the planets can be usefully explained if we begin with the classical idea that the Earth is the centre of the solar system. In reality, individual chimps have their own *personalities* – and the personality of the leaders hugely affects the fate of the whole. So as the Cambridge psychologist (Sir) Patrick Bateson told me in the 1980s *(pers comm)*, 'Sensible anthropomorphism must now be seen to be heuristic'. Thus liberated, other biologists since Jane Goodall's pioneer studies have opened whole new dimensions. Animals now truly are emerging as fellow creatures, and fellow sufferers.

2. Molecular biology has similarly been opened up. The whole subject has become hugely more complex and is raising questions of a kind that science as commonly perceived – the kind based on experiments that lead to conclusions of a kind that can be falsified – seems inadequate. Thus, it's clear that Crick's proposed 'dogma' --- 'DNA makes RNA makes protein' does not tell the whole story. Far from it. For one thing the proteins that are made by the DNA (via the various RNAs), and other molecules that the proteins in turn help to create – can and do in turn affect the *modus operandi* of the DNA. That is, there is constant feedback. So it was that in his enormously influential best-seller *The Selfish Gene*, published in 1976, Richard Dawkins presented the DNA as a kind of dictator, esconced in the nucleus of the cell and issuing orders to the organism at large. But now we can see that in truth the genes are engaged in constant dialogue with the rest of the cell and so with the whole organism. They are not so much dictators as librarians, storing the information that the organism as a whole has accumulated over evolutionary time, and indeed during the lifetime of the host organism, and doling out this information as required. All this is beautifully described in Denis Noble's book of 2006, *The Music of Life*. Indeed, as his title suggests, it seems that to describe

the mechanisms of nature adequately – or even half-way adequately – we must venture beyond the normal vocabulary of science and invoke the metaphor of music: concepts that seem to belong to a different sphere – rhythm, melody, counterpoint, harmony.

3. Indeed, this line of thinking – the idea of a two-way conversation between the genes (DNA) and the rest of the organism – has given rise to the whole new science of *epigenetics*; the study of the many mechanisms that influence the behaviour of DNA. Among much else we can see now – very much contrary to mid-20th century thinking – that the experiences of mothers, not least during their own childhood and pregnancy, are passed on to their offspring, via the genes – or rather by the mechanisms that influence the way the genes behave' and it seems too that this effect may last for several generations. Thus, it seems, the reason that English women of my mother's generation (she was born in 1910) averaged only around 5 foot two or so inches in height (~ 158 cm) was partly because they didn't usually get a great deal to eat when they were young, but also because – importantly! – their mothers *and grandmothers* had had even less to eat. Thus working class women in 19th century Britain were lucky to reach five foot (~ 152 cm). Yet modern western women commonly top six feet (~ 183 cm) – partly because they are well fed during gestation and infancy but also because their mothers and grandmothers were well-fed. The same applies to men of course. I am taller than my father was but am dwarfed by my son. It will be interesting to see whether future generations will grow taller and taller if the high plane of nutrition continues. Will seven-footers (two metres-plus) be commonplace? Of course the genes are key determinants of height. But genes are influenced by experience – and they pass on the memories of their own experiences to the generations that come after. All this is very well summarised by Nessa Carey in *The Epigenetics Revolution* (2011).

4. There's been a huge shift too in the attitude of biologists towards microbes – bacteria and archaeans – and indeed towards viruses: their role in our own lives, and in the ecology of the world as a whole. For instance: when I first studied nutrition in the 1950s and

early 60s the hosts of microbes that lived in the gut were seen in effect as spivs. They just lived in the colon as 'commensals' – uninvited guests – which usually did no harm but sometimes got out of hand and made us ill – sometimes fatally so. Infant diarrhoea in poor countries where the diet is inadequate is a prime cause of death. Indeed in the early 20th century it was briefly fashionable to remove the colon altogether – an organ that was seen to do more harm than good. Now it's clear that the gut microbes are key players in animal – including human – nutrition. To stay healthy we need to maintain their diversity and keep them happy, and of course to keep the colon in good health. All is described in Tim Spector's *The Diet Myth* (2015).

5. The same kind of principles apply to the soil and to the nutrition of plants. The early nineteenth century saw the first stirrings of agrochemistry – the first artificial fertilizers; and by the mid-twentieth century agrochemistry was equated with modernity. Agrochemistry entered a golden age. It was known in particular that plants above all need nitrogen (N), phosphorus (K) and potassium (K). Farmers the world over – those who could afford it, and even those who couldn't – were encouraged to ply their crops with artificial fertilizer delivered in bags marked 'NPK'. Insects were zapped wholesale by new generations of pesticides of which DDT was the harbinger, while 'weeds' (a term that included and includes all wild plants) were seen off with a new range of herbicides.

But then it became increasingly clear at least to those who cared to look that life is not quite so simple. As Rachel Carson so memorably described in *Silent Spring* in 1962 the pesticides that killed the pests also killed the birds that hitherto kept the pests in check. And pests and weeds quickly developed resistance to the chemical agents that were meant to kill them. Now it's clear too that the fertilizers and various '-cides' between them kill off the soil microbes that had been assumed to be of little or no account, plus all the other creatures (worms, protozoans, arthropods) that between them keep the soil 'in good heart' (as farmers say). Thus, a good, truly fertile soil has an intricate architecture – able to hold both air and water with all its dissolved nutrients, in perfect balance; and this architecture is maintained by the myriad creatures that live in it. Wipe out the microbes and the soil fauna and the architecture collapses. The soil is reduced literally to dirt: powdery or baked hard when it's dry and to mud when it's wet, and always liable to blow or wash away. Soil degradation and erosion now affect up to a third of all agricultural land.

The lesson is that soil biology (on which in the end we all depend) and nutrition (of plants and animals, including human animals) *cannot* be conceived simply as exercises in chemistry and in simple cause-and-effect. Though agrochemistry still rules – abetted these days by biotech in its various forms – the thinking behind it can now be seen to be naïve in the extreme. Soil science and nutrition in all creatures should now be seen as an exercise in *ecology*. 'No man is an island', said the seventeenth century English poet and cleric John Donne; and now we can see that the principle applies to all life. All Earthly creatures including us depend in the end on all the others, including an untold host of microbes, most of which are hardly known at all. The wellbeing of each depends on the wellbeing of the whole – on the diversity and abundance of all the players, or at least a great many of them, at any one time and place. Ecology thus evokes the metaphysical – spiritual – concept of *oneness*, as in the Sanskrit *advaya* and the African concept of *ubuntu*.

But it's here, in the vital but much neglected and seriously under-funded science of ecology, that we are brought, starkly, face to face with the depths of our own ignorance.

What do we really know about our fellow creatures?

Ecology begins with an inventory: a *Who's Who*; just finding out what creatures live in any one place. But although many millions of expert people over the past 100,000 years or so have spent their lives trying to find out – hunter-gatherers, farmers, apothecaries, naturalists, explorers, and scientists (who now operate in international teams) - we still don't know *even to an order of magnitude* how many different species share this world with us. Fewer than two million have been formally described and named (which means several per day for the past 200 years). But even among the best-known and best-studied species – birds, mammals, frogs, fish, insects, flowering plants – new discoveries are still being added, probably faster than ever. So modern scientists now estimate that the true number of living species could be anywhere from five to 30 million – or 100 million-plus if we include bacteria and archaeans. Eight million is a conservative ball-park figure. So *at best* we have observed and formally described less than a quarter.

However, 'formally described' does not imply deep insight into ways of life. The inventory of species is only the cast-list. What matters are the way creatures live and the relationships between them, where 'them' includes us. As Hamlet commented (Act 2 Scene ii) 'the play's the thing'. But if our knowledge of the cast-list in any one ecosystem is sparse, our understanding of their interrelationships (and, vicariously, their impact on our own lives) is miniscule.

Consider, for example, the forests of the neotropics, from northern Mexico down to northern Argentina and Chile. They contain an estimated 30,000 different species of trees, out of an estimated global total of around 50,000 – and note 'estimated'. Each one interacts with a host of other creatures of all kinds, from bacteria to epiphytic mosses and ferns and pineapple-like bromeliads to frogs, bats, monkeys, birds, insects, arachnids, and everything in between. One study revealed over 4000 different *species* of insects on just one individual kapok tree. The number of possible interactions between all these creatures is literally infinite – and any one set of interactions may be hugely complex, as illustrated not least by the Almendro tree of Panama.

The Almendro is a 'legume': it belongs to the family of the acacias and the laburnum, and of peas, beans, and clovers. As a legume, it harbours bacteria in its roots of the genus *Rhizobium*, which 'fix' nitrogen: turn the ubiquitous but fairly inert atmospheric gas into soluble ions that the plant can use as nutrients. And like all trees of all kinds, and indeed like all the perennial plants that I know about, it depends on mycorrhizas – intimate associations with soil fungi that hugely increase the range and efficiency of its roots.

But it's in its reproduction that we see the full range of the Almendro's interdependencies. For after the spring rains the tree produces festoons of pink flowers which give rise to seeds that are contained within hard pods that have a fleshy exterior. Many different animals feed on the pods and seeds but the ones that matter to the trees are the fruit bats, which carry the pods away from the trees (otherwise they are ambushed by owls) and scatter them far and wide. The bats eat only the flesh around the hard pods and drop the pods with their cargo of seeds to the ground, and so the seeds are efficiently dispersed. But they are left on the surface, still within their wooden pods, where they cannot develop further.

Enter then the agoutis, local rodents like large guinea-pigs. They crunch away at the pods to get at the seeds. They eat some of the seeds – it's their reward – but then they bury, or cache, a fair proportion of them, like squirrels caching acorns; a store for later when food is scarce. Later they come back to dig up the seeds – but not all of them. Their memories are not 100 per cent. So some of the seeds – not many, perhaps, but enough – are left to germinate. Yet the game is not over for when the seeds do germinate the agoutis come back and eat the shoots – and so, it seems, the Almendro tree still misses out.

But there's a third player. The middle-sized spotted cats known as ocelots. They prey on the agoutis: not enough to wipe them out but enough to ensure that there aren't enough of them left to eat all the Almendro shoots. They are natural agents of pest control. So by the unwitting cooperation of bats, agoutis, and ocelots the next generation of Almendros is first widely distributed and then is effectively planted and protected. Human beings are now spoiling the arrangement in various ways – not least by killing the ocelots – but that is how the system has worked for many thousands and perhaps for millions of years.

It took decades of research by scientists at the Smithsonian Institution in Panama to work all this out. Yet over the whole neotropics there must be hundreds of thousands or millions of such scenarios being played out – some of which are already known to be even more complex than the tale of the Almendro. Books of biology – guides to identification; the accounts of naturalists; and a plethora of scientific journals – fill entire libraries. Yet what we know compared with what there is to know is minute. Furthermore, if we spent half the nation's GDP on ecological research we still could not get to the end of it. However much we know, or think we know, there might always be something we've missed. And as the former US Secretary of Defence Donald Rumsfeld famously observed, in addition to the things we know we don't know (like how many different kinds of tree live in Amazonia) there are bound to be a whole number of things that we don't even know we don't know (what he cryptically called 'unknown unknowns').

Furthermore, *it is logically impossible to gauge the extent of our unknowingness: our 'ignorance'*. We could not logically judge how little we know unless we were already omniscient, and so could compare what we do know (or think we know) with all there is to know. You may still feel of course as Michelson apparently did about physics that the main ideas of biology are already in place and there's only the details to fill in – but this is no more true in biology than it proved to be in physics. For one thing 'the devil is in the detail', as the expression has it. More broadly, some of the shifts in understanding we have seen over the past few years are not matters of detail but require a completely new mindset – including the idea that the science of nutrition is an exercise in ecology and not simply of chemistry; and the realisation among those who care to take note that ecology as a whole – wild nature – is far more cooperative than it is competitive: the complete antithesis of the idea that has prevailed since the mid-nineteenth century when Alfred (Lord) Tennyson spoke of 'nature red in tooth and claw' and Charles Darwin wrote *Origin of Species*. The false idea that nature is one long punch-up is deeply pernicious. It is used to support the idea that the ultra-competitive 'neoliberal' economy that now prevails is natural and is therefore morally justified, or at least is just the way of the world (but that's another story).

In short: for all our wondrous intelligence and scholarship and our powers of communication we remain profoundly ignorant in the simple sense that we know only a minute fraction of what there is to know – and it is logically impossible to judge how ignorant we really are; and, in the spirit of Socrates, the most expert experts are the ones who are most aware of this. True expertise is humble. The arrogance of *some* scientists and a great many entrepreneurs and politicians – their assumption that we already know all that is worth knowing and thus are able and have a right to re-design the world as we see fit – is ignorance in full flight.

Yet there is worse.

How can we be sure that anything we think we know is actually true?

We, human beings, like to think that we know a lot – and of course we do; enough to fill whole libraries and to dominate the Earth. Yet we cannot be certain that *anything* we think we know is actually true – and, of course, 'truth' is itself an elusive concept. Often we do feel certain, and *some* scientists and philosophers and religious evangelists are certain that what they say and do is *right*, factually and morally. But we can never be certain that our certainty is justified. It is very possible to be absolutely certain about things that later prove to be untrue, or that at least tell only half the story – and of course, much of what we believe is never shown to be untrue or incomplete because no-one ever gets round to looking, and often we have no means of testing our convictions even if we do get round to examining them.

The truth of all this is revealed by reference to the Logical Positivists (LP) – a group of philosophers centred on Vienna in the early twentieth century who argued in effect that the best ideas of science could be demonstrated beyond all possible doubt, and that any idea that could not be shown unequivocally to be true was mere 'gibberish' (logical-positivists liked the word 'gibberish') and should be dismissed out of hand. This included all metaphysics, including the core ideas of religion.

Their reasoning seemed impeccable – though this, I suggest, serves only to show that what is generally meant by 'reason' does not and cannot lead us to perfect understanding. Thus, the LPs insisted that all our ideas should be rooted in observations of the observable universe that could be reliably repeated, and measured. Observations of a kind that seemed undeniable, and were measurable, were deemed to be 'facts', and 'facts' were all that could or should be taken seriously. But facts *per se* are just shopping lists. What matters is to explain the facts – to provide narratives, accounts, of a solid kind known as *theories*. Many philosophers have felt that with enough facts the explanations would naturally follow – the idea known as 'induction'. But by the twentieth century it was clear to most philosophers that induction does not work. The explanations do not fall out of the woodwork. Indeed as Isaac Newton had observed in the seventeenth century, 'no great discovery was ever made without a bold guess'.

The necessary guesses are known as 'hypotheses', which are then tested by rational thinking and by experiment, always abetted as far as possible by mathematics. The whole process is said to be 'deductive', as opposed to inductive. Basically, the scientist says: 'if my idea is true then such-and-such a thing should happen'. Then he or she does an experiment to see whether whatever has been predicted does, in fact, happen. If the prediction is borne out then the hypothesis is supported. If not, then it's back to the drawing board. The maths – often of a statistical kind – that is used to test the ideas cannot be wrong. Maths can *prove* that its pronouncements are true, beyond all possible doubt. Done properly, maths is infallible. Or that was the assumption.

Doubts were raised when logical positivism was still in its infancy, from the 1920s onwards. First the Austro-Hungarian-American mathematical genius Kurt Godel showed that all mathematical statements that are not mere tautologies (in effect, matters of definition) contain presuppositions that are not themselves provable. In other words, even maths has a subjective element. Then in the 1930s the Viennese-British philosopher Karl Popper showed that whereas it is possible to show beyond all doubt that a particular hypothesis is false, it is not even theoretically possible to show that any one hypothesis is unequivocally true. For example (it's not a great example but it will do) it is possible to disprove the hypothesis that all swans are white. One black swan would put paid to that. But it is not possible to prove that all swans *are* white, because however many you observe there may be one lurking somewhere that's some other colour (and indeed there are black swans in Australia). That is: science is *not* composed of theories that have been shown unequivocally to be true, but of explanations that have not yet been shown to be untrue. But all our explanations are precarious, waiting to be knocked off their perch; and all are partial – never more than part of the whole.

Then in the 1960s the American philosopher Thomas Kuhn argued that science does not build an inexorable edifice of truth, stone by stone, as was often supposed (and still is). Instead at any one time scientists share a worldview – what Kuhn called a 'paradigm'; but as new observations and ideas came on board the paradigm begins to look more and more shaky until, at intervals, the whole edifice is shattered and a new one takes its place in what Kuhn called a 'paradigm shift'. The expression 'paradigm shift' is now used (and over-used) to describe changes of ideas and attitudes in all fields, and not just in science.

Finally, I do like the idea of the zoologist Peter Medawar -- that science in the end is and can only ever be 'the art of the soluble'. That is, scientists achieve the certainty they seem to do only by focusing on problems that they think they can solve. The really big problems, like 'why does the universe exist at all?' and 'does the universe have purpose?' and 'is there an intelligence behind it all?' is outside their field of inquiry. Of course, though, this does not stop some scientists from speculating, usually in the hard-nosed style of the now philosophically defunct logical positivists. But in such matters they have no special authority, though they commonly speak as if they do.

In short: ignorance in the 'neutral' sense – lack of knowledge, or at least of complete knowledge; and only partial understanding – is our lot in life. It goes with being human, or indeed with being mortal.

So where does this leave us?

Many people seem depressed by our inescapable ignorance. How terrible that we can never really claim to know or to understand *anything*!

But I don't find this thought – which I didn't fully appreciate until recent decades – at all depressing. Indeed I welcome it. I relish the idea shared by the 'Romantics', that life in the end is a mystery, beyond our ken. It's often said that scientists hate mysteries. But as Einstein, one of the greatest of all scientists, observed in *The Living Philosophies* (1931):

> The most beautiful thing we can experience is the mysterious. It is the source of all true art and science. He to whom the emotion is a stranger, who can no longer pause to wonder and stand wrapped in awe, is as good as dead —his eyes are closed.

I like, too, the notion that we cannot hope to reach understanding of all but the most circumscribed problems – the ones that Medawar said are soluble – just by being 'rational'. As Dostoyevsky observed in *Crime and Punishment* (1866): 'it takes something more than intelligence to act intelligently' - and that extra 'something' is in the realms of the mystical: seeking as far as possible to tune in directly to whatever it is that enables the universe to exist, and drives it; making use of all our faculties to see beyond what is immediately apparent, as best we can. Perfect knowledge and understanding are indeed beyond us. But it's the search for them that is truly exciting.

The other meaning of 'ignorance' – deliberately blinding ourselves to observations and ideas that disturb our own favoured view of life, aka bigotry – seems to me to be not only crass, but wicked; the height of irresponsibility. Yet bigotry has played a huge and often decisive role in human history and still does. It is manifest in racism (some people just can't bear to accept that people who are different from them may be just as worthy), or sexism, or snobbery. It is obvious too in climate change deniers – and also in those scientists and entrepreneurs and politicians who seek to replace traditional farming, which often demonstrably works, with high-tech GMOs and all the rest which look more 'modern' and promise short-term profits. Very obviously, some of the world's most powerful people in all walks of life – science, politics, economics, religion -- are bigots. One thing we can be certain of is that however open-minded and scholarly we may be, we can never arrive at perfect truth. But at least we should try.

THE CAN OF HAM

James Brooks

I'm writing this sitting alone on the eighth floor of the Can of Ham. You may have guessed, even if you don't keep up with the vernacular names of the latest office towers to sprout in the City of London, that yes, it's a building – so-called for its planar ovoid shape, redolent for British people of a tin of Prince's Cured Ham.

The offices are new and the whole space is immaculate. I am sitting at a bare table in the middle, facing the window. On both sides and behind me are banks of desks fastened with computer terminals, their screens black. The overall feel is 'business-class austerity'. Everything is straight lines and right angles, and the palette runs from charcoal to pastel grey. The air conditioning emits a hush of white noise, keeping the temperature lightly chilled and at odds with the early summer, early evening heat that has turned the sky a rich blue. The office seems hermetically sealed off from outside, as if two unrelated worlds have been brought into contact by reinforced plate glass, like in an aquarium. On my side, all is calm. But this is not the reflective calm of a monastery; it is the dead calm of a morgue. Apart from a few trays of leafy plants that I just had to check weren't plastic, I am the only macroscopic organism here. The offices are so spotlessly, antiseptically clean, I wonder if there are even any microbes around. It's six o'clock on a Friday and everyone else has left. For the next few hours (for me) or the next twenty minutes (for you) it's just the two of us.

I don't know who you are. Me, I'm a higher-education and science journalist. When I joined the company I work for, it was one of the few remaining independent specialist news publishers in the UK. Our offices used to be in a spacious but crumbling former Victorian workhouse where every six months there was a leak, or a power-cut, or a lump of fallen plaster appeared on someone's desk in the morning, and repairs were necessary. Then we were bought out by the higher-education arm of a big IT firm, but rather than joining them in their headquarters, we stayed put. Then came the pandemic and another buy-out, and we were folded into a bigger and swankier tech firm that acquired these big, swanky offices in the Can of Ham.

I am clueless about tech. I'm one of the last people under eighty not to own a smartphone. But even I could grasp the core of our first corporate buyers' business. They mostly sell software, especially indexing software for academic libraries. Their corporate branding is suitably slightly dated: simultaneously blocky and slightly fussy in the early noughties style. Our new owners are a more modern concern with their operations tightly yoked to scientific research. Their main trade is in processing, filtering, and analysing the digital era's preeminent product – data. The company's promotional videos play silently on a loop on a handful of flatscreen TVs around our offices. They feature clean, elegant branding with text promising 'solutions' and 'innovation' over stock video of pristine test tubes being loaded into a machine or medical equipment carefully being affixed to a patient. It's hard to grasp what is actually being sold if not some vague sense of progress towards a cleaner, invisibly managed future – of better living through data. On the other side of the plate glass, as if you didn't know, life expectancy is in retreat and the healthcare system sinks ever deeper into perpetual chaos.

In these videos, faith in knowledge to bring about positive change reigns supreme. At play here is a curiously desiccated, depersonalised version of what I'll call factual knowledge (philosophers have had other names for it) which is arrived at without much human intervention. You just need the right programme, or algorithm, and you can 'let the data speak for itself'. For sure, most data scientists would dismiss that phrase as naïve, but it remains a vital subliminal message in the marketing material of powerful IT companies like the one I now work for. Perhaps not unrelatedly, it has also come to underpin modern secular myths of progress and innovation now that huge, faceless institutional projects and giant computer systems have replaced alleged lone geniuses at the forefront of science. In this contemporary configuration, computer programmes comb over huge masses of fine-grained data to eke out patterns and correlations that are unattainable via conventional hypothesis-based trial-and-error testing.

Knowledge is produced, and you didn't need a felicitous flash of individual inspiration at three in the morning to obtain it. In this paradigm, or myth, the knowledge will then be applied to produce 'progress', 'innovation', 'solutions' – take your pick – and better living for all.

The Can of Ham claims to be rich with this kind of oddly outsourced factual knowledge. But it forgoes another kind: experiential knowledge (this time, philosophers also call it that). This is the type of knowledge that has got humans through the majority of their two-hundred-thousand-year existence. For most of that time it was transmitted orally. Unlike factual knowledge, it is highly resistant to translation back and forth from data. It still grounds us in our day-to-day lives. When we say we know someone, we are not saying we are familiar with certain facts of their life, or that we recognise their physical appearance. We are saying that we have *experienced* their character, or rather their being, in some way. Maybe even in the way that 'Adam knew Eve his wife; and she conceived...' (Genesis 4:1) or in which the mystics of all religions have known God, where to know God is to experience Him/Her/It. I'm not sure I'm making sense, but experiential knowledge is tough to describe. If you know, you know – you know?

Experiential knowledge may accumulate within a person to make them wise, and this wisdom has long been prized in our societies. But not here. In the Can of Ham, as elsewhere in the west, experiential knowledge is surplus to requirements, or must be subservient to factual knowledge. Sections of the professional managerial class may claim to value the 'lived experience' of those below them in the hierarchy, but this is just a socially advantageous mask for class-condescension and fundamentally untrue. They don't value it at all. Returning to science, the move towards patient inclusion in medical research is more genuine – and has proved more fruitful – but is done so that patients can furnish the factual machine with better prompts; the experiential knowledge isn't valued for itself. In the quotidian, we live permanently tethered to an infinite repository of factual knowledge via the internet, unable to cut the cord even for an hour or two. Today, social human experience and shared flights of imaginative fancy must always be curtailed; somebody must always whip out their phone to check a fact.

Well, not me. Just for a while I want to resist the tyranny of silicon-stored data. I've turned the laptop internet connection off. I bundled a few references – a note of the Genesis verse, a couple of statistics and quotes – into a Word document before I sat down to write. I want to speak directly to you, to write from my own subjective experience – from the heart, if you like.

I've stayed in the office to write not just to be embedded within my subject matter, but for the aircon. A heatwave that has grown in intensity across mainland Europe, with record monthly temperatures breached for many regions, has begun to gently bake the UK. It's around 31°C outside according to the last weather report I saw. When I sampled the fume-heavy London air at lunchtime it felt even hotter but now I'm back in the office and under the discreetly efficient aircon, I've put a thin jumper on and 31°C is just a number to me.

As are the other, lethal temperatures recorded elsewhere in the world this month. France hit 40°C yesterday, as did parts of central and southern US. Yesterday evening I watched an horrific Twitter video filmed from a car as it crossed farmland in Arkansas. For 40 terrible seconds, the camera panned across dead cattle arranged in blocks of a hundred or so, their bellies bloated, their legs up in the air, cooked alive by the relentless heat. Swathes of north, central and east Africa, the Middle East and south Asia have endured even more lethal extremes, breaking 50°C in some places. For inhabitants living there, far less respite from the heat will be available than in France or rural Arkansas, and daily life will require much more arduous exertion. The heat will have been acutely lethal to tens or hundreds of thousands of people. We don't yet know how many, and worse is yet to come. After three years of extreme and unpredictable weather, East Africa is already suffering from famine. Using UN data, the charity Save the Children estimated that around a quarter of a million children died of hunger in East Africa in 2021. (That bears repeating – a quarter of a million *children*.) This latest wave of brutal heat has decimated local crops and livestock once again but, worse still, coincides with the war in Ukraine – the most important exporter of grain to east Africa – and similarly agriculturally disastrous weather across Asia. In late May, the Indian government said it would block wheat exports after having promised to increase them last year. India is not a major wheat exporter, but this move further drove up grain prices and points to wider crop failures and further restrictions. In these sentences I haven't even begun to describe the climate crisis as it is currently unfolding. It is a crisis that has placed millions of people in or near the tropics 'in the mouth of the wolf', to borrow a French expression. They languish in the animal's fetid maw, unable to escape, their only goal survival when the jaws slam shut. Each time this happens, thousands disappear.

In the Can of Ham, as in all the other comfortable, air-conditioned enclaves of the global north, people continue, untroubled, to go about their business – the very business that caused the crisis. The deaths go unnoticed and the victims' stories unheard, even though they have been told for years. I do wonder when I hear the opinion, angrily directed at climate activists holding up traffic, that 'everyone *knows* climate change is a problem; blocking a road won't help', what that person does actually 'know'. Especially if they think climate change can adequately be described as a 'problem'. Certainly, very little experiential knowledge will be involved. But their factual knowledge will be scant and, crucially, will resemble belief rather than knowledge. They will say they *believe* that what scientists say is correct: that the planet is warming, that this is caused by 'human activity', and that this is indeed a worry ('for future generations' maybe).

I know all this because occasionally I am one of those climate activists holding up traffic and I have heard or read these words more than once. A few elements are worth noting. First, that our partially imagined person believes what *scientists* say. Not people living in Bangladesh, or the Maldives, or Mozambique, or in any number of locations in the tropics being battered by climate breakdown, but scientists. Such framing reflects the western media's presentation of the climate crisis, foregrounding scientific studies, and rarely covering the various climate-related catastrophes as they unfold in the global south. That framing informs everything people 'know' about climate change, including their focus on the planet *warming*. The word is so prominent in climate discourse it can be hard to imagine discussion without it. And yet, imagine if the protest-protestor (and the rest of us global northerners) had been informed by the relayed experiences of those on the climate frontline rather than a heavily media-filtered scientific consensus. In that case, the humanly imperceptible overall 'warming' of the planet by barely more than 1°C would hardly be at the forefront of the person's mind, whereas the disruption of the weather systems that are indispensable to agriculture might be. 'I believe that climate *chaos* is happening,' they might say. Instead, it's 'warming' which, for those accustomed to British weather at least, sounds rather welcome.

This person's claim to 'believe what the scientists say' is another profession of faith in outsourced factual knowledge. It echoes a slogan deployed by Joe Biden's team – and frequently used by now-vice-president Kamala Harris – during the 2020 US presidential campaign: 'believe the science'. With these three words the Democratic hopefuls sought to differentiate themselves from the ignorant, climate-denying, Covid-conspiracist Donald Trump in the minds of the educated, middle-class electorate. The slogan did its bit for Biden's eventual triumph. Then, within months of entering office, Biden had declined to halt oil drilling projects in Alaska, allowed one of the biggest ever auctions of oil concessions in the Gulf of Mexico to go ahead, and given another funding uplift to one of the most carbon-intensive, climate-wrecking organisations on the planet – the US military. But nobody apart from a few pesky climate activists cared much about this. For both the protest-protestor and Biden, the profession of belief itself performs some sweet magic; all of us believe the same thing, all shall be saved! Why are you protesting?

Such thinking, with its likely Christian roots, was summed up by the late cultural critic Mark Fisher (following a line of thought from Slavoj Žižek) in his short 2009 book *Capitalist Realism: Is There No Alternative?* In Fisher's words:

> Capitalist ideology in general [...] consists precisely in the overvaluing of belief – in the sense of inner subjective attitude – at the expense of [...] behaviour. So long as we believe (in our hearts) that capitalism is bad, we are free to continue to participate in capitalist exchange.

Fisher was discussing the supposedly 'anti-capitalist' movement when he wrote this. Obviously neither our protest-protestor nor Joe Biden are likely to concur with the statement that 'capitalism is bad', but that's by-the-by. What's important is the magic potency of belief in the late-capitalist psyche to absolve all sins. Possessing the supposedly correct belief means you are among the good guys, no matter your actions. Our protest-protestor is therefore free to carry on their car journey, pumping clouds of poison gas into the air, and Joe Biden can further entrench the global climate crisis with his policies.

It's worth noting just how far we've come from the factual knowledge which supposedly drives operations in the Can of Ham, and the techno-capitalist project more broadly. Neither Biden nor the protest-protestor claim to know much themselves, and make no real arguments based on their knowledge, but instead defer to knowledge held elsewhere ('science'), and by others ('scientists'). This is redolent of operations in the Can of Ham, with its eternally looped videos professing faith in the power of a knowledge that none of its employees possess. That sounds harsh, but it's the business model; the computer programmes get to work on decontextualised data, and no subject-relevant human expertise is called for. The work conversations I hear in the Can bear this out. They're mostly about business, or organisational management, or very occasionally some technical issue. They're not about any field of knowledge at all, they're about growing the company, which is another way of saying 'making money'. The genuine subject-focused discussions, when factual knowledge comes into play, happen, I imagine, in research departments as scientists pore over the analysed data before publishing it in journals that no non-scientist will ever read. Again, this sounds churlish, but isn't it true? And then there's the extreme stratification into minutely circumscribed subspecialties that most areas of scientific research have become subject to. So the scientists who do read those journals will mostly be expert in the same ultrararefied field, which most non-scientists will be unaware even exists. The factual knowledge that the techno-capitalistic system encourages such faith in is accruing, but diffusely, like microplastic in the ocean. We're still swimming in a sea of ignorance, and sea-levels are rising.

I called the feel of these offices 'business-class austerity' but there are signs that design consultants tried to inject some brand identity. There is art on the walls, mostly of the 'corporate unobtrusive' school, and there are also prints of successful modern scientists which make much use of white space and fail to capture anything of their sitters' personalities. Impersonal blandness is the order of the day. The company runs a 'hot-desking' system where employees book desks before coming in to work. Nobody leaves any personal items on their desk. There are no silly knickknacks, no piles of paper, no photos of family. Nothing to show that humans, rather than robots, work here.

The dominant western cultural narrative of technological progress and advancing knowledge has blinded us to the growing impoverishment of our everyday experience, which has in turn diminished our knowledge and understanding of the world in which we live. Socially, fewer and fewer of us are active in the kinds of complex interlinked, multigenerational communities that have typified human existence since the birth of humanity. We have so much less of the experience of our neighbours and relatives that comes from living cheek-by-jowl with them. Even at work, collective endeavours have been slowly replaced by tasks performed singly by members of a 'team' (the currently fashionable corporate buzzword intended to infuse a certain collegiality among an individualistic middle-class workforce). Or those not in a team at all. The advertised ideal of computer programmes combing vast virtual expanses of data unaided by human hand is a myth. It ignores the estimated twenty million people around the world who do the lonely grunt work that keeps the digital revolution going. This is 'microwork', and it typically involves tagging, cleaning and annotating the data that underpins almost all digital operations. The data is usually decontextualised which makes microwork mind-numbingly tedious, and also means it can be performed by anyone with an internet connection. It is therefore largely outsourced to the global south, and paid at shockingly low piecemeal rates. In his book on the subject, *Work without the Worker*, the British digital-economy researcher Phil Jones estimated the average hourly wage for microwork at less than $2 an hour, but added that because of the power of microwork platforms, up to 30 per cent of microworkers regularly go unpaid. The anonymous bedrooms of the global south where microwork is performed thus represent new 'zones of confinement', to borrow the sociologist Zygmunt Bauman's phrase, in which capitalism's dirty work is carried out, while the bourgeois western consumer carries on oblivious. Honestly, who even knows that 'microwork' exists? I couldn't tell you how much of it is being farmed out from the Can of Ham. And I don't know who could.

If most westerners' social experiences have been impoverished by techno-capitalistic 'progress', our experience – and knowledge – of the natural world has degraded to almost zero. Nowadays, it's as if a zone of confinement surrounds everything outside the man-made domestic, professional and consumer environments in which the western middle-class exist. Items – clothes, food, tech gizmos – appear on supermarket shelves as if by magic and we know little of the farms, mines and then factories from which they sprung. We know even less of the seasonal biological or geophysical systems that brought them into being. Our ancestors possessed this knowledge, intimately and experientially, and indigenous communities around the world still do, as outside industrialised society it is vital to survival. Among the general public today it has nearly vanished.

What are we filling our time and heads with? In a word, screens. So many of us spend the near-entirety of our waking lives staring at the things. 'Near-entirety' isn't even hyperbole. A UK study published in March estimated that half of UK adults now look at screens for eleven or more hours a day. Only the most evangelical Silicon Valley zealot stepping off a time machine from 1996 could argue this is time well spent, and that we are efficiently informing ourselves about the world. (Even then, is that any kind of substitute for experiencing it? Just for a few hours, at least?) No, most of that time we are passively absorbing the news and entertainment spectacle, communicating with colleagues or friends (often rather than speaking directly to them), or performing work that was, until at most fifty years ago, done otherwise but is now done onscreen. We forget that the word 'screen' also denotes a solid barrier that shields what is beyond it from view or reach. We're all looking at screens now, not the real world beyond.

We have become as the inhabitants of Plato's cave who think that the shadow-play unfolding on the wall in front of them *is* the real world. Like them we are alienated from the knowledge – experiential or factual – that would reveal the dancing silhouettes as an elaborate ruse. And this, as we have seen, at a time when the real world is in a state of profound existential peril. But we shut out the screams of those condemned already to the abyss, ignore the – admittedly quiet – voices of the scientists saying, unanimously, that we are on 'a fast track to climate disaster' as the United Nations secretary-general António Guterres correctly surmised, and remain glued to our screens and the frivolous shadow-play they display.

How does the climate crisis feature in the onscreen shadow-play? Mostly bizarrely transmuted into propaganda to the greater glory of western civilisation – as a 'problem' that the west can solve if it puts its mind to it, with cleaner, greener technology and a dash of political will. The speech of His Royal Highness, Prince William, Duke of Cambridge, at the Platinum Jubilee celebrations for his grandmother, may represent the apotheosis of this tendency. The scion of a dynasty in whose name so many genocidal, ecocidal atrocities have been carried out, a man who probably has a personal carbon footprint to rival a small African nation's, William approached the lectern with images of verdant foliage projected on the façade of Buckingham Palace behind him. He started with a brief history-rewriting routine which aligned the world's pre-eminent colonial family with the efforts of environmental activists. Then we were on to the 'unimaginable technological developments and scientific breakthroughs' of the last seventy years with the observation that 'when humankind focuses its mind, anything is possible'. Predictably, there was no mention of fossil fuels, or hyper-consumptive, hyper-mobile western lifestyles, or the neo-colonial resource extraction that serves it. There was just the promise that if we do 'harness the very best of humankind, and restore our planet' all our children and grandchildren 'will be able to say – with pride at what's been achieved – "What a Wonderful World"'.

William's speech was not followed by howls of derision and scorn. No mainstream commentator piped up to remind His Royal Highness that in many countries of the Commonwealth the children are unlikely to join in the chorus of Louis Armstrong's soothing psalm, for they had already perished. Obviously not, for Willliam's speech was emblematic of mainstream climate discourse in so many ways: in its presentation of climate breakdown as a problem for the future, in its unswerving faith in technology, and of course its blindness to reality – be that the one experienced by those on the frontline, or evidenced in scientific data.

And there's the thing, the laws of physics dictate that the climate crisis now ravaging the tropics can only worsen and spread. Carbon dioxide, the most common greenhouse gas, stays for several hundred years in the atmosphere. On a human timescale, therefore, emissions are effectively cumulative. Yet carbon emissions are not only rising, they are doing so at close to the highest rate ever recorded. To date the actions of major governments amount to no more than, to quote Guterres again, 'broken climate promises' and 'empty pledges'. On all the evidence, this will not change. We cannot imagine the horror that we have locked in. Climate collapse will not stop at the Mediterranean, or the Mexican border.

When the cataclysm hits the global north with the force that it is now unleashing in the south it will come as a brutal, terrible surprise. Even though we were warned – by millions on the frontline and by the science that we place so much faith in – we ignored those warnings and lost ourselves in a haze of self-aggrandising delusion and fantasy. The products kept appearing on the shelves and we never asked from where they came or how they got there. The real world stopped being real to us.

I imagine a climactic scene from the 2006 film *The Last King of Scotland* playing out on the carpet behind me. Nicholas Garrigan (James McAvoy), an idealistic young doctor working in Uganda who falls into a role as the personal physician and adviser to Idi Amin (Forest Whitaker), has incurred the formidable wrath of his employer. After a severe beating from Amin's henchmen which has left Garrigan bloodied and broken, Amin enters and confronts him. Eyeing Garrigan's pitiable form, he spits: 'Look at you! Is there one thing you have done that is good? Did you think this was all a game? "I will go to Africa and I will play the white man with the natives." Is that what you thought?' Yes, Amin senses, that is what he thought. He speaks again, as if to an idiot. 'We are not a game, Nicholas. We are real. This room here, it is real.' And then he delivers a strong contender for what will be the west's epitaph: 'I think your death will be the first real thing that has happened to you.'

It is dark outside, but the office is bathed in efficient, unobtrusive strip-lighting. The aircon whispers away and the air remains perfectly fresh. It's getting close to office closing time. I don't know if one of the staff on the front desk downstairs will come up and throw me out or whether the lights will automatically shut off and the door will lock and I'll be stuck here for the night. I'm going home. What you do is up to you. But know this: if you stay in the Can of Ham, however calm and comfortable it may be now, you're dead meat.

RIGHT TO IGNORANCE?

C Scott Jordan

Many questions have kept me from the release and peace that follows my head hitting the pillow at night. More recently, I have spent many a twilight hour pondering if Russian President Vladimir Putin has ever read Sylvia Plath.

It has recently been revealed to me that there is little doubt that Putin, like a good upstanding Russian boy growing up in a Soviet world, has delighted in the words of Alexander Pushkin, Sergei Yesenin, and, of course, Leo Tolstoy. It is also said he enjoyed classic Russian novelists like Fyodor Dostoevsky and Vladimir Nabokov. Even Russian fairy tales have stuck with Putin, such as those collected in the *Kolobok*, which make the most unforgiving that the Grimms had to offer, along with all of the Penny Dreadfuls, look like Baby Shark. When he is not filling his head with the dangerous-nonsense philosophical musings of Alexandr Dugin or 'the modern-day Rasputin', Vladislav Surkov – who believes Ukraine does not exist – Putin instead tops up with other worldly classics like the *I-Ching*, the *Book of Change*, a much more astrological book than I would think fitting his tastes, and Ernest Hemingway – oh the things you learn when you ask for whom the bell tolls! His admiration of Antoine de Saint-Exupéry's *The Little Prince* and the novels of Alexander Dumas makes me rethink my own readings of and admiration for these works. Perhaps he could do us all a favour and take a page from Hemingway's advice on mixing spirits and longing gazes down the end of a double-barrel shotgun. That was dark, but such is the case when we explore the sources of another's knowledge.

While it is not exhaustive, we can tell a lot from what a person reads. To begin, we can see what knowledge they may have or at least have been exposed to. But more importantly we can see what gaps leave room for uncertainty and ignorance. We put almost all of our epistemological efforts into trying to understand what others know. While this can be a most fruitful quest, we often, incompletely, refer to this as education. In actuality, it is only one side of the coin. Agnotology, the study of ignorance, can be equally as revealing and simultaneously self-revelatory as to what we ourselves do not, and perhaps cannot, know. So, instead of trying to sort between what Putin has read or what his media apparatus would like to have people think he enjoys reading, I wonder what exploration of ignorance Putin himself has taken on. This is where Plath comes in. In fact, after considered thought, had I the opportunity, I would not really wish to speak with Putin, simultaneous translation can be a bit of a headache, instead, I would gift him Plath's only novel, *The Bell Jar*.

Specifically, I might bookmark a passage found within the seventh chapter. She writes, 'I saw my life branching out before me like the green-fig tree... From the tip of every branch, like a fat purple fig, a wonderful future beckoned and winked.' She goes on to describe several of these fat purple figs. Various professions such as an editor or a professor, along with family opportunities of children and the options she had thus far been presented with as choices for a husband. She even describes an off-hand, girlhood dream of being an Olympic women's crew champion. She continues,

> I saw myself sitting in the crotch of this fig-tree, starving to death, just because I couldn't make up my mind which of the figs I would choose. I wanted each and every one of them, but choosing one meant losing all the rest, and, as I sat there unable to decide, the figs began to wrinkle and go black, and one by one they plopped to the ground at my feet.

It is a rather relatable passage, especially for those of us caught up in our postnormal times. Our constant, instant updating and overstimulating climate of information leaves us with a wealth of options when we contemplate the future. Only the slightest whiff of despair has our opportunities rotting before we can harvest their potential. At first glance, it feels like a trap, one all too relatable and challenging for the futurist who is constantly scanning the upcoming horizon for what is coming but is unable to cope with the recombinant complexity, chaos, or contradictions that come with each new horizon.

Geopolitically the trap is none more real than to Mr. Putin, I presume. Whether his fat purple figs were Odessa, Mariupol, Kyiv, or even Snake Island. Or even the death of NATO, control of Ukraine without invasion, doubling down on Belarus and Chechnya, or drawing together the Collective Security Treaty Organisation (CSTO) or the Eurasian Economic Union (EAEU), making them forces to be reckoned with. The restoration of Russia to global influence as seen in the Czarist days of old and the flexing of Russian culture and power in Europe, Asia, and beyond plopping to the ground at his feet.

To read this passage out of context, one is left with a rather simplistic view of the future, more specifically what futures can tell us. The future is a vastness of choices and when we make one, some are nullified – also the essential mechanic for the 2022 film *Everything Everywhere All at Once*. For those who are aware, we are left to either accept or mourn our potential possibilities. But, you see, that is not quite what this passage is about. Unfortunately, it is often read out of the context of the novel, aided by the fact that the novel is fairly autobiographical, and instead read in the context of the world in which Plath brought about this work. I am referring to what would take place on 11 February 1963, within a month of the publication of *The Bell Jar*. Plath herself woke up early, she had been waking unusually early due to a bad bout of insomnia. She moved into the kitchen, sealing it off from the room where her two children slept with clothes, towels, and tape. She then proceeded to turn on the gas and place her head deep within the oven. By nine in the morning, she would be found by the nurse hired to assist her daily with the children as she adjusted to a new antidepressant. She was thirty years old. And thereafter, every word Plath had ever written must have been a window into her most unfortunate end, right? Can it not be so simply written off? Well, I suppose it could be, but what a tragedy. Another hysterical woman incapable of reconciling the real drag reality tends to be or hormones, case closed. Not quite.

Let us look back at the novel. Granted, it is a rough read dealing with issues of mental health and sexual violence that we still, today, not only meteorically under-appreciate but grossly misunderstand. And perhaps we cannot separate the clinically diagnosed depression of the artist from their work, I am not particularly interested in weighing in on one side or the other here. Indeed, the main character, an obvious analogue for our writer, Esther, is committed to a mental institute where she undergoes electroshock therapy. In fact, on a troubling number of incidences throughout the novel, Plath uses electricity as a metaphor for or association with something good or progressive – in other places, Plath has indicated the successes of her own electroshock therapy. But, then again, this could have well been an effect of the treatment. When we look at the endgame, questions abound. And I'll even do you one better, one proposed title for the novel early on was *Diary of a Suicide*. But I do not think this was just a book about the value or inevitability of suicide as some would have it. Rather, *The Bell Jar* is a book about change and more importantly, what we look like as we go through it and once we have reached the other side of it. Depression and suicide are without a doubt a part of this, but not the emphasis and certainly not the apotheosis. And for a novel written at the beginning of the 1960s when the times were indeed a-changing, the novel embodies this, taking a pretty drastic flip a third of the way through. Think of the difference between what the library of National Lampoon's films tells you American universities are like (shenanigans, copious volumes of alcohol, and full-frontal nudity) versus the image painted by various exposes into sexual crime, hazing, nepotism, and corruption that really go on in the Ivory Towers. And the passage above is placed almost right at the moment Plath's novel takes this epic flip.

Prior to chapter seven, *The Bell Jar* is a pretty interesting slice of life depicting young women having fun in New York, working for a professional women's interest magazine, and getting into all kinds of harmless trouble and frivolity. And without the apologia of having to say look at the contrast between what men and women go through, in order to make the same point, Plath simply shows us. Look at all the wonderful things women can do beyond being a secretary or typist. It's rather refreshing, that is until it is not. Just when Esther is under the impression that she is charting a new course of independent and capable women, fully equipped to do anything a man can do, she realises she is still in the confines of a rather messed up normality. After learning that her de facto fiancé, Buddy, was not a virgin, she learns that he has had numerous affairs and that society does not seem too concerned about it, while had their situation gone the way Kate Bush suggests and been switched, the centre would definitely not hold. In the novel's first major comparison of what men can do and women cannot, she questions how the conservative American family could exist amid such an inequality-inducing hypocrisy. So, in sticking to the motif of independence and trendsetting of the first part of the novel, Esther contemplates having an affair of her own.

In recalling Buddy's shockingly unchaste reveal, Esther is faced with Constantin, a foreigner who works as a translator for the United Nations. She delights in the fact that he could physically pass for any old American, but that a certain exoticism in his action and demeanour makes him most definitely not an American. It's problematic, but at least it is honest. It is a wonder what a little honesty could do for our present world. While debating whether or not to take the leap and let Constantin deflower her, she ponders the passage above. But not directly in the way one analogises an existential crisis. Instead, she comes about it more organically in that stream-like way one happens upon thought or revelation. But first, in spending time with Constantin – which makes her happy – she notes that she had not been that happy since she was nine years old, the age when her father passed away and her childhood effectively also died.

In the most eloquently written description of boredom I have yet come across, Esther's mind begins to wander while attempting to listen to the multilingual and rather dull debate of delegates on the UN floor. She is attempting to find the root of happiness. Unable to decouple happiness from action, she begins devising a list of all the things she cannot do. In each ability's contemplation, she considers what happiness would be denied or accessed with a knowledge or skill of each said capacity. It is not far into the list of her incompetence that she feels dreadfully inadequate. And then comes the vision of the fig-tree. But what remains is the happiness, uninhibited. It is interesting because each thing she cannot do is something suggested to her by a variety of elders who in their own pursuit of these necessary skills, have lost their happiness. So, she is better off, at least for the hedonist or utilitarian, having ignorance in these areas. And when we return to her vision of the fig-tree as future, her anxiety is not whether or not she can stomach eating all the figs at once, but if, in the end, they will increase this feeling of happiness she has recently rediscovered, like an old friend not spoken to for an extended period of time having suddenly shown up at her front door.

Plath even goes on to write off the fig-tree metaphor within a few paragraphs when Esther and Constantin head to a Greek restaurant. The whole pseudo-nightmare might well have just been the ruminations of a hungry stomach. She cannot quite remember what they ate, but food essentially drowned out her feelings of insignificance. Where earlier she felt she was not worthy of the esteemed Constantin with his linguistic skills and swagger, she leans into a made-up dream, saying she wishes to learn German (the language of Plath's father she sort of develops a love-hate relationship with throughout her poetry) and become a war correspondent. Maybe a lie, maybe a justification, but as she spills out the fubar to Constantin, she feels validated and the ignorance-is-bliss carries her through the courses of their dinner. By the time she reaches the yoghurt with strawberry jam, she is prepared to allow Constantin to 'seduce' her.

Ignorance-is-bliss has gained a significant currency in recent times even though it is antithetical to our fundamental nature, if Aristotle or Descartes are to be heeded. From the perspective of futurists or political junkies or anyone with concern or care for what is happening in the world, from a whole range of academic levels, it makes some sense. The phrase 'no news is good news' is the new political zeitgeist in a world full of politicians who cannot make heads or tails of the day. Ironically, they cast old playbooks and codes of ethics to the dustbin, diving into ignorance, for maybe in that some knowledge can be gained. Bottomline is the world is rather depressing, so why not live in a bubble. Maybe it would not be so bad to be plugged into the Matrix or Robert Nozick's Experience Machine. We know it is a cop out, but we cannot break from it and worse, we cannot keep but from making excuses for its allowance. It begins as those white lies we tell our loved ones or those we have empathy with. You look great, I love that top, did you get a new haircut, Dad-bods are the new black, and all the other rubbish we tell to make each other feel better. But half-lies or any other fractional partition of the truth is that – a diminishing of the truth. Why are we sometimes okay with it and sometimes not? Because the other side of the coin is, these guys have Weapons of Mass Destruction or these guys are Nazifying the place, so we better kill them before they kill others or worse, kill us. So fellow countrymen lend me your anointed fully automatic, precision scoped, heat seeking, customised rifles (which are totally necessary for weekend deer hunting) and your holy hand grenades, its clobbering time!

But wait a minute, are things not getting a bit appley and orangey here. Complimenting a friend who is wearing a less than flattering outfit or telling my mother she is looking majestically regal when she feels and presents somewhat less is not even in the same ballpark as the ignorance traps of George W. Bush and Putin which ended up getting their respective citizens (and frankly the rest of the world who would rather not have had to be bothered over the matter of revenge or whatever fluffy language you want to hide that motive in) into kerfuffles that last well beyond their expected due dates. But is it? It is the problem of little lies, we can forgive one here or there, but we all know well and good that little lies become historical inaccuracies or even propaganda and all the nastiness that follows in their wakes. And these extremes, though I hesitate to call them that, are bridged by the little lies we allow or that we are simply ignorant to. Increasingly, our lives are inundated with the lies of algorithms, what we see, what we are told we want, and even our motivations are driven by algorithms that have been shown time and again to be shamelessly lathered in bias and fascistic tendencies toward xenophobia. The more you think about it, the more it becomes clear that these little lies are not some exceptions to the rule or mild bending therein, they are the rule themselves. Rather, society seems to accept the norm that lying is acceptable except in the cases where you may get caught or cause harm to the one or the many. And this is solidified in one simple, but no less dangerous, thought.

Well, at the end of the day, is it not simpler to let people be as they wish, think as they like, and live in the bliss and warm comfort of their ignorance. Why not raise the stakes? Do certain people have a *right* (divine, natural, or constitutional) to their ignorance and who are you, bastard, to interfere in their feigned tranquillity? And this brings to mind my grandparents and the television phenomenon brought into this world by Gene Roddenberry in 1966, *Star Trek*.

Growing up a Midwestern American kid surrounded by the uterine safety provided by American exceptionalism and the laurels of having won the Cold War, I am no stranger to ignorance's blissful properties. In fact, the doubt of the truth behind America's being the best nation in the world and whether or not the Cold War could end (how were we to carry on without hating on the exotically familiar Russkies?) fuelled the caffeine like surges of patriotism that punctuated 1990s middle America. Nothing like a diarrhetic to keep you drinking from the hose. But the greatest lie came in that we now lived in a more civilised age, having defeated all our old flaws. Academics called it the end of history, but commonly our education system fed it to us as the sentiment that we had reached the mountain top. Race, sex, disease, inequality, poverty, technology, barbaric primitivity, language games, difference, it had all been beaten, or at least we had it all under control. The late great American writer, Michael Crichton, wrote extensively on this notion of control which was, in reality, a lack thereof. But this spoon-fed medicine, followed with a spoonful of sugar, has made us none the wiser and as a growing boy I had this thrown in my face with visits to my grandparents, where the generational divide was clearly shown to me to be alive and well.

While both my father's and mother's parents came from different midwestern towns, their towns told the same story. All from rural areas that were never too far away from the big city, a terrifying notion that they grew to loath as they aged, resenting anything that dragged them into the wretched suburbanism of midwestern cities. Raised on the poverty of the Great Depression they got by fine on what they could get (my grandfather often threatened to serve us dandelion soup or various road-kill centred delicacies for dinner). Too young to join the gung-ho jubilation of World War II and too old to experience the transcendent horror of the Vietnam War. The Midwest, often described as Fly-Over country, remained relatively isolated not only from the rest of America but the greater world. Although segregation was history for them, the lines that once were upheld, remained firmly in the subconscious of urban development and civic planning. Yet, despite their being 'cut off' from the outer world, all four grandparents were avid fans of history and travel. So, to say they were your average midwestern 1990s grandparents would not quite do it justice. There was no strong devotion to a family business or duty to serve one's country or even to religion or the church. They also broke from the stereotype in being rather loyal Democrats, hold overs of Franklin Delano Roosevelt, renewed by John Fitzgerald Kennedy's zeal, and hatred for Richard Nixon. While neither was impressed or disappointed by Jimmy Carter, who couldn't love Bill Clinton, he is that ideal flawed American who excuses the rest of us for our all-too-human existences. Ironically, many of their children grew up to be card-carrying members of the Republican Party. Perhaps this is what youth's rebellion against the parents gets you in late twentieth-century America. And while they would openly praise Al Gore, their politics as time went on revealed some murky bits.

Conversations with my grandparents were never a stranger to flirting with and even down right diving into the realm of what today would be considered 'not PC'. Often times, I think my grandparents would do this on purpose, prototypical edge lords, attempting to get a rise out of little Mr. Progressive. Indeed, my grandparents were far more open-minded and progressive than most of my peers, but in certain linguistic details, a contradiction arose. Many of my grandparents' stories had an element of the fantastical, a sort of mystical realism that you find in the concept of a tall tale. And certain minority characters would be described with certain terms that I would rather not utter here as they do not entirely serve much of a purpose. But I knew my grandparents were not racist per se or even prejudiced. My grandfather himself was often grouped in with the Irish in an age where being Irish was not very fortuitous in the Midwest, without having much of a pedigree to put him in that group. Social exclusion makes strange bedfellows. Yet he slung around racial slurs without vitriol or much concern. The dreaded n-word was thrown around without any sort of emphasis or sentiment of belittlement. The endemic ignorant pacificism behind that word in the context of my grandparent's world was brought to life to me when my aunt once told the story of an awkward encounter where she was not sure what to call Brazil Nuts at a social gathering, as back home they had always been referred to by a moniker one would be best to avoid in polite company.

It's a strange sociolinguistic evolution that allows for words and sentiments born out of anger, hatred, and othering to be pacified. Thus, a speaker can give power to an endemic xenophobia without holding the sentiment themselves. And beyond just the racialised language other contradictions could not help but slip out. Though they were still ardent supporters of the Democratic Party, well Hilary could not make a great president, you know, she's a woman. And well, Barack Hussein Obama, even after we navigate the minefield that is his name, he is after all... It was always weird to hear my grandmothers use the argument that men are more fit to rule than women when there was no doubt that their own households would be unable to last for a few seconds without their management. And there was always this defensive walk around language to justify which just made it all the weirder. And it was not that I would love my grandparents any less for their opinions. In fact, I think the greatest threat to global society today is whatever keeps us from learning to love those with different ideas than ourselves. The contradictions, at least at the time, of one's language and one's sentiment were unascendable. And this might well be at the heart of the United States' contemporary condition. What deeply troubles me is not that these contradictions exist, but that we excuse them with one simple idea. That is just how they were raised. They are of a different time. Something equating to the inability one will experience in teaching an old dog new tricks. And the kicker is that my parents would say we have to let go and forgive what they say, they know not what they do I suppose, but that we, my brother and I, were to, under no circumstances, use certain words, phrases, or sentiments my grandparents uttered lest we face the wrath of a mother's fury.

Before I even knew the term, cultural relativism was deemed the best way. Even if it felt kind of wrong. In high school I joined the American football team. At my particular high school there were three men on the football team with the surname Jordan (and as far as I can tell none of us are related, but Jordan is a rather common last name in the US) which creates a dilemma as it is convention for American athletic coaches to refer to teammates by their last name. And all three of us were linemen, so to distinguish us was no simple task. While one of us was tall, the other two were equal height, so the typical prefix of 'Big' or 'Tall' to Jordan only did a third of the job. And our skin tones only differed ever so slightly depending on how far through the season we were after long sun-exposed practices. So, our lineman coach took to breaking convention and calling us by our first names. The only issue was, he had gotten them wrong and we, mere mortals, dare not break decorum or stand up to the intimidating presentation of this particular coach. So, for two years, after school I became 'Andrew', sometimes 'Drew' and my fellow Jordans followed suit with their new football names. One day, this coach learned of our ruse when an ignorant wide receiver called me Scott in his earshot. I was called into his office the next day and given my weight in being told off along with the promise of extensive push ups and laps to run for punishment for making the coach look like an idiot. I tried to explain the web of respect, subordinance, and lack of care for whatever people called me I was attempting to navigate. In response, he gave me sporty platitudes that normally make me vomit in my mouth, but he had a point. 'Would you willingly tell a teammate something that would make them screw up out there on the field, just to make them feel better about themselves?' Ah, yes, as they say the truth hurts, but it shall set you free. This highlights the dilemma I have grappled with for most of my life. How could I allow my grandparents who I love and respect dearly to live in ignorance like that? Similarly, this conflict arises in my travels and interactions with a variety of cultures, norms, and ways to life. Truth must exist, God willing. Otherwise, what are we doing? Throw it all away if the inverse is the case. Yet to speak out against certain cultures can easily come off as racist or insensitive. Perhaps, but is not the greater racism in allowing another to be othered in such a way, to be left to the fate of ignorance, something that cannot possibly hold in perpetuity?

And here is where the *Star Trek* franchise refracts an interesting insight and reveals the wider scope of the trap we find ourselves in concerning the ignorance of others. Through its various permutations, *Star Trek* follows the crews of various space exploration vessels on a mission 'to explore strange new worlds, to seek out new life and new civilizations, to boldly go where no man has gone before'. These crews are military installations working under the command of Starfleet, the space force controlled by the United Federation of Planets in the twenty-third century. Critical to all operations, missions, and adventures undertaken by the characters in *Star Trek* is the Prime Directive. Also referred to as Starfleet General Order 1 or the non-interreference directive, the Prime Directive 'prohibits Starfleet personnel and spacecraft from interfering in the normal development of any society, and mandates that any Starfleet vessel or crew member is expendable to prevent violation of this rule'. This rule sort of waxes and wanes in its importance from episode to episode as writer's digression allows and series to series, sort of presently on a downward trend. But what a strange rule for Roddenberry to build into the foundation of this science fiction series. Perhaps it is a ready-to-hand exit clause whenever the show decides to start playing with space-time. More easily, it has been labelled as an allegory, if not effect of the history of international doctrines between the eighteenth and twentieth centuries to regulate the practice of imperialism. But when I look at the Prime Directive, my parent's response to my grandparent's inconsistencies, a wave of the flag to postmodernism's relativity ad infinitum, I see something deeper at play. Interesting that Starfleet would not want other civilisations to be saved or advanced. It would be more difficult to control them were that the case. But, of course, Roddenberry comes out of that generation looking to respect others, loving them to death to a certain extent. Respecting them so much that we prevent them from changing with time and, whether intentional or not, maintaining their otherness. Not that the show does not do its work. A multitude of episodes address the violation of the Prime Directive, where one race is given an unfair advantage to another or where Starfleet officers are worshipped as divine, God-like beings. Interestingly, the concept is further complexified when Starfleet characters run into what are essentially God-like beings that have no regard for revealing the ignorances of the crew, often for self-gain. But while it is a fun think-piece that has produced some beautiful television and films, I think it has darker undertones that need to be surfaced.

Roddenberry developed *Star Trek* just as postmodernism was picking up steam, right at the cusp before it started infiltrating a variety of areas of thought and expression. Roddenberry clearly had in mind the hope of envisioning a better future for humanity. And he made no small contribution to thinking about how we could better ourselves, the show itself breaking a lot of ground for racial, sexual, and xenophobic progress towards ultimate harmony. This is brilliantly displayed in the third season of the original series in an episode titled 'The Savage Curtain', originally airing in the woeful year of 1969. The crew of the USS Enterprise lead by Captain James T. Kirk, in the course of their travels, come across a figure claiming to be none other than former US President Abraham Lincoln. After being brought aboard the bridge, Lincoln is introduced to the crew including Communications Officer and Translator, Lieutenant Uhura (whose name is Swahili for 'freedom'). Overcome by her beauty, Lincoln utters 'what a charming negress,' which he immediately retracts realising the error he made. He apologises realising that from his time, that term was often used as a description of property. Uhura responds asking why she should be offended in this time noting how in the twenty-third century they had moved beyond fearing words. Racism or at least racial slurs were apparently so buried in history that the crew of the USS Enterprise would not know where to begin in registering such types of hatred and the offense therein. While indeed much of the vision put on by Star Trek is firmly held within the realm of what postnormal times literature describes as Familiar Futures, discussions and thought inspired by the show have pushed people to consider what we might call Unthought Futures.

Unfortunately, Roddenberry and those behind the *Star Trek* franchise are unable to think of a future beyond postmodernism which has and continues to do quite the number, colonising and trapping certain potentialities in all our futures. A key issue with postmodernism comes in its very definition itself. The argument goes that there are no grand narratives, which is a grand narrative in and of itself. The problems only compound from there. But the critical feature which has made it so attractive to thinkers and those trying to heal certain historical wrongs is this notion of a fundamentalist grade of relativity. While this relativity makes significant steps in opening the discussion for respect of and appreciation for others' cultures and worldviews, it lacks a guide rope and too often allows us to fall into the crevasse of tolerance. I can recognise and acknowledge your way, but I am not required to go beyond this in attaining understanding or acceptance of anything you have to say or decide to stand for. Relativity dictates that you must allow me to do as I please just as I allow you to do as you please. The fracturing of any hope for a tranquil society is evident as culture itself becomes a nonentity, political and social systems will be confounded trying to adjust and correct for it, and any hope for an ethical system falls at the waist side. Where do we even begin to judge right from wrong where these items are now completely and utterly subjective and individual beliefs demand supremacy. Critical thought cannot lay down roots in this environment.

Infected by postmodern apologia, whether intentional or not, the Prime Directive and this great future of Star Trek has some issues. First off, the modernist propensity for exploration, bathing in all of modernity's flaws without any critical reflection, underlines that a certain imperialism, colonialism, and, with all the militaristic structures, even a certain level of fascism exists in this future. To simply wash this away with a rather flimsy policy of half-baked respect seems very problematic. In fact, the Prime Directive presents as a giant literary 'we're sorry' for the White Man's Burden but without actually doing anything to change that train of thought or make restitution for the wrongs it has perpetuated. The biggest issue I have been discovering in postcolonial history, particularly from the British perspective, let us call it the dismantling of the British Empire, is that this dismantling was done as passively as possible so that it could continue to exist in all but name and be remembered as a success in civilising the primitive native. The White Man's Burden, which was used as a justification of imperial brutality and colonisation, survived the fall of the British empire nearly unscathed, it just could not call itself that anymore. Who are the British to dictate what is civilisation and progress, so let us not challenge ourselves to think of a new way of looking at progress, let us just take the easy way out and say, well it is all relative when you think about it, really. The Prime Directive is a nice pat on the back to the United Federation of Planets. Our way is obviously the right way and it is our right to learn as much as we can, but if some aliens – natives – are not on our level yet, we shall just wait until they come around to seeing things our way. And it is not just *Star Trek* that carries forward this problem left undealt with.

While postmodernism has reached its pinnacle in architecture, art, film, television, and music, it not only runs out of its own tired cliches but perpetuates this necessary little lie. In fact, while a film may not be entirely postmodern these days, it still reeks when an unsatisfied ending is delivered. The audience learns a pivotal unknown just as the so-called protagonist does, only to see it as his or her undoing. Far too many stories, explicitly postmodern and otherwise, are contingent on a necessary ignorance of the protagonist. If the protagonist is to learn the ignorance too soon, the film cannot happen, so for some reason (sometimes justified and other times left, hoping the audience does not think or ask questions) the protagonist walks on in the dark until the plot deems it necessary for them to learn and hopefully become a savoir. I will not get into whether or not the people he or she is supposed to be saving needed or wanted his or her salvation. So, it has become endemic in the art of storytelling; and technologically advanced and progressive society (mostly of the northern and western variety) not only allows, but even encourages the little lies.

But some of the best of what Christianity has to offer tells me to love my fellow humans, while some of the best Islam has to offer asks me to know my fellow human beings. And while I can love people who disagree with me, it is very hard for me to justify leaving people I love or grow to care for in blatant ignorance. And perhaps you might ask, well why are you so worked up. This is just a few stories or a backwards generation or group that eventually will reach an end and what will it matter what they knew or did not know. Well, as is the case in postnormal times, things are happening faster, in a more simultaneous manner, and in our own confounding complexity. It does not take much for simple ignorances to become societal undoings. A few harmless little lies could easily turn into personal or societal (or both at the same time) threats.

Our most recent societal enactment of John Carpenter's 1982 film *The Thing* – where each character is reduced to being incapable of trusting the other characters as they try to figure out who is the monster hiding amongst them – was the recent global Covid-19 pandemic. Who has it, who is positive, do you trust everyone you have been in contact with, have you noted everything you've touched today, when was the last time you washed your hands, dare you make contact with someone you might put at risk, was that a cough, a sneeze, or the scourge virus itself? The paranoia was real, and a certain degree of trust was necessary, for governments, organisations, and businesses to do right with the vast swaths of power instantly given over and for citizens to keep themselves well, clean, and be vigilant so that the virus could be quickly added to the annals of history. And perhaps if an individual was found to be an agent of biological terror, licking public utilities or sneezing in the general direction of the innocent, then perhaps mob justice would do some good and see to the tarring and feathering of the superspreader. Sounds ridiculous, but is it? Let us not forget the mass chastisement of Asians in the US and UK for their role in spreading the disease, regardless of whether or not they, their parents, or even their grandparents had been born anywhere other than within the borders of the very country they are being reminded that some do not give them welcome within. And of course, once we were done blaming the Chinese or anyone resembling whatever that quintessential stereotype of the Chinese Asian boogie man has run its course, what other dirty people's spread virus. Of course, refugees or immigrants of whatever variety you prefer based on the home country you are looking at. There's some fun relativity for you. And then the LGBT communities and specifically the clubs and social centres friendly to these groups. If one is so liberal and open with their sexual practices, then it must be the same with their hygiene. Of course, all this hate and the flawed logic used to bring it about are utterly ridiculous and mostly ignorances compounding and complexifying other ignorances. Lies upon lies and it is not long before we are giving credence to the words of Nazi German propogandist Joseph Goebbels concerning lies turned truth.

I wonder how many people lied to themselves and others throughout the pandemic about how they felt because they wanted to see a friend or needed to get a bit more work done or because they found themselves trapped. I wonder if we can reflect on these moments and really take a more serious approach to ignorance. Be that the ignorance we maintain for ourselves, impose upon others, or allow to reign in a world with far too little truth. I have always been hesitant about calling this the post truth age, not because I do not think the truth is threatened, far from it, but because this age has been a slow build up, from the Enlightenment and modernity, through the turbulence of postmodernism and it is my hope that we take a new approach to it with the postnormal times we are given.

Interestingly, the global pandemic has had a few positives, among them, a renewed interest in medicine and fighting some of the diseases and disorders we have been plagued with over the last century. HIV is one that has witnessed leaps and bounds of research progress, even a new vaccine against this viral threat is progressing through the preliminary testing phases. And after we hang up the face masks for good and stop excessively applying hand sanitiser every two minutes, those inflicted with HIV are still faced with the paranoia and questions of ignorance the rest of us only dabbled with for a few years. HIV and other sexually transmitted diseases (STDs) give us a real and present need to rethink our attitudes towards ignorance. And although progress has been made, with the recent declaration of monkeypox as a global health emergency, we see how much slower sentiments change than science as the same HIV/AIDS script is having a second reading in all its ignorant glory. Who has a right to know, who has a right to their privacy? And although these diseases are not necessarily death sentences anymore, the stigma still remains, which makes the issue far more complex than Covid-19, where if you got it no one was going to think any differently of you, just wish you to get well soon. What a refreshing future that may be, where an HIV victim is met with empathy and care as opposed to judgement and even fear. It is not an easy road to such a future and awareness is definitely needed up front. But we also cannot be so naïve as to think that ignorance and knowledge necessarily hold such a simply polar existence, but that there is profound complexity in navigating between the two that is going to take entirely new ways of thinking to appreciate and then understand in the hopes of changing for the better.

In this exploration I am left thinking that no one has a right to ignorance, but actually, that is the wrong way to think about it. Ignorance as we know has a dark side of the moon if you will, as our ignorance of ignorance leaves as much for us as what knowledge lies in wait for us to attain or build. And in so doing, we can start by really exploring why we lie to ourselves and others and what fragile little systems we build upon castles of sand because, like it not, they will eventually buckle.

One last interesting insight is left by Plath towards the end of the seventh chapter of *The Bell Jar*.

Just before the book shifts hard into darkness, Plath embraces the Bell Jar she finds herself in and she rewards Esther for doing the same. Esther later wakes to Constantin asleep beside her, still fully clothed, the happiness maintained and hope for humanity and the world somewhat renewed. Constantin did not take advantage of the situation presented when caution is thrown to the wind (this sadly does not become a theme throughout the rest of the book). He compliments her hair and then drives her back to her hotel. Interestingly when she woke up next to Constantin, she describes hearing the 'the sound of rain', but after returning to her hotel room, while lying in bed, the rain stops sounding like the rain, instead 'like a tap running'. Her leg bone aches, as old wounds ache with changes in barometric pressure. She remembers that Buddy, that de facto fiancé of hers, had made her originally break the leg in some distant past. But that is a lie, and she quickly recants, saying she broke it herself over feeling utterly disappointed with herself. The Bell Jar is fragile, but Plath and by way Esther, used it as a crutch. It traps us within our thoughts and within societal norms, but once the cracks begin to form, try as we might, and some spend their whole life trying to keep the cracks from winning out, the Bell Jar is doomed to break. So why not let it shatter. But be prepared for the cuts that follow glass shards let loose.

A KEY TO ALL CONSPIRACIES

Robin Yassin-Kassab

1.

Now here's a strange coincidence. In the summer of 1994, after a year living in Rawalpindi and working for *The News* – the English-language sister of the Urdu *Jang* – I spent six weeks travelling in the high mountains of the Pakistani north. I hear the area has since been opened up for tourism, but in those days, it was the very definition of isolated. You were unlikely to meet even a Punjabi up there, let alone a group of Scotsmen, let alone a group of Scotsmen from the specific part of Galloway in which I'd passed a large part of my childhood. And yet that's what happened: in Mastuj, on the Chitral side of the Shandur Pass, I bumped into three sons of Galloway, artists, fishermen, farmers, and they were called Robin, Robert and Richard.

Brought together for a few hours there in a dip between the Karakorum and the Hindu Kush, we marveled at our common Gallovidian connections and the strange similarity of our names, and drank several cups of tea together, and shared several Chitrali cigarettes, then slept side by side on the floor of the tiny village's one-room accommodation. The next day we continued on our respective ways – I towards Chitral, and they in the direction of Gilgit.

Soon the encounter was lost in the stream of events; that is, I more-or-less forgot it, until one afternoon fourteen years later, when I had recently returned to Galloway, and there was a knock at my door.

It was Robin. The other one.

'I saw you in the shops and followed you home,' he said. 'We met in Pakistan, years ago now. You're Robin, I think.'

What were the chances of that? Not only of the meeting, but of the re-meeting too. In the following weeks I also re-met Robert and Richard.

And Robin introduced me to others, in Galloway and further afield. A good part of my current social life owes to him, or to that serendipitous meeting in Mastuj.

What should I make of this?

Our storytelling minds always look for correspondences, for patterns. Through them we find rhyme and rhythm in reality. By them we make sense of what otherwise seems senseless.

Different people will approach patterns in different ways. Someone who sees no patterning at all in their life – and perhaps no meaning – stands at one extreme. A paranoid schizophrenic stands at the other. For such a person, every detail of life is meaningful, each atom contributes to an overwhelming plot. And the schizophrenic is personally at the centre of the plot as the prime or sole victim, the reason the conspiracy was born. A run-of-the-mill conspiracy theorist stands somewhere in the middle, making a very normal effort to understand life's strangeness.

But back to the meeting in the mountains. How to understand this unlikely intertwining of Robins? In retrospect, the meeting was a convergence which seemed predestined. Had it not happened, so many more events would also not have happened. Everything would have turned out differently. So can I say it was meant to be? Was it written into the fabric of creation? Or had it been planned on some lower level? Did some dark Gallovidian intelligence send the Scotsmen to find me? And to what end? (The lack of a punch line to the story makes it a poor candidate for this kind of reading. Had I or the Scotsmen disappeared after the meeting, or suffered some dramatic sudden change, then the plot would need to thicken...)

What kind of agent was at work? If the meeting occurred by God or nature's arrangement, it was a fateful correspondence, a matter of destiny. If by human plot, a conspiracy. Though the thing about conspiracy theories – for those under their fictive sway – is that they are bigger than human, very often they render human efforts redundant.

2.

In upper Chitral we weren't very far from Khyber Pakhtunkhwa (in those days still called North West Frontier Province), which at the time was becoming a heartland of various conspiracy theories surrounding the polio vaccine. According to these tales, the vaccine's true purpose was to render Muslim women infertile and thus to prevent the birth of future Muslim generations. The top level plotters were Americans, Israelis and UN officials, but the foot-soldiers were the Pakistani doctors and nurses who administered the vaccine. Several of these health workers were shot dead.

The conspiracy theory persists, and today Pakistan and Afghanistan are the only countries in the world not to have eradicated polio. The result, as well as dead doctors, is lives blighted by disability. But the explanatory power of the theory overcomes everything else. 'My child has stopped praying since you last administered polio drops,' complains a parent in 2022.

How do these theories work? The perpetrators of the conspiracy keep changing to fit culture and context. They may be witches, Catholics, Freemasons, Ahmadis, the Illuminati, the lizard people, the EU, George Soros and his minions, or the Bill Gates Foundation. Whoever they are, a specified group of humans is conspiring against the rest of us. Yet the theory divides humanity not into two, but three. First there are the conspirators, with their evil plan. Then the victims, the conspired against, are split into two: the ignorant herd, almost always the vast majority, suffer from but are blind to the conspiracy; but the awakened few, who have access to the truth, are to some extent redeemed by knowledge. One undoubted benefit of being a conspiracy theorist is the sense of specialness that true sight conveys. To understand the conspiracy is to claim membership in the elect, the one right sect. In this informational if not moral righteousness, there are many echoes of religion.

It should be admitted here that conspiracies do in fact exist, and are in fact very common. Whenever two people conspire against a third, there is a conspiracy. Everyday family politics is full of conspiracy. So is the world of business, and no doubt governments, political parties, militaries and intelligence services are fairly constantly hard at work conspiring. The trouble with the conspiracy theory is that it over-simplifies, over-generalises and over-explains. It assumes that one specific conspiracy wields the power to cancel out all others. It reduces the dazzling complexity of reality. It seeks to boil everything down to one key factor. It sees one overarching plot rather than a jumble of a trillion. The conspiracy theory, to borrow the title of Edward Casaubon's failed book project, seeks to provide 'A Key to All Mythologies'. Casaubon is the pedant and failed husband in George Eliot's novel Middlemarch, and his book title is a pointer to his narrowness of vision, his attempt to force a poly-angular world into the square-shaped hole of his preconceptions. And so a child's refusal to pray can be put down, very simply, to polio drops.

Pakistan is located in what used to be known as the third world, and polio thrives in the least developed parts of Pakistan. So it's tempting – at least it was then – to believe that conspiracy theories are caused by underdevelopment. That they inhabit the minds of people who lack good information or proper education, people unequipped to understand how the world works.

Two things must be said: conspiracy theories concerning vaccinations are as old as vaccinations themselves, and they started in Enlightenment Europe. When – in eighteenth Century England – Edward Jenner inoculated patients against smallpox with a cowpox vaccine, critics claimed that the vaccinated would grow horns. Second, false narratives can be reinforced by idiotic interventions by those who are advanced in technology but undeveloped in wisdom. The CIA organised a fake vaccination programme in Pakistan's Abbottabad as part of its hunt for Osama bin Laden, seemingly confirming to local conspiracy theorists the notion that vaccines were a front for foreign imperialists.

The prevalence and salience of conspiracy theories rise and fall across time in cultures, rising particularly when people are confused and frightened by rapid social change. They are quite possibly catalysed by novel communication technologies. The spread of the printing press throughout Europe, for example, coincided with a witch-hunting mania of mass-murderous proportions. (One of the most popular and most frequently reprinted texts of the period was *Melleus Maleficarum* or 'The Witch's Hammer'.) Through the twentieth Century newspapers and radio helped define national saviours and enemies and potential scapegoats. And today social media creates instant communities of conspiracy theorists across national borders.

The ideal conspiracy theorist is someone who feels impotent amid the onrush of change. Someone who senses others are directing the changes, not him, and that none of them work in his interest. Someone who lives under dictatorship fits this profile particularly well. This suggests that political underdevelopment specifically may promote a conspiratorial atmosphere.

In its appetite for conspiracy theories, the Arab world is very similar to Pakistan, and very possibly worse. Pakistan is a seriously flawed but nevertheless working democracy. None of the Arab states are democracies – with the partial and precarious exception of Tunisia since 2011. In Arab capitals, until 2011 at least, conspiracies were usually how politics was done. The people of the area had no influence at all on the management or even the formation of their states. The borders were drawn by unannounced foreigners. Coups and counter-coups were organised by competing intelligence services and secret military committees. Nobody knew who was actually doing what, or why, so stories grew to fill the gaps.

In the Arab states, there's always a lot going wrong, and always, therefore, a lot of blame to be allocated. Rather than blame economic, military and political failures on the regimes in power, or on generalised corruption, or on ourselves, it's easier to blame the hidden machinations of foreign powers, or sectarian minorities, and best of all – as traditional anti-Semitism meets outraged anti-Zionism – the Jews.

In frustrated, censored, fearful spaces, stories epitomising local concerns proliferate and grow until they perform as impossible explainers of the largest global events. So, while it may be reasonable to worry about the Israel lobby's influence on American policy in the Middle East, it isn't reasonable to blame the Jews for the collapse of the Soviet Union, or for the failure of the Arabs to organise themselves into one mighty super-state. I've heard both of these theories from the mouths of café philosophers in Syria. In Damascus, copies of the *Protocols of the Elders of Zion* are reliably on sale, without any introduction to inform the reader that the text is a forgery penned by Russian secret policemen in the nineteenth century.

Of course, the anti-Semitism is state-sanctioned. The ignorance and prejudice of the powerless is exploited and directed by the powerful, who will always do what they can to deflect popular anger. A typical if somewhat extreme example is Mustafa Tlass, Syria's defence minister from 1972 to 2004, writing and publishing 'The Matzah of Zion'. The book rehashes the 'Damascus affair' of 1840, which was itself a rehashing of the medieval European 'blood libel' against Jews. In 1840 Damascene Christians accused Damascene Jews of killing a monk in order to bake Passover bread with his blood. The accusation was adopted by the French Consul, who convinced the Egyptian governor of the city to arrest some unlucky Jews. Confessions were extracted under torture, and were taken as firm evidence then, and once again by the Baathist Tlass a century and a half later.

It doesn't matter how far the theories stretch credibility; they'll always find an audience. Lebanon's Hizbullah started the story that thousands of Jews were warned not to go to work in the World Trade Centre on 9/11. Jews are presumably so loyal to their central command that not one of these thousands spilled the beans (except perhaps to Hizbullah; otherwise, how would Hizbullah know?) I've been told over the years, by different people in different Arab countries, that the Saud family, Colonel Qaddafi, Hosni Mubarak, and Yasser Arafat were in fact secret Jews. This approach certainly obviates the need for political analysis, and suggests – optimistically – that to achieve success the Arab world only needs to find some actual non-Jewish leaders. As well as simplifying, these stories soothe wounded pride. It's not so much of a failure to be defeated by an omnipotent global conspiracy – indeed, without divine intervention, no other result is possible. And the stories are also very flattering – for how important and frightening our nation must be if the Jews, the Freemasons, American capitalists, and assorted others in concert are constantly plotting to keep it down.

During the Syrian revolution, the regime generated an endless string of conspiracy theories to explain the trouble it was in. Apparently Saudi intelligence chief Prince Bandar bin Sultan, the Zionists, and al-Qaida were in bed together, and were paying protestors to take to the streets. Apparently protestors were fuelled by thousands of imported LSD 'pills', some of which were intercepted and displayed, each pill branded with the Al-Jazeera logo. Apparently Al-Jazeera had built stage sets of Syrian cities in the Qatari desert, and actors were performing as Syrian soldiers shooting at other actors performing as Syrian civilians.

Revolutionaries on the ground, meanwhile, laughed at the silly tales. Having broken with the regime's alternate reality, they were taking responsibility for their own lives. They were organising their neighbourhoods, working with their neighbours, working for a better future. They were taking power.

3.

Now I live again in Scotland, in Galloway, where the infrastructure is well developed, the economy healthy, the education universal. In Galloway we are free of war and state violence. We can vote. We can say what we like.

Twenty seven years after our initial meeting, what has become of Robin, Robert and Richard?

Robin is of an older generation, less internet-influenced. His fishing line keeps him down to earth.

Robert, on the other hand, is a deeply invested conspiracy theorist. He believes that Princess Diana was assassinated. He believes that 9/11 was an inside job. He believes these conspiracies are obvious, if you only choose to look. He has YouTube videos to back them up. He insists that you watch and listen. He that hath ears to hear, let him hear. He waxes passionate. If you demur, he flares into anger.

His theories exaggerate intentionality and underestimate the arbitrary. In his world view, things can't just happen by themselves. Cars don't just crash; terrorists don't just get lucky. To explain such events, he asks the question *cui bono*, or *who benefits?* Somebody must – and that somebody must be the person who has caused the event.

This fallacy has often been used to deny the evidence of regime chemical attacks against civilians in Syria. These must be false flag attacks, goes the argument, staged so as to provoke western intervention. The rebels benefit, therefore they (or their supposed allies in the Turkish, or perhaps French, states) must be the ones who carried out the attacks. The same argument was used many times to cover many different attacks – and long after it became evident that there would be no meaningful western intervention. Of course the rebels didn't benefit from seeing their families choke and convulse to death; whereas the regime did benefit by spreading panic in revolutionary neighbourhoods and breaking the force of rebel offensives. And of course the rebels didn't have the means to store or deploy chemical weapons, and no Turkish or French planes were flying anywhere near the vicinity of the attacks. But all this is irrelevant. The story is what matters, not the facts, and certainly not the dignity of the victims.

When Robert began repeating the Syrian conspiracy theories, I had to ask him to be quiet. Not in my presence, I said. Not about Syria. I can't bear it.

What about Richard?

Richard is a man who talks with exclamation marks. For instance: 'The carbon thing? That's a hoax. A hoax! They're saying climate change, yeah? Well of course it changes! If it didn't change, it wouldn't be climate! But you can't say it. It's like the Holocaust – you can't talk about it!'

Does that mean you can't talk about the Holocaust being a hoax? Better not to ask. Better to keep the conversation on those things right beneath our noses, because Richard has reliably outrageous takes on anything more distant. On things of which he has no direct experience, he has sudden enthusiasms which lead him immediately into a confidence as deep as the deepest abyss.

He was briefly – after listening to a podcast – an expert on Bolivia. When President Morales resigned amid protests over disputed elections in 2019, Richard was certain this was part of a secret American plot – known only to the plotters themselves, and the listeners of the podcast – to deprive China of Bolivian uranium. Another time I ran into him, he was an expert on gay men. Didn't I realise that they were gay because the government was funding them to be gay? Before this recent funding opportunity, gays didn't really exist.

Fortunately the expertise concerning the gays lasted only one day, as far as I could see. On Covid, however, Richard has been a consistent expert since the beginning of the first lockdown. He knows for absolute sure that the disease doesn't exist, and that if it does it's no worse than a cold, and that vaccination is a ruse for gathering the population's DNA, and that the vaccine is also designed to kill. 'It's a cull!' he exclaims. 'That's what it is!'

When a wave of Covid hit India so badly that the crematoria were overwhelmed and people resorted to sailing their relatives' corpses down the Ganges, I thought that at last Richard and people like him would have to accept that the disease was real. But I was wrong. He brought the subject up as soon as we next met, along with a ready-made explanation for the deaths. The Indians were dying not of Covid but of hunger and thirst, because the Indian government had stopped the food and water supplies. It had done so because it wanted to create the impression that Covid was killing people.

I didn't ask how he thought the Indians could be so stupid as to believe they were dying of a virus when they were simply starving. I did question his wisdom on the gays, and I do sometimes tell him to change the subject, but usually, I'm afraid, I just nod and smile and wait for him to finish.

I'm not sure if this response is cowardly or tolerant. If I came across such a person on social media, I'd block them immediately. In the virtual world, such people enrage me. All I know of them are their statements, and their statements make a mockery of both truth and human suffering. They are statements which lead, before too long, towards the justification of all sorts of madness, up to and including genocide.

But this isn't social media, and Richard is in actual fact a nice guy. He's always been good to me. When I tell him it's time to change the subject (because what he's saying will lead us into dispute), he does change the subject, and does so with a smile. Besides, he's too unconnected to power, or to anyone beyond his own small circle, to do anyone any damage. And within his local sphere of practical knowledge, he's actually pretty impressive. He rebuilt his house around an enormous wood-burning stove, for instance, and is now entirely self-sufficient in fuel. He grows vegetables, raises goats, chickens and geese, and cuts his own hay with a scythe. He's built a tower from tree trunks, and attached gargoyles to his roof. He's obviously a great father to his son.

On the other hand, he isn't much of a critical thinker. In terms of internet media, he's largely illiterate. 'The word on YouTube is….' he declares, unironically, not understanding how the YouTube algorithm works. How it works is this. Videos are selected and presented to the user according to the user's search and watch history. So watching a video which questions vaccines leads to a selection of videos condemning vaccines, and eventually to videos claiming that vaccines are designed by Bill Gates to cull the population and engineer a great economic reset. Soon each video presented is more extreme than the last, and no video is presented which might provide a counterweight. This creates the impression in the viewer that the videos and the conspiracy theories they express are not extreme but mainstream. After that, confirmation bias kicks in. This is a mental rather than digital algorithm, by which a person registers only that information which confirms a pre-existing belief. So if someone suffers a heart attack, and was vaccinated in the months previous, Richard reasons that the heart attack must have been caused by the vaccine. The smoking, drinking and cake-eating have nothing to do with it.

Usually conspiracy theorists are eager to explain that they aren't conspiracy theorists, simply observers of the truth. Richard, however, claims the label with pride. 'I'm a conspiracy theorist, me!' he roars. 'I swallowed the red pill early!'

The openness is disarming, and makes him seem like a special case, but Richard's mental habits, though not generally owned up to, are remarkably common. Our aged neighbour, for example, knows that Covid is real, and isolates himself for fear of it. But he won't take the vaccination for fear that the government will murder him. He also has fixed ideas concerning the Arabs. 'They are divided,' he told me over his garden wall, 'into Sunni and Shia. That's why they need a strong leader to stop them fighting. That's why Qaddafi did so much good for Libya, and why it's chaos there now he's gone.' I pointed out that Libya isn't actually divided by sect, given that the Libyan Shia population is tiny to the point of insignificance. Without missing a beat, Monty shifted to his next stock explanation. 'It's Israel, then. Whenever there's trouble in that part of the world, Israel's the one behind it.'

Reader, you can leave the Arab world behind, but these days it will follow you.

A friend who isn't a conspiracy theorist visited a friend of his who is. When he said he'd been vaccinated, his friend not only told him he'd been injected with a microchip, he even brought out a device to locate it. This was a tool he'd purchased through the internet. When it didn't provide a reading, he grew upset. 'O well,' my friend said, smiling gently. 'The chip must have embedded itself in my brain by now.' But the conspiracy theorist said that couldn't be the case. 'It stays in the arm. It doesn't move around.' He threw his tool to the ground. 'It's broken,' he announced. 'I'll ask for a refund.'

You can laugh, but you can't escape these theories. You can laugh until you grow tired of laughing, until your cheeks hurt, and still the theories come.

Someone I know visited the local reflexologist. During the friendly chit-chat accompanying the foot massage, she was informed that Putin had invaded Ukraine not because he wants to recreate the Soviet empire, not even because he's disgruntled by NATO expansion, but in order to break up paedophile rings.

I'd just noted down this list of local conspiracy theorists when my wife and I decided to drive into the nearby town to buy a kebab. While waiting for our order, we each opened a copy of the free newspaper which lay on the counter. It was called *The Light* (with the strapline: The Uncensored Truth). In previous decades a free newspaper available in a public place, if not advertising products, would likely have advertised religion, or perhaps workers' rights. *The Light*, however, is a publication serving 'the truth movement'. Most of it covers what it calls 'the covid coup', but there are also articles on 'the fake war between Russia and Ukraine, deliberately triggered by the conspirators' and 'weaponised LED 5G streetlights'. Products are advertised too, mainly things you can ingest or wear to protect your health if you're not gullible enough to submit to the vaccine.

One of *The Light*'s columnists warns of 'the conspirators' blood-thirsty ambition to reduce the world's population by 90%,' and ends his piece thus: 'whenever anything bad happens, ask yourself "What is the most sinister reason for this?" … Eternal paranoia is now the price of freedom.'

4.

I'd like to believe that conspiracy theories are particularly prominent in this particular part of Scotland (as well as in the Arab countries, and Pakistan), and not everywhere else. That perhaps isolation renders rural people more paranoid than the average, or more vulnerable to the algorithmic rabbit hole. But when I look out into the world – metropolitan as well as rural, western as much as eastern – I can't see anywhere free of the curse. Because once again we are in the midst of an age of conspiracy theories. They determine our high politics as well as our popular culture.

The Global War on Terror, reducing dozens of conflicts to a decontextualised, homogenised story of good warriors versus evil plotters, was somewhere between a conspiracy theory and a slogan. That's how our century began.

Two decades on, and Donald Trump has proudly performed the first social-mediatised post-truth presidency. His original move from real estate and reality TV into real politics was via Birtherism, the unevidenced belief that Barack Obama wasn't born in the United States and therefore was ineligible for the presidency, and that this secret was being hidden by scheming liberal elites.

Following the populist playbook, Trump, an enormously rich and privileged man, presented himself as a man of the people and a victim – like the people – of various malign cliques, most notably the 'fake news' media. In this way he neutralised the truth-telling potential of investigative journalism – he simply declared the truth to be fake, and his own lies to be truths, even when they contradicted each other. He also profited from the QAnon movement – an interlinking set of conspiracy theories which hold that establishment figures including Hillary Clinton are engaged in the trafficking and sexual abuse of children, and are also conspiring against the Trump presidency. (The Scottish reflexologist's story about Putin battling Ukrainian paedophiles seems to be a variation on the QAnon theme.) Trump's biggest conspiracy theory, and the most damaging to democracy, was the story that the result of the 2020 presidential election was falsified by the Democrats in league with shadowy deep state forces. According to a Reuters/Ipsos poll, 53% of Republicans choose to believe this lie. That's many millions of people, many of them armed. The full ramifications have not yet played out.

Underlying a great deal of Trumpist politics – the Birtherism, the border wall, the travel bans – is racial resentment, and specifically the American version of the Great Replacement conspiracy theory. This story is about the Democratic Party and other liberal plotters destroying America's white majority by 'replacing' white people with non-white immigrants (many, no doubt, originating from 'shithole countries'). According to YouGov, 61% of Trump voters and 53% of Fox News viewers believe this stuff. Tucker Carlson of Fox News has referred to the Great Replacement on his show more than 400 times. The most extreme iterations of the theory deploy the term 'white genocide', and often identify the liberal plotters as Jews. This is why the marchers at the Unite the Right rally at Charlottesville, Virginia in August 2017 chanted 'You will not replace us' and 'Jews will not replace us' interchangeably.

The European version of the Great Replacement theory focuses in particular on the supposed Muslim demographic threat. Hungary's authoritarian prime minister Viktor Orban frequently refers to it, and it was bandied about during the recent French presidential elections, not only by the two professedly far right candidates, but also by the centre-right Valérie Pécresse as she attempted to compete on the far right's territory. 67% of French people say they are worried about the Great Replacement. The Bosnian-Serb general Ratko Mladić justified genocide against Bosnian Muslims by stating that the Islamic world is armed, if not with an atomic bomb, then a 'demographic bomb'. Burman Buddhist ethnic cleansers in Myanmar imagine their Rohingya victims – poor farmers and fishermen – as the striking arm of an organised demographic threat which has already wiped out Buddhism in parts of Asia including Pakistan and Afghanistan. Hindu nationalists in India see love affairs between Muslims and Hindus as a 'love jihad' conspiracy, an attempt to subdue India by non-military means. (And these replacement stories travel to the strangest places. Sometimes Muslims will pick up an Islamophobic conspiracy theory and repurpose it as a wish-fulfilling dream. A Syrian once told me – a little over twenty years ago – that within twenty years Europe would have a Muslim majority.)

Renaud Camus, author of the 2011 book *The Great Replacement* – the text (in French) which gives the conspiracy theory its current name – routinely refers to non-white immigrants in Europe, those arriving from ex-colonies, as 'colonisers'. And so, by these rhetorical turns, even the powerful can recast themselves as powerless. The victimisers, confused and frightened by rapid social change, turn themselves into victims.

In Britain, Brexit, while containing many dimensions and motivations, was built on a foundation of national victimology. Great Britain, it was sometimes implied and sometimes openly stated, was being held back by European bureaucrats and all kinds of immigrants. Control – or sovereign power, or liberty – had been snatched from British hands. The solution was expressed in the free-floating three-word slogan 'Take Back Control', and then, when nobody could agree on what taking back control should actually mean, in the even more brutally uncomplicated three-word slogan 'Get Brexit Done'.

Not the climate crisis, or increasing poverty, or rising strategic threats, but this politics of myth and bruised identity is what dominated British public life for over half a decade. It was a diet of dreams, perhaps expressed most clearly by a man seen on TV, interviewed in a pub on Tyneside: 'What do they mean we'll be isolated after Brexit? Of course, we won't. This is the British Empire! There are billions of people in the British Empire.'

It was a remarkably stupid thing to say, but also remarkably revealing of what lay beneath the surface of more intelligent pro-Brexit commentary. The bar-side take, about three quarters of a century out of date, expresses nostalgia for a time when Britain did rule the waves, just as the Trumpists of the United States dream of a time when the ruling classes were entirely white, and Black people knew their place. Most British people and most white Americans in fact had far shorter and poorer lives in those times, but the burnished image of those times, their happy representation, shines brightly when compared to the troublesome global complexity of the present.

Indeed all this reaching for walls, reinforced borders and simple certainties, the isolationism and protectionism, could be understood as an angry reaction to our internationalist reality, in which waves of trouble, ideology, wealth, or democratisation starting in one part of the world may quickly wash into another. Those white supremacists who marched at Charlottesville had almost as many opinions on the politics of the Arab world as on immigration policy in the United States. 'Support the Syrian Arab Army!' they shouted (and I quote:) 'Fight the globalists! Assad did nothing wrong! Replacing Qaddafi was a fucking mistake!'

These talking points – support for Syria's Assad regime and the conspiracy theories which absolve it of blame for mass murder and ethnic cleansing, the Islamophobia which underpins these theories, the notion that 'globalists' staged the Arab Revolutions, and the idea that the Libyan revolution was entirely a foreign plot – are shared to some extent or other by much of what remains of the left.

Because it's not only the right. The conspiratorial mode of thought, the radical overgeneralisation and oversimplification of the world, is every bit as common on the left. Partly because the left is in deep historical trouble, but mainly because the reductive habit of mind is universal, conspiracy theory is prime left-right crossover territory.

Having failed to adequately update its economic and social models to adapt to the current age, having failed to reckon with the legacy of left-wing authoritarianism, having despaired of the hope that people ('the masses') would ever rise up to effect radical change, far too often the left has turned from hard analysis to demonology, and from a focus on the struggle within states to an obsession with the struggles between states. But it's a mythic, storied struggle, because the analysis is so poor. The world view which describes itself as 'anti-imperialist', as espoused by leftists such as Jeremy Corbyn or Noam Chomsky, first identifies its villains, the bad states – the United States, the United Kingdom, Israel, Saudi Arabia. Then, by crude binarism, any state deemed to oppose, or to be opposed by, the baddies, becomes one of the goodies. The first set are imperialists (or perhaps, in the Saudi case, a tool of imperialists); the second set, therefore, are anti-imperialists.

The world has never been as simple as this schema assumes, and it certainly isn't today. Leftists who begin at the position that every problem originates in American imperialism will not be able to understand, for instance, that Iran is both a historical victim of western imperialisms and a contemporary perpetrator of imperialism (in Syria, Iraq, Lebanon and Yemen). Similarly, they were unable to understand (or admit) in the 1990s that the immediate danger to Bosnians and Kosovans wasn't NATO but Serb fascism. Corbyn scornfully referred to the organised slaughter of Kosovan civilians and the burning of their villages as 'a "genocide" that never really existed'. Serbian president Slobodan Milosevic and his allies murdered almost 58,000 Muslims in Bosnia and over 11,000 in Kosovo, as part of a concerted effort to permanently destroy Muslim existence in the Balkans.

For these self-proclaimed anti-imperialists, anything outside the framework of active American oppressor and passive third world victim does not compute, and must therefore be either ignored or re-imagined to fit the established narrative, even to the extent of genocide denial.

So, taking American empire as the key to all mythologies, they argued that the Arab Spring, when it spread beyond those states with obviously pro-American regimes, was an attempted replay of the 2003 Iraq invasion. They failed to recognise the popular revolutions in Syria and Libya, preferring to see western 'regime change' operations. They shut their eyes to the evidence and their ears to the voices of Syrians and Libyans. They implied that the Syrians and Libyans struggling against tyranny either didn't exist at all, or did but only as putty in the foreign plotters' hands.

This denial of agency is racist, and plainly absurd when people are facing bullets. The implication is that these backward fools are so hopelessly under the sway of the clever American that they will risk death again and again because the CIA has somehow got through to them. It's a stupidity reminiscent of Richard's imagined Indians, dying of hunger and thirst but believing they're dying of Covid. Once again, it's the story that's important, not logic, not facts, certainly not human suffering. It's as if the people involved aren't real, but only pawns in the plotline.

The UK's Stop the War Coalition never marched against Assad's barrel bombs or chemical attacks, or Iran's starvation sieges, or Russia's levelling of cities, but they marched against any proposed western action against Assad. 'Hands Off Syria!' they chanted then. This kind of leftist usually agreed with the fascists on the basic Syrian tropes: Every oppositionist is a Saudi-funded jihadist. The White Helmets are an American-funded al-Qaida front. An Arab regime possesses the sovereign right to deal violently with its population. 'Assad did nothing wrong.' Alleged atrocities are 'psy-ops'. Alleged victims are 'crisis actors'.

This last phrase was attached by American conspiracy theorists to the bereaved relatives of the children and teachers murdered at the 2012 Sandy Hook Elementary School shooting, which they held was a hoax orchestrated by – *cui bono?* – those wishing to implement gun control laws. Some were so certain of their story that they tracked down and berated as liars the weeping parents they'd seen on TV.

Here we enter the territory of esoteric religion, in which apparent events are simulacra, facades conceal secret meanings, trickery is a divine principle, and only the select can see through the veil. And then, as the human mind's basic storytelling urge meets propaganda and post-modernity, we move beyond even that territory into a realm where meaning breaks down completely. Here nothing is true and everything is possible, because the purpose of contemporary propaganda is not to establish a particular story as the single truth, but simply to confuse, and therefore to undermine any possibility of positive action.

A few weeks into the full-scale Russian invasion of Ukraine, a Pakistani friend sent me a clip of Russia's chief diplomat Sergei Lavrov engaging in such bluster. 'If you cannot sleep because of Russian Ukrainian conflict,' Lavrov said, 'there are some advices to calm you down. First, imagine that this is happening in Africa. Imagine this is happening in the Middle East. Imagine Ukraine is Palestine. Imagine Russia is the United States.'

Such a strange logic is implied here. Lavrov is saying something like: 'Yes, I'm a murderer, but that guy over there is also a murderer.' And his implied audience is nodding and smiling, patting him on the back. His implied audience doesn't stop for a moment to consider that Russia is currently killing civilians in Syria, which is in the Middle East, or that the Wagner Group, mercenaries closely linked to the Russian state, is currently killing civilians in Libya, Mali and the Central African Republic, which are in Africa. His implied audience – which is real, and enormous – follows the logic that we shouldn't complain about the Russian invasion of Ukraine because in 2003 America invaded Iraq. Forget about the rights of Ukrainians. And look what happens when we keep the logic going: We shouldn't complain about the invasion of Iraq because the Russians destroyed Chechnya. We shouldn't complain about Chechnya because the Americans violently intervened in Central America. We shouldn't complain about Central America because the Russians invaded Afghanistan. We shouldn't complain about Afghanistan because the Americans bombed Vietnam. And so it goes on. Forget everybody's rights. Just talk about the chess game.

Lavrov says such stuff because he knows that it works. He knows his audience, and the power of binarism, and the human need to see goodies and baddies.

So Kémi Séba, a Franco-Beninese pan-Africanist, describes the invasion of Ukraine thus: Putin 'wants to get his country back. He doesn't have the blood of slavery and colonisation on his hands.' This betrays ignorance of the long history of slavery (or serfdom) within Russia, and of the continual outward expansion of the Russian state to absorb the Muslim lands of the Caucuses and central Asia and the Buddhist and animist territories of Siberia and east Asia. It betrays ignorance of the many genocides perpetrated by Russian imperialism on non-Russian peoples, and most pertinently of the Holodomor of the 1930s, in which four million Ukrainian peasants were starved on Moscow's orders.

'Anti-imperialists' like to remind us that Crimea used to belong to Russia. They don't remind us that Crimea used to belong to the Tatars, a Muslim people deported en masse from their homeland by Stalin's imperialist terror.

According to the 2022 Democracy Perception Index, Egyptians, Saudis, Moroccans and Pakistanis have a net positive view of Russia – not only after the burning of Ukraine, but after Russia's recent mass slaughter of Muslims in Syria, Chechnya and Afghanistan.

This turns the notion of Muslim solidarity across the *umma* into a ridiculous joke.

5.

We used to have better stories.

We were once sustained by the classical religions. These soothed our confusions and explained our pains by situating them within an overarching plot. Plot then meant a purposeful storyline, an arc tending to justice, designed by divine love. But the classical religions in their traditional forms collapsed. In their traditional forms they were unable to adapt to scientific and social modernity, and so perhaps they collapsed for good reason. But still people needed to fit their fragile, temporary, fractured lives into a larger story. Without a larger story, there is only despair.

One way of understanding our post-religious history is as a series of failed attempts to produce alternatives to religion. In the twentieth Century the old faiths were generally replaced by ideological grand narratives, that is by the nationalisms and political faiths which found virtue in shrinking or even erasing the individual. 'The ideal subject of totalitarian rule,' wrote Hannah Arendt, 'is not the convinced Nazi or the dedicated communist, but people for whom the distinction between fact and fiction, true and false, no longer exists.'

Under Communism the story was of the proletariat marching forward to a classless society under the benign direction of the party elite applying the supposed science of dialectical materialism. Though progress was inevitable, it was also beset by scheming saboteurs. The Soviet system identified and eliminated class enemies (particularly kulaks, or peasants who were slightly better off than the rest, resisting agricultural collectivisation, and nomads, who happened to be Muslims, resisting urbanisation and proletarianisation), as well as national enemies (the Soviet Union's Poles, Ukrainians, Chechens, Tatars, Koreans, Jews, and others). Lest their imagined plotting ruin the bright future, millions upon millions were variously starved, shot, imprisoned or deported.

Under fascism the proletariat was replaced by the people, or race, in their monovocal state, and dialectical materialism by the pseudo-science of social Darwinism. Conspiring enemies were as central to the fascist vision as the pure race they supposedly victimised. Nazi pogroms against Jews were presented as self-defence, and the Holocaust was kicked into overdrive in 1941 when Germany failed to win a quick victory over the Soviet Union. What else could explain German reverses than the eternal perfidy of the Jews? What else could explain Communist Russia, capitalist America and imperial Britain working together against Germany except, once again, the transnational scheming of the Jews? Every Jewish woman shot, every old man gassed, every child burned, was therefore a practical part of the war effort, a necessary blow against the conspiracy.

There were also the Romani, and the disabled, and Ukrainian and Belarusian villagers, and the inhabitants of Leningrad, and of Warsaw, and the millions of Soviet prisoners of war deliberately starved to death. The Nazis designated these groups as different breeds of subhuman, not part of the same species as Germans. Soviet Communism did not speak such a racialised language – though it certainly oppressed non-Russian nationalities – but it agreed with the Nazis on the basic premise that human beings should be thought of statistically, as resources or as obstacles in the way of the future, not as complex miracles of consciousness, not as fully real.

And let us not imagine that the non-west escaped the phenomenon. China, deifying party and leader, produced its own totalitarian victimology, and dozens of millions of corpses. Ba'athism, replacing the Qur'anic message with the 'eternal message of the Arab nation', did similar damage, if on a proportionately smaller scale. Even in those countries considered to be still religious, religion has been repurposed to fit epic national stories and to scapegoat or demonise epic national enemies. The BJP's very post-colonial, very materialist, very paranoid Hindu nationalism bears little relation to the Hinduisms of earlier epochs. Likewise, the various Islamisms of the last century have been inextricably wrapped up with arguments concerning the postcolonial nation states, and have worried inordinately about plotting foreigners and fifth columnists. In an ever more toxic mix, Marxism and fascism have been amalgamated with Islam. At the furthest extreme, the ISIS phenomenon set its tone more by computer games, action movies and gangster rap than by medieval theology.

ISIS pushed through the boundary from modernity into post-modernity, and absurdity. It was a twenty-first century phenomenon, born in an age which had lost faith even in political religions. Communism was the god that failed, and fascist governance tended to make the walls fall in, even on the master race. Epic turned rapidly to tragedy, and so, like the classical religions before them, the grand narratives were defeated, or at least hollowed out, to become parodies of their earlier selves.

What is left to fill the gap? Apart from the instantly evaporating stories of consumer capitalism, and celebrity iconography, and virtual reality, and drugs. What else? Only conspiracy theories in greatly reduced, non-epic, but nearly ubiquitous forms.

That copy of *The Light* picked up in our local junk food outlet contains the following letter: 'Knowing few other awakened souls, condemned by my family and losing my fiancé, I have felt desperate at times, but persevered, hoping that a newspaper such as *The Light* would appear....'

This is a religious language of exile and homecoming, of fallenness and redemption, and aptly so, because conspiracy theories manifest the return of religion in the most debased shape yet. They provide a kind of community and a sense of right and wrong, but they are poorly written. Plot no longer means the story which writes the universe, but the skulking cabal of enemies conspiring. There is no gospel, no good news, only bad. Even the enemies have been shrunk in size – no longer the Jews but only George Soros; no longer the machinations of international capital, but only Bill Gates.

All this is disempowering. The feeling that justice is continually squashed, and of impotence in the face of powerful forces, leads to a performance of gestures, a half-hearted role-playing, and an undirected anger which can explode in random violence.

But people love their stories, however shoddy they are. They turn them into positions, which they stick to. Their positions constitute their identity, which is something they'll fight to defend. Here is the new sectarianism.

No remedies immediately present themselves. Perhaps in the future our cultures will write better stories, or reconstitute the old ones in more satisfying ways. In the meantime, we need at least to remind ourselves and those around us, as often as possible, of certain facts. That things can happen 'by themselves', or according to logics too complicated for us to follow. Life is infinitely more complex – thank God – than our conceptions of it could possibly be. That nobody is in absolute control, at least not in this sublunary world. That there are no absolute goodies or baddies but only human beings. Those who are good in one respect may be bad in another. Those who are good at one moment may be bad at another. That everything is in flux. That there are no short cuts to thinking things through.

And when we think, we must make the search for truth our central motivator. We must respect truth, but not 'the truth'. We must prioritise the process of approaching truth, the investigation, but not hold onto a particular conception of the truth, the self-satisfied certainty.

'Thinking does not lead to truth,' wrote Hannah Arendt; 'truth is the beginning of thought.'

ARTS AND LETTERS

}

A HISTORY OF FORGETTING AND IGNORANCE

Alev Adil

This is a history of forgetting, of my father's unravelling mind, the memories blanketed by a fog of emptiness, but also of the willed forgetting that each generation of Turkish Cypriots have enacted, erasing and retelling the path as they attempt to forge a new identity that will enable them to survive as a community. And this is a history of ignorance, my ignorance, the things I didn't save from furnace of time and death, and how little I understand the objects that did survive. It is an ignorance that I am still in the process of disentangling and illuminating, both through archives and libraries. Excavating my own heritage and family history.

I am ambivalent about that ignorance. I was brought up to see ignorance as a mark of shame, something to be overcome. I was supposed to come first in the class. I came second once and my father said, 'My father used to beat me if I didn't come first, but we are modern, I won't beat you for it.' He was very disappointed though. He used to like to test me, times tables, flags, my favourite was being tested on the capitals of the world. I liked the sounds of all those names.

Uruguay? Montevideo

Armenia? Yerevan

Yugoslavia? Belgrade

There were the tricky ones like Australia (Canberra), USA (Washington) Turkey (Ankara) where I had to remember that the first cities, Sydney, New York, Istanbul were not the capitals; easy ones like Mexico City, Brasilia, Luxembourg, Djibouti, and then there were cities with names like jewels: Luanda (Angola), Kinshasa (Democratic Republic of Congo), Asmara (Eritrea), Bamako (Mali), Lusaka (Zambia), whose names I learnt by heart but couldn't always locate on the map. It was a game I thought I enjoyed at the time. It thrilled me to have earned his attention, and approval when I got it right. I was supposed to grow up to work at the United Nations and solve the Cyprus Problem. But now if someone asked the capital of... I'd seize up; I'd say I don't know before they'd finished the question. Am I forgetting too? Or is it just the sense of being a disappointment, not working at the United Nations, having failed to solve the Cyprus Problem?

I first came across the term 'memory palace' in the historian Frances Yates' ground-breaking work *The Art of Memory*. The memory palace is a mnemonic technique first described by Cicero in 55 BCE in his *de Oratore*. The method involves recalling a real or imagined architecture and placing the facts to be recalled in specific locations. Everybody can build their own memory palace, a place to archive their memories and facts they might need to retrieve at some later date. Some choose a memory of their first home, or build a grand imagined space in which to contain their memories. There is an architecture to remembering. Memory needs a landscape in which to grow, to take root.

Cicero credits the poet Simonedes of Ceos as the originator of the system and recounts the story of the first memory palace. Commissioned by Scopas, a nobleman to compose and chant a eulogy at a banquet in his honour, Simonedes included an extended passage of praise to Castor and Pollux, Spartan brothers, those famed Argonauts, horsemen and pugilists who were hatched from the same brood of eggs laid by their mother Queen Leda when she was a swan. Perhaps Simonedes dwelt on how the brothers were hatched from eggs and destined to become stars, the constellation of Gemini, which could only have made a workaday mortal plutocrat like Scopas look dull by comparison. Whatever the fashion in which Simonides chose to eulogise them, it is perhaps not surprising that the lengthy digression offended Scopas' vanity 'whereupon with excessive meanness' he told the poet he would only pay half the agreed fee for the lyric.

Later that evening, during the feast, Simonedes was informed that two young men were waiting outside to see him. He could find no one outside. During his absence the roof of the banqueting hall collapsed, crushing Scopas and his guests so completely that none survived and their mangled remains were unrecognisable. Simonedes 'was enabled by his recollection of the place in which each of them had been reclining at a table to identify them for separate interment; and that this circumstance suggested to him the discovery of the truth that the best aid to clearness of memory consists in orderly arrangement'. Cicero goes on to tell us, 'he inferred that persons desiring to train this faculty must select localities and form mental images of the facts they wish to remember and store those images in the localities, with the result that the arrangement of the localities will preserve the order of the facts, and the images of the facts will designate the facts themselves, and we shall employ the localities and images respectively as a wax writing tablet and the letters written on it'.

The memory palace is a technique borne out of tragedy, vanity, magic, and mystery. It is no accident that Memory, Mnemosyne, is the mother of the Muses. It is She who generates poetic action. There is poetry at the heart of the memory palace, and death. Death always lurks close by, memory and death, and the death of memory, the ruins of a palace in the mist. My father has forgotten so much, but he remembers reams and reams of Turkish poetry, a ruined library full, a library on fire. He doesn't usually remember the names of the poets, but he remembers flowing verses of poetry. Both his formal education and his personal passion for poetry involved much learning by rote; or rather I prefer the expression, learning by heart. For the poetry is a gift of love he can still offer me, and the poem animates his poor soul and sense of self, becoming erased by the relentless deluge of the great forgetting.

My father has forgotten so much. Sometimes, I know, he isn't quite sure who I am and I always announce myself, 'Hello Mustafa, it's your daughter, Alev' as soon as I enter their house. But sometimes I'm slow, or delayed in calling out whilst unpacking his favourite trifles and fruit jellies and putting them in the fridge and he'll ask my mother, 'which one is this?' for there is a roster of agency carers now from Khartoum, Mogadishu, Rabat and Kabul. I am one of the carers, Alev from Nicosia.

The memory palace is a ruin now, though its lineaments are still grand and imposing in the dewy mercury clouds that wreath the grounds. Whatever the season or time of day it is always misty in the gardens. The ivy is overgrown, propagates vigorously whatever the season, locking garden doors, covering crumbling brickwork, working their tentacles across the cracked glass of the windows. These ruins. The memory palace I speak of now is not a place where I am training my memory; it is the ruin where my father is losing his. When you enter this memory palace you are never entirely sure what you will find, sometimes only emptiness, the wind howling, leaves blowing on dark days, death knocking on the window, or is it just the branch of a tree? But sometimes, on better days, I emerge through the fog to find there is an octogenarian gentleman in his plaid pyjamas playing backgammon in the atrium of an old Mediterranean mansion, whilst the BBC news plays constantly in the background, *The Times* newspaper at his side. He wanders unsteady through the treacherous structure of the ruined palace, through corridors and corridors of doors as he recites word perfect renditions of the Epic of Köroğlu, poems by Yunus Emre, Yahya Kemal, Nazim Hikmet, Orhan Veli, and many more shards of verse whose origins I cannot identify.

While so many doors in the palace are locked, others swing open to reveal a terrifying chasm of blankness. Some of the corridors are on fire, or blanketed by drifts of snow, in others it's always raining. The floor gives way beneath him and we are somewhere else entirely. It's a lonely place though people come and go, a crowd of people, carers in the present, ghosts and guests from long-ago, but everyday, sometimes incrementally, at others suddenly, the phantoms of the past become fainter and fainter, some barely wisps of smoke, others become heartbreakingly familiar strangers. This ruin of a memory palace, it is my family home now, my past, my heritage collapsing and being demolished too.

My father Mustafa was born in Famagusta, within the old city walls. He grew up amongst the glorious Lusignan and Venetian ruins of a once magnificent port that is said to have rivalled medieval Constantinople and Venice. The city is the setting for Shakespeare's *Othello*. The Lusignan Cathedral of Saint Nicholas in Famagusta's main square was the site for the coronation of the kings of Crusader Jerusalem. The Venetians rechristened it as Saint Sophia Cathedral after their occupation of the island in 1489. After the harrowing eleven-month siege of the Venetian port and the Ottoman victory in 1571, the Cathedral became the Saint Sophia Mosque of Mağusa and since 1954 has been called the Lala Mustafa Pasha Mosque. Just over three centuries after the Ottoman conquest my maternal great-grandfather Mustafa Nuri Effendi was to become the Imam of that mosque. My father never met the grandfather he was named after. Mustafa Nuri Effendi died in his early forties when Fatma Hanum, my grandmother was only ten years old. His funeral filled the piazza outside the Gothic splendour of the mosque where he had been Imam.

Imam Mustafa Nuri Effendi circa 1915

My grandmother was a religious woman, but only very quietly so. She boasted that my father was a remarkable hafez as a child; he could memorise and recite extended tracts of the Qur'an when he was just three years old, but he was raised as and remains a lifelong strident atheist. My father, born in 1934, was of a generation of Turkish speaking Cypriots born and raised as an ardent Kemalist. The cultural revolution that Kemal Atatürk brought about in the new Republic of Turkey founded in 1923 not only changed the alphabet from the Arabic script of Ottoman Turkish to Latin, it taught the younger generation that religion and spirituality were no more than backward superstitious nonsense that had no place in a republic that embraced modernity and occidental values. His generation enacted a kind of Nietszchean forgetting. The past was a foreign country they had no interest in, the history of the Ottoman Empire, religious piety, the Arabic script of Ottoman Turkish all that was put behind them. They were part of a new Turkish identity that rejected imperialist ambitions, that wanted to be a modern nation state, part of the 'civilised' Western world, under the rule of Law, not the whims of Sultans, subject to science and industrial capitalist values not superstition and tradition.

Izzet Bey in his suit (sixth from the left) and his sons Naim and Mustafa (curly haired child in light coloured coat)

Turkish speaking Cypriots in the main embraced the Kemalist revolution with great enthusiasm but the family's antipathy to religion had a personal dimension too. Despite the fact that my father's maternal grandfather Mustafa Nuri Effendi was an Imam and his paternal grandfather, Naim Bey, a Qadi (Judge) was founder of the then new-fangled Bahai faith in Cyprus, the next generation of the Adiloğlu family was avowedly atheist. My grandfather Izzet Bey, scion of a prominent feudal landowning Famagusta family, a handsome man with the greenest eyes, had been blinded after falling off a wall as a child. Nothing, not even a pilgrimage to Vienna to consult the foremost ophthalmologists and neurologists of the time, could restore his sight. A spirited character he didn't let his handicap curtail him and usually took daily, often unaccompanied, walks around town, tapping his way with his silver tipped cane. 'The streets of this town carry the names of my family and I will walk them', he told little Mustafa. Izzet Bey had a very personal grudge against God, 'if Allah exists why would he blind an innocent child?' he would rail, 'There is no such thing as the will of

Allah'. So it is unsurprising that I found it anachronistic that a portrait of a gentle bearded Imam graced our atheist living rooms. Mustafa Nuri Effendi was a gentle ghost from another era, someone none of us had ever met, whose own daughter, my grandmother, had known for all too short a time. He was a foreigner to us.

Izzet Bey and Fatma Hanum and their children Naim, Münüre, Mustafa and Ayşe in 1938.

Mustafa Nuri was born in Nicosia in 1875, at the very end of Ottoman rule in Cyprus. He was just three years old when the island became a British Protectorate, a price the Ottomans paid for their alliance in wars with the Russians. The British arrived with three British Regiments in June 1878, shortly followed by 8,470 soldiers from the Indian Army, from the Bombay, Bengal and Madras Cavalry and Infantry. My father insists that he is a Londoner now. He has no desire to return to Cyprus, however much I have begged him to return. The care would be much cheaper, we could afford more of it, and it would be much easier for me to find people to play backgammon with him. But he is adamant London is his home now, it has been for nearly fifty years, though he still loves the old walled city of Mağusa very much, and sometimes remembers its sprawling castle, the beautiful Gothic, Genoese and Venetian architecture, the yellow Venetian sandstone house he grew up in. The British were unenthusiastic about the city of my father's childhood. Sir Garnet Wolsey, the first British High Commissioner and Commander in Chief, was not at all enchanted by Famagusta, its architecture does not even warrant a mention in his journal. Cyprus was just a military outpost for the British Empire. On Monday, 4th November 1878, he recounts:

> In the afternoon we had a conference: Stanley, Smith, Hornby & self about Famagusta: it was pronounced by Hornby to be well suited as a coaling station for a fleet watching Port Said or Alexandria. The inner harbour to be dredged out, and a pier to be run out from the mainland beyond the outer walls of that place into the outer anchorage. Hornby imagines that trade will follow after a good harbour, but my argument is that trade has all reasonable facilities at Larnaca now, & that it is already established there: the houses are good & the place comparatively healthy, whereas there are no houses at Famagusta & the place is pestiferous. However, if the marshes outside can be drained and plenty of trees planted there, the climate may have its character entirely altered.

During the period of the British Protectorate, my Ottoman ancestors continued their, now somewhat constrained, Ottoman lives, the paternal side of my father's family as Qadis and ağas (judges and landowners) incrementally losing power and wealth, whilst the young Mustafa Nuri went off to Cairo for his religious and pedagogic education and settled in Famagusta on his return where he became the Imam of the magnificent Saint Sophia Cathedral turned Mosque, head of the Madrassa, and sat on the board of the Famagusta Vakf. Mustafa Nuri was a member of the Committee of Turkish Cypriots who met with Winston Churchill on the 9 of October 1907 on the British ship the HMS Venus to represent Turkish Cypriot protest and counsel against growing Greek demands that Cyprus be ceded to Greece.

But the winds of change were blowing and they brought war. When the First World War broke out and the Ottomans declared themselves against the Triple Entente, the status of British rule in Cyprus changed from that of a Protectorate, nominally leased from the Sultan, to one of military occupation. The Ottomans of Cyprus were no longer merely quasi-comic oriental colour; they had become the enemy within. Famagusta became the site of a prisoner of war camp for captured Ottoman soldiers from Gallipoli. Conditions in the camp were dire and many prisoners perished in an outbreak of meningitis. Little archival evidence exists from this period. No natives were allowed cameras and Turkish Cypriots were forbidden to visit or to send food or medical aid to the prisoners of war.

An exception was made for Imam Mustafa Nuri, who was allowed to visit the camp to offer religious instruction and spiritual comfort. He was known for his beautiful voice and lyrical Qur'anic recitations during the funeral ceremonies he conducted (British records show 213 prisoners perished in the camp between 1916 and 1920). He complained to the British authorities about the ill treatment of prisoners, that they were blindfolded when taken out of the camp to perform manual labour mending the old walls of the castle, that the prisoners were malnourished and fed only a diet of red cabbage and barley soup, and poor-quality bread. Nuri Effendi was accused of trying to help captured Ottoman soldiers by smuggling in food and allegedly aiding prominent Ottoman feudal families (including my paternal great-grandfather's family) plan the escape of prisoners from the camp in Famagusta. He was arrested on a charge that would lead to capital punishment by hanging, at the behest of a Greek Cypriot policeman called Delivano, and the testimony of several Greek Cypriot merchants and an unnamed Turkish Cypriot witness. Despite being acquitted after a court case that lasted for two months, upon his release he was rearrested and interned without trial, with fourteen other prominent Turkish Cypriots, in Kyrenia Castle in 1916.

Kyrenia Castle, originally built by the Byzantines in the seventh century was enlarged and fortified by the Lusignans and then the Venetians. It is, like the grand architectural heritage of Famagusta, magnificent but now rather forlorn and neglected. The *kalabents* (an Ottoman term for those imprisoned in a castle) were kept in small dank cells, one of which now serves as a desolate gift shop, selling faded postcards, curling up in the fetid airless room that still smells of dust and damp. One of the cells has a rather half-hearted display about the prisoners.

I have not yet found any trace of the *kalabents* in British archives or the work of Greek Cypriot historians. Turkish Cypriot historians who are not of a nationalist bent have little interest in them too, indeed the eminent historian Tuncer Bağışkan has a much more class-based reading of the imprisonments, and posits that rather than heroes helping the former empire against the new imperial regime some, or at least one, was a feckless feudal lord betrayed to the British by oppressed villagers. He recounts that one of those arrested, the ağa Ali Effendi Hüseyin Babaliki, was set up and informed on by local villagers because he had sexually harassed the wife of Abdullah Havaca, a local villager. Even who exactly was imprisoned in the castle is not securely established or properly proven Bağışkan told me.

I am certain that Imam Mustafa Nuri Effendi was imprisoned though. I'm not relying on the work of historians with any axe to grind, or only the recollections of my grandmother, whose marriage to Izzet Bey was arranged by her father and Mahmut Bey, (Izzet Bey's older brother from another mother) whilst both men were incarcerated in the castle. I'm not relying on my faded memories of the stories my father told me, that he can only remember now when I retell them to him, 'ah yes, that's right...' he says, but can't recall unprompted. Before she died my grandmother gave my father a tiny notebook that the Imam had made whilst imprisoned. The notebook is small, an A5 size handmade artefact, and its pages are fashioned out of an illustrated English journal *The War Pictorial* from 1917.

Over ten years ago, when the memory palace was a secure stone fortress of patriarchal pomp and splendour, my father first showed me the slim homemade notebook by the imam that his mother had bequeathed him. Fatma Hanum gave it to him because the Imam had been a poet, like my father. The notebook covered that crucial and tragic period of Mustafa Nuri's life, whilst imprisoned in Kyrenia Castle between 1917 and 1918. 'You are poet too and it will be yours when I die' my father told me. It is a visually arresting object, the pages hand cut and sewn together, with curling written in the empty spaces between images, different sizes and styles of Ottoman Turkish script in red and black ink, sometimes in pencil. The juxtaposition of English text and images of the First World War is enchanting, especially for an ignorant great-granddaughter who, like all those who learnt to read and write in Turkish after 1928, is utterly unable to read Ottoman Turkish, and even to understand the rich Persian and Arabic inflected vocabulary of scholarly Ottoman Turkish speech and literature of the turn of the twentieth century. My father couldn't read it either. 'We should get it translated', I suggested. He agreed, 'but it's so hard to find someone we can trust with it,' he said. I thought he meant someone to trust with the artefact itself, so small, fragile, so strange and beautiful. I knew that wouldn't be a problem. My mother made a DVD scan of the pages. But my father still seemed reluctant to release that too. Perhaps he was reluctant because it is such a sad story. Mustafa Nuri Effendi and the other prisoners were released at the end of the war due to a lack of evidence against them, but he died shortly afterwards at the age of 43, his heart broken by his wife and youngest child's death whilst he was imprisoned, his health broken by the harsh conditions in the old castle. He died of the Istanbul sickness, that's what the Ottomans of Cyprus called it. My English great-grandmother died of it in Oxford in the same year; they called it the Spanish influenza there. Anyway, I didn't push my father to find a translator, and then events overtook us.

My mother had a heart attack in September 2008, a massive cardiac arrest. She was dead for ten minutes whilst the paramedics pumped her

A Glimpse of Orders, a page from Imam Mustafa Nuri's Prison Notebook

lifeless body with electric paddles. They got her heart working again but she was then in a coma for four days. My father insisted on demanding the doctor tell him the prognosis. She was very unlikely to regain consciousness the matter-of-fact Polish doctor replied, his professional demeanour quite unmarred by any emotion. The Jamaican nurse grabbed my father's hand. 'You can't know that', she told him, 'God works in mysterious ways, we must pray hard for your wife'. 'I can't' he told her, 'but yes, please, you pray'. Her prayers, my friends' and mine too, worked and my mother gradually regained consciousness although she returned to us diminished, blurred and vague, a Persephone who had eaten too many pomegranate seeds in the darkness. She was not quite there, is not quite here. She remembers us, and sometimes makes cogent coherent conversation, but she was never to paint again (she was an artist) or to care passionately about anything but my father. 'I love you Mustafa' she says many times a day, 'are you happy?' They have always been deeply in love.

I don't know what happened to the DVD but I became increasingly fascinated by the images of some of the pages that my mother had shared with me. My ignorance, and my father's, our absolute rupture from the recent past fascinated me. My inability to read the images textually made them all the more visually compelling. They represented my undeciphered heritage, not just yet to be deciphered but undecipherable perhaps. The break from an Ottoman Islamic world view to a Kemalist modernist Turkishness, trying to enunciate itself in a British colony, where the majority of the population wanted not independence but to be united with a Greek mainland over a thousand kilometres away. And so the Turkish speakers decided they wanted to be Turks, no longer Ottomans, and to be united with the Turkish mainland two hundred and fifty kilometres away. The Greeks had history on their side and the Turks geography. Everyone's mind was elsewhere, no one was much interested in being Cypriot.

My father Mustafa Izzet Adiloğlu was a poet. His favourite memory, which he would recount repeatedly until just a couple of months ago, and which I now cheer him up by recounting to him, is from when he was just nineteen, in 1954 when the bust of Namik Kemal was unveiled in the main square outside the mosque where his grandfather had been Imam. Namik Kemal was an Ottoman writer, a democrat and reformer of the Tanzimat era who had been exiled to Famagusta between 1873-76. Nationalism was on the rise in Cyprus in 1954, EOKA, Εθνική Οργάνωσις Κυπρίων Αγωνιστών, the National Organisation of Cypriot Fighters; a paramilitary group that sought to establish Enosis, union with Greece had just been formed. Famagusta was a hotbed of EOKA supporters and fighters. Nikos Sampson, a Greek Cypriot, just a year younger than Mustafa Izzet, was also born in Famagusta, and also a keen writer and footballer. Unlike my father he was an active member of EOKA, a fascist killer too. His gory endeavours were later to earn him the nickname 'the butcher of Omorphita' after he led the ethnic cleansing of a majority Turkish Cypriot neighbourhood in Nicosia in 1963. After the Greek Junta-led coup against Archbishop Makarios in 1974, Sampson became President of Cyprus for eight days, until the dictatorship in Greece fell, days after Turkey invaded.

In 1954 the Turkish Cypriots were embracing a more vigourously Turkish identity too, though it was to be another four years before they set up their own fascist nationalist paramilitary organisation TMT, *Türk Mukavemet Teşkilatı*, The Turkish Resistance Organisation. But most of the bloodshed, ethnic hatred and division that was to dominate my father's life and then mine too was yet to come that year, the year that the Saint Sophia Mosque of Famagusta was renamed Lala Mustafa Pasha Mosque, after the Ottoman general who had conquered Famagusta in 1571 after a ten-month siege and a bloody battle with the Venetians that had culminated in the flaying of poor Marco Antonio Bragadin. There was still an innocence to the nationalism on display, a sense of forging a new modern identity beyond the failed Ottoman empire and the fading fortunes of a shrinking minority community: approximately 30,000 Ottoman Cypriots had left the island between 1881 and 1927.

The ceremony to unveil the small bust of the exiled Namik Kemal, attracted a huge crowd, several hundred people overflowing the piazza right up to through the arches of the old Venetian palace. The ceremony began and ended with the local Lycée band's rendition of the Turkish national anthem and consisted of poems and short speeches about Namik Kemal. My father, a great orator, made a huge impression when he recited his poem. The crowd cheered enthusiastically, a young woman cried out, 'He's my lover you know'. 'A pretty girl' my father giggles, 'but I didn't know her at all'.

In 2009, I returned to Cyprus with my father. It was to be his last visit to his homeland. My mother wasn't well enough to travel after that, and they didn't want to be separated. We went for a walk around Kyrenia harbour and stopped outside the castle. 'How do you feel about it all?' I

Mustafa in Famagusta circa 1953

asked him. 'About the twists and turns of history? Your grandfather was imprisoned and suffered at the hands of the British, and yet you went on to marry an English girl, and your grandson is three quarters British?' 'At least they had their day in court' he said, 'they had some sort of legal process, and they were released. Their families could send them food and visit them once or twice a year. Look at the poor people being tortured in Guantanamo Bay and Abu Ghraib now, not charged with any crime, with no promise of due process of law, no prospect of release. The world is even more savage now than it was then'.

My great-grandfather's notebook became more and more important to me, and as the years passed I became more and more entranced by how much my ignorance of what the words said revealed to me. My ignorance gave me a humility that revealed the absolute alterity of our ancestors;

Mustafa outside Kyrenia Castle, 2009

whatever stories we turn them into. It revealed how absolute the breaks and shifts in history can be, the chasms of forgetting and ignorance between generational points of view. My ignorance of the script made me reflect upon how my father and then I, how many in Cyprus, had made the journey from Ottomans of Cyprus, to Turkish Cypriots, and then after all the wars, and despite the international embargoes and increasing dominance of Turkey, the long deferred and dashed hopes of peace, had become Turkish speaking Cypriots who longed for the reunification of the island, not for saviours, colonisers or patrons from elsewhere. And as these changes ensued how much has been lost, as well as found.

In my ignorance of the meaning of the words he wrote, the images, the strange and astonishingly original juxtaposition of text and image, of English and Ottoman Turkish, became all the more powerful. The little prison notebook was made in 1917, as the Dadaists were meeting at Cabaret Voltaire in Zurich. His work seemed to be to something quite other, more melancholy, gentler than theirs but nevertheless informed by the same artistic zeitgeist, an Hüzünist modernism all of its own. And much more than melancholy here was the courage inherent in creative self-expression in the most challenging of circumstances. I saw the line that bound me to him, of poetry and image, the reverie and concentration that my ignorance bestowed on me revealed that Mustafa Nuri was an artist with a singular modern visual language as well as a poet and a notable religious and community leader.

As I wrote articles and made art about the notebook, about my undeciphered heritage, several people sought me out, some wanted to claim him as a hero for a nationalist Islamic Cypriot identity that is highly unusual amongst Cypriots in Cyprus itself, more commonly found in the children and grandchildren of those who emigrated from the island, especially to the UK, or immigrants to Cyprus from Turkey. Mustafa Kureyşi, a young British Muslim of Turkish Cypriot descent, approached me wanting to translate the notebook. The polite young man translated one of the pages. 'The Great British' is the printed headline, and a picture of a harbour, the Ottoman script is the other way around. Whichever way you look at it, the page is upside down to someone. In large script Mustafa Nuri wrote 'my wife Ayşe Hanum's death Wednesday, then in red smaller script Wednesday 6 Rebi'ül-Ahir (the fourth Ottoman month of the year) the year 1335. In smaller black script he writes 'my tiniest daughter Ayşe's death 26 Receb, year 1336, and under that 7 May 1918'. The Great British is a diary of loss. Ayşe Hanum died in childbirth, her baby namesake a year later, and her remaining four children, Fatma, Osman, Emine and Asım were to be become orphans soon after.

The young man shared a colourised version of the portrait and a brief biography of the Imam on the Facebook page of group called Cezire Derneği (the Island Association). A teacher from Trabzon, the Black Sea region of Turkey, who now lives in Cyprus, wrote under the post: 'I wonder which impudent smart aleck who swears at religion, who says that Tayyip is Islamicising us by force is his grandchild...' The Association replied, 'Imam Nuri Effendi lived and protected the authentic pure and innocent Cypriot identity. If there is anyone with his identity and way of life on our island, I wonder how Cypriot they are considered.' Incensed I messaged the chair of the Association: 'Are you responsible for the horrible post and comments on your association's page. I am appalled!' He responded, 'as a gesture of goodwill I have had the messages deleted and

The Great British is a Diary of Loss, a page from Imam Mustafa Nuri's
Prison Notebook

apologise for any offence caused'. But he defended the teacher from
Trabzon; 'he didn't direct it at anyone specifically. It was a general
observation to those that hold views that serve to polarise our community,
trying to hide our heritage under the carpet to further their own interests.
Not to a particular individual and certainly not to you or your family'.
Perhaps to someone who grew up in London or Trabzon, such an attack
could seem general, but in a tiny place like Northern Cyprus, within the
community such attacks are always personal, everybody knows each other,
personally. I responded, 'Yes, I understand that but he should have the
intelligence to understand he is insulting the Imam and his descendants as
well as all modern Cypriots generally. May Allah protect us all from the
likes of him.' My great grandfather had become the site for competing
narratives, identities and loyalties, beyond my nene's childhood memories
of her father, my father's understanding of him as a poet, mine of him as an
artist and heartbroken husband, he had become a poster boy for a new
nationalist fundamentalism.

Someone from Trebizond, the site of Armenian massacres in 1895 and 1915 and fierce fighting between the Ottoman and Russian armies during the First World War, was claiming the Imam as his own, supposedly protecting him against my father and me. During the Turkish War of Independence many Pontic Greek communities rebelled against both Atatürk's army and the Greeks who came to proclaim national revolution. The city still has a sizeable Greek speaking Muslim community. Why didn't he engage with his own complicated post-Ottoman history I fumed to myself, though it would have been unfair to further burden the young translator who had so respectfully memorialised my great-grandfather and lovingly colourised his portrait for the Facebook post with my observations. After all, it wasn't his fault that others in his association wrote hateful comments.

Anyway, on reflection, my reaction wasn't consistent. I thought the ignorant teacher from Trabzon should engage with his own history and not write inflammatory posts about Cypriot historical figures and yet I was equally perturbed by the growing number of young London Cypriots I saw on social media who didn't connect with London culture and engaged with their own version of what they considered an essentially Turkish, not particularly Cypriot heritage. They insisted on 'a pure and authentic' Muslim way of being Turkish Cypriot, and found Cypriots actually born and brought up on the island and who lived in Cyprus lacking in religious and national fervour. Some posted Ottoman versions of the Turkish flag and dreamed of the day all of Cyprus would be under Ottoman rule again. Unlike most young Turkish Cypriots on the island, they vehemently oppose a peaceful settlement between the two Cypriot communities or secular rule of law, and dismiss those who want a reunified island as not of 'pure blood', as 'linobambaki', Greek Cypriots who converted to Islam in Ottoman times. I had come to understand all too well my father's former apprehension that it would be hard to find someone to trust with the Imam's notebook. He was not ours to hide in my father's dossier of important documents I knew that, but I wasn't ready to see him made a puppet for the new fundamentalism. The time would come, for now we would rest in gentle, loving ignorance.

I approach the grounds of memory palace nervously, through overgrown jasmine bushes to a ruined pool, the fountain is broken, and dragonflies are dancing on the surface of the water. It's a shard of an early childhood memory I realise, my father's or mine, I'm not sure which. Today the roar of the sea is loud, my father thinks that he is in the old Turkish quarter of Mağusa, on the castle ramparts; I think I'm on the battlements of Kyrenia castle. Whichever it is, we're both looking out to sea and the memory palace is made of yellow sandstone. I think of Mustafa Nuri on his deathbed, little Fatma watching from the doorway. The things we remember, the things we imagine and can't imagine, the things we forget, they are all part of the history of ignorance. I hold his hand. 'Let's go back to Mağusa soon' I say, 'let's go and see that bust of Namik Kemal. You know you were just nineteen, the piazza was full of people…' He chuckles, 'The crowd was huge. I didn't even know her you know, I'd never even seen her before, that girl who shouted, "he's my lover"'.

ON MY SOLE

Tam Hussein

I understand why you slammed the door shut in my face. This sort of stuff is hard to process for anyone, let alone seeing someone that looks like your twin brother. You must be sitting there in your room trying to understand what is going on. I must admit that I too was quite shocked to find you there in my flat, but I have also figured out how all of this has come about even if you haven't, especially as you are still new to this world. So I wrote this account from A to Z for you to take in all of this in your own time and then perhaps we can figure out how to proceed. Please excuse this lengthy account but I feel it is important for both of us to understand what has passed.

I was quite taken aback when I received a direct message on Facebook from a friend I had never met before, never had coffee with, or whose voice I had never heard. I accepted his 'friend' request and we became friends. We never talked of course, but we were friends. He would like my stuff and send me emojis whenever I posted something and I would in turn reciprocate even though I didn't like his posts. But this time, Danny, for that was his avatar, wrote: 'Wow, this is amazing! You are having a relaunch?'

Me: Relaunch? Relaunch of what?

I sent him an emoji. He sent back a LOL. I sent back a GIF. He responded with a meme and once this cycle of formality was complete, he sent me the link with a simple 'TC' and I didn't bother responding. He took no offence to such online behaviour.

In truth, I had become engrossed with the link. Waterstones, that vast book shop in Green Park was holding a relaunch of *The Travels* again and of the author it declared: the notable scholar and traveller George Richard

Sole will be delivering a talk on the book that he has translated from the Andalusian scholar and polymath Ibn Fudayl.

This was strange. Why would someone impersonate a character that I had conjured from the darkness of my imagination? Why would someone relaunch a book which had been written in jest and only sold three hundred copies or so? Was it a ruse or a marketing ploy by my publisher?

I called Evan, who usually didn't respond to my calls on account of my queries about that royalty cheque he was meant to send which always tended to get lost in the post. But eventually when I called his house in Primrose Hill, he negated the assertion that this relaunch was a marketing ploy by his publishing house.

'Mate, can you imagine how much money it would cost to do such a gimmick?'

'That's what I thought, I told him.

'Was there anything else?'

Before I raised the matter of my pitiful royalties again, he had put the phone down on me saying, 'Maybe you have *one* fan?'

A fan? *Moi*? Can't be, not me, but then again, why not? There are some authors who have a cult following. Chuck Palahniuk or Elmore Leonard are good examples. There were tribute bands for Queen, ABBA, and Michael Jackson, so maybe this was the literary equivalent?

So there was nothing for it but to attend this relaunch of my book.

I decided to go early to Waterstones. It was a bright sunny day and Piccadilly is lovely in spring. I wanted to pop into Hatchards, that beautiful bookshop that reminded you of what bookshops were meant to look like. It always had delightful books in there. And I also wanted to catch this impostor who had appropriated my *nom de plume* and maybe have a conversation about this wonderful marketing opportunity. He had after all succeeded in doing something which I had failed to do – to promote *The Travels* – so it would only be right that I introduce myself to this mystery fan or man, sign a few copies in gratitude and also, I should add, to encourage sales.

He was not there when I arrived half an hour early. I found my book piled up in rows. There were middle-aged women already sitting in the chairs which had been arranged in a U shape. In fact, I heard the assistants discuss how the chairs were to be arranged for the presentation. One of them said:

'Professor Sole likes to walk among his audience, so why don't we make it into a herring-bone shape? He can walk down the middle if he wishes to. I'm sure the translators would love to be able to engage with him in close quarters.'

The second assistant, who appeared to be the more senior, said: 'Quite, but Professor Sole prefers the audience to be around him. He has a passion for the dramatic, so let's give him a stage.'

'Doesn't he! He's quite the performer!' giggled the first as if she had a crush on her English teacher.

By the time the relaunch was about to start, there were no seats to be had and people were forced to stand. I had managed to weasel myself into the front row, having got myself some elderflower juice and seized the last chocolate chip cookies just before a well looked-after pensioner was about to get his paws on them. I heard the excitement and the conversation from the audience who were mostly translators and academics, but they were talking about this conjuror as if he was Indiana Jones delivering a lecture.

He did not arrive on time, and one of the book sellers wearing a frumpy dress and spectacles said that Professor Sole had a penchant for the dramatic and was running somewhat late. It did not annoy the audience but seemed to gladden their very souls. It was annoying because I only had four people, excluding the publisher turning up to my book launch. For me, it gave me pleasure to hear such heartfelt praise for *The Travels*.

When he finally entered, he was exactly as I had conjured him in my mind's eye, his hair was cut in the classic style and pomaded. Although he was elderly, he looked youthful for his age. If Oscar Wilde's *Picture of Dorian Gray* wasn't fiction, I would have thought that Dorian Gray was indeed him! His eyes were piercing blue, he displayed his mustachio the way a walrus might make a show of his tusks by way of a mating call. He wore an Oxford shirt with a tie unknotted and collar unbuttoned showing the hair sprouting out of his fulsome testosterone-filled chest, contained only by a mustard tweed blazer. He wore blue hardy trousers and shoes. He was everything I was not; from a different era – a different century. The sort of man who didn't watch women's football, who assumed that women drank shandy and men drank whiskey, the sort of man who still wore leather gloves when he drove and did not make any allowances for pronouns or what anyone felt, declaring: 'I shall not butcher the English language, Sir.' That was it. You felt that if you pressed more, you would be duelling in St James's Park. Sole felt no compulsion in ordering a bloody steak or asking if there were any bars in Mecca. And yet, I noticed that despite this, the ladies giggled in expectation as soon as he stepped in.

Sole did not apologise for his arrival and his performance, I must admit, was quite magical. Whilst the first book launch I presented of *The Travels* was bumbling and often confusing for the listener, Sole's presentation was lucid and clear. He explained the political climate in Medieval Spain, the Taifa period, Andalusia and the *Reconquista* with ease. He explained it so simply that even a child could comprehend the topic, and yet none of its depth and profundity was lost in making it simple. When he flitted from Spanish, Arabic and Persian, the translators – mostly female – gasped, as if he had made love to each and every one of them and had finished with a twizzle of his mustachio.

He belonged to a different time, an old school Orientalist, like a Snouck Hurgronje who could at once study the peoples of the Malay Archipelago with wonder and curiosity, yet also devise and submit dastardly plans for the Dutch East India company to exterminate the indigenous population in order to get hold of the spice. He had true cold objectivity. I could see why men and women could love him and yet hate him. And I could see why many of these translators who would otherwise be offended by his opinions and ideas excused him as being 'old fashioned' as he explained the journey of my character, Ibn Fudayl, in Andalusia.

I had written this character initially as a rant against the attitudes that I saw in some of the scholars when they dealt with the likes of us. I suppose I and my fellow students resented being looked at as a separate species by these learned old fogeys. The first story of this character was received well, and so, influenced by academic writing and Pierre Bayle no less, I wrote the book in my own time putting into it all the vitriol I felt for some of these scholars whose lectures I attended.

It was merely a bit of fun. I circulated it amongst my friends at the School of Oriental and African Studies, SOAS, as we discussed the various texts, and they too made their additions and it became known as *The Travels* amongst us. But it seemed Ibn Fudayl started his own life and decided to leave his creator. For whilst I finished my postgraduate studies, spending an enormous amount of money so that I could have the title 'Dr' to my name and become what we call a 'high value' man, I ended up eking out a living on a zero hours contract at the same institution that paid minimum wages despite its leftist credentials.

Ibn Fudayl ended up in the inbox of Evan, my future publisher, and it was he who got in touch with me. Introducing himself as Jerry Evan, he said he ran a small publishing house and wondered if I might be interested in publishing the book. Surprised and flattered by the proposal, I accepted and the book took on a life of its own. At the very least amongst my friends, most of whom had abandoned their doctoral studies to become civil servants and tax officers. The most successful as I could gather was Eesa, who went from being a cult leader of sorts, pickup artist, and then Google executive – which seemed to crystallise all those talents in one job, except he also made loads of money unlike me. I was a purist, though, and remained in academia. I would keep up the fight against the powers that be. I would enlighten the youth so they didn't become slaves to corporate media and think for themselves.

But I hoped that Eesa might be able to persuade someone with Search Engine Optimisation experience to perhaps manipulate the algorithm so my book would be at the top of the search page.

'Can't do it,' Eesa said, taking me to a gentleman's club. He drank a scotch and tried to break it to me gently. 'Google is about fairness, ethics and corporate responsibility – think about the optics if this came out.'

'Yes but, that motherfucker WD Allen from *World Literature Review* wants to destroy me. Can't you just bury the review in a mass of Google pages? C'mon man! We've been friends for years. The motherfucker called the book "tedious". "Tedious"!'

'Dude, listen to me, it would be against freedom of speech to suppress this. It's immoral. Chill man, who knows who WD Allen is? No one gives a fuck. Look at her! She's lovely.'

I left him trying to get with one of the exotic dancers writhing on a pole and headed back to Senate House. As I left, he said, 'Don't worry about paying me man! I'll expense it as client entertainment.'

Still, three hundred books sold wasn't that bad.

When the Q&A started and everyone raised their hands with a multitude of questions for Professor Sole, I thought about interrupting him and confronting him about this relaunch. But then I thought about standing up and praising him for his acting and presenting myself in front of the ladies and saying: 'It is I, the writer, the creator of that book.' But then I noticed how my mind raced to make quick profit-and-loss calculations. Surely it would be better to confront him alone? For this ruse, this subterfuge, this deception would result in greater sales. I was torn between telling the truth and book sales and I did not know what to do, until a quiet voice within whispered in my soul. Why had you written this tale under a *nom de plume*? My rational self responded: 'To protect myself from the religious zealots, so they do not come after me.' I decided that this deception and increase in sales was worth paying for if it meant that my safety was not compromised. Although there wasn't a religious zealot about in Waterstones, nevertheless health and safety considerations and precautions had to be taken into consideration and I didn't reveal myself to the public.

The book signing went well. I estimated that we sold about three hundred books that day. A whole stream of mostly ladies queued up to have the book signed. I was only annoyed that the selfies this impostor took with the translators excluded me. Often, if they were still young, he would touch their shoulder as he stood next to them or even clasped the side of their hips and they didn't seem to object. In fact, they gave him their number in order to discuss, as he put it, 'translation theory in practice and the second sex or, as I like to call it, the fairer sex'.

The translators were not offended by such remarks and they walked off positively reinvigorated by the encounter. If I did that, I'd receive a slap.

And so, having grabbed the last book, I waited for my copy to be signed and when I came up to his table, he had his fountain pen open and erect, ready to sign my book.

For a moment his piercing blue eyes, it appeared, recognised me the way a son may recognise his father. Then there was some dismay as if I was some effeminate boy, as if only women were permitted in this line and if it was a man, there was something wrong with him.

'Yes,' he said, 'To whom shall I make it out to young man?'

'You know who,' I replied.

'I beg your pardon, I do not. I have not had the pleasure,' he said.

'I am the author of *The Travels*.'

He looked around as if I was a mad person.

'Good God,' he seemed to say to himself, 'I think this fellow is mad.'

'You mean to tell me that you really *believe* you wrote this?'

'I do not believe, I know.'

'But I am the author of this book. I conjured Ibn Fudayl and George R. Sole from my mind. It's a play on the word "arsehole".'

'No, I am afraid you have lost your mind. I am its author, George Richard Sole esquire.'

'Look, with all due respect to your mother, but George R. Sole is a bastard. I'm his father. He's a figment of my imagination, I created him, I wrote the whole story. Everything, absolutely everything. From the footnotes down to Ibn Fudayl. You are taking this a bit too far.'

'A bit too far, sir? It is you who insult me, now I would ask you to leave me alone.'

I didn't like the way he looked at me, as if I was a peasant or some poor Indian worker in Dubai. I started to clench my fist. 'Now look here you fucking bastard...'

But Sole called security and a large Nigerian fellow, presumably doing a master's degree part-time, approached us. 'Sir, would you kindly escort this gentleman out, he's causing me a bit of bother and I don't wish to box his ears.'

'Box my ears! Ha! Just you try it. You are my son. You have no mother.'

I was subsequently escorted out by the polite Nigerian man and I found myself outside of the bookshop.

'I am going to sue you and Waterstones!' I said, as the security guard stood outside with his arms crossed as if to say: you shall not enter.

God's honest truth, I was incensed by Sole's response. He needed to acknowledge me. I was his creator. His utter refusal to recognise me made me immensely upset. Sole would have been nothing had I not conjured him. He was merely a caricature until I gave him flesh, and now he was an open enemy to me. What was even more upsetting was to see the sales on Amazon skyrocketing. *The Travels* only had two reviews, but now I noticed that the newly reissued book had three hundred reviews. Three hundred reviews! Gushing with goodness. It looked like the reviewer had been boned by Sole. I needed to confront him with the absoluteness of the truth. So I sent off several Freedom of Information Requests to the Foreign Office inquiring about the incident I had written about in the 'about the author' section: 'releasing a greased piglet into a ballroom of diplomats' in Oman. I expected the Foreign Office to reply with a negative. After all, I had made it all up. But after several weeks, they replied:

Dear Sir,

Thank you for your query. Your request has been handled as a request for information under the Freedom of Information Act 2000 (FOIA).

Whilst the full detail of your query cannot be answered due to it being covered by the Official Secrets Act 1989, however, we can confirm that the incident did indeed occur.

It is on public record where we made a statement saying how deeply sorry we were regarding the incident as it violated the Sultan's and indeed the country's Muslim sensibilities.

Yours etc,

I was flabbergasted. My head spun. How could it be? How could this character outsmart me? But then I thought about it. Was it not true that I had made him thus? That I had envisaged him to have the panache of a Flashman novel or a Richard Burton who had the boldness to measure a Sudanese man's member without batting an eye lid? Or perhaps he could outsmart me because I was part of him and he knew me too?

Or this must be some elaborate plot. But why? Why exactly would he or anyone want to do that? I was too insignificant, broke, with only the title 'Dr' to my name, which would make most men, unless you could stitch them up or give them a medical diagnosis, assume that you were one of those professors concerned with Marxism or feminism and all of its ugly sisters.

But still, I was now pitted against him. I needed to outsmart him. I could not simply allow this to pass. So I began my inquiries and took the Oxford Tube up to Balliol. I had written in my book that he graduated from Balliol and, as expected, the college had no record of such a distinguished alumnus.

And yet, when I searched his name in JSTOR, the electronic repository for academics and their articles, there they were – all of his numerous articles and publications. They were erudite and learned and some had been peer reviewed. 'From the proto-Semitic the pro-biotic in nature. The origin of Akkadian, Ugaritic, Aramaic, Urinic and the diuretic language groups', by Professor George Richard Sole, had been published in the *Bulletin of the John Ryland's Library*. So I called the editors of the journal up in Manchester, and there they put me in touch with the previous editor, John Mcteague.

Mr Mcteague remembered the Professor well for his article, on publication, had caused quite a stir amongst them. Especially as Sole had just returned from the Empty Quarter.

'He,' said Mcteague, 'had turned up with a savage young fellow, Hanzala, and lectured us for two hours on the article he had written for us. I never thought such an obscure topic could receive a standing ovation but it did! He was a bit of a rascal with the ladies too.'

'So you saw him?'

'Well, why of course,' Mcteague was quite puzzled, 'why would I not have?'

'Could you describe him?'

'A tall fellow with piercing blue eyes, a bit excessive on the Brylcreem maybe, but a dashing splendid fellow. We went out for some wine and cheese afterwards – as I said he was a rascal with the ladies.'

I was mystified. This couldn't have been an act, or could it? My imagination must have brought him to flesh, perhaps in the way God says: 'Be!' and it is. But then, how come I could not bring other things to life in my imagination? Why couldn't the most brilliant minds of the age bring their characters and protagonists into the flesh? Even Michelangelo, the supreme artist, had demanded that his creation walk and yet it could not. Was this some sort of madness? Narcissism?

That night like I was Dr Frankenstein, I sat in my room trying with my mind to conjure Bethany in front of me. I closed my eyes and focused on her totally, her womanly figure, her brown hair, her hips, her fleshy body – but nothing came forth. So I thought: well, Bethany is a living person, it does not do. She must be totally imaginary. So I began to create the character of Isabelle, the beautiful nymph. She was the most exquisite creature I could think of who did, I must confess, mirror Bethany in many ways, but she was not her. Imagination and writing are, after all, based on the author's experiences, just like George Richard Sole was, and yet for the life of me she did not appear in front of me – even after I dressed her more modestly.

Then I thought, it's because she is a woman. Whatever Tolstoy or Flaubert write, these men cannot fully create a true woman, they can only write about men. So it follows that, since I am a lesser author than them, I must create a figure who is a man, for my imagination can fully create such a character in the way that I cannot do so with a woman. Hemingway's way is the best – let it be from the perspective of a man, let me create a character who occupies a world that I understand. So I tried to imagine a man and drew together all the powers of my experiences and imagination, hoping to bring him forth. But it was to no apparent success. I went to bed hoping that perhaps this new character that I had created needed to percolate in the recesses of the microcosm of the self in order for it to come forth. After all, I did not see George – he simply appeared in the world like a malevolent sprite ready to torment me. So, I reasoned, this is how it shall be with my latest creation too.

When I woke up next day, I didn't find him sitting on my desk reading a book. No, my small single room, and now yours, in King's Cross was pretty empty. I was disappointed. I had lectures to prepare, and so I took myself to university to do some work for the undergraduate class. The day would have been miserable had I not found Bethany in the staff room reading. She was wearing an expensive purple wool jumper I had given her and she had tinted her hair slightly auburn. She looked so feminine. I sat next to her as she was reading a book. She ignored me – she always did when she was reading. It was always her way – the page had to be finished before she spoke to me. When she had finished, I asked her for permission to buy her coffee. She gave it. I went to the machine and got both of us coffee.

She took hers with a frown. 'No sugar,' she said. I got up and got her two sachets and stirred them in to her coffee. I prayed to God she wasn't going to complain yet again about where all the nice guys had gone. She was blind. They were all around her, confined to the 'Friend Zone' and she needed merely to go there.

'What are your plans today?' I asked.

'I have to organise an event for the Syriac society.' She had the look of annoyance that made her even more delectable.

'Do you want me to help?'

'No, no, it's fine. It's only right that I do it. I don't like the organising but hosting the lecture is going to be great. You should be there.'

'Do you want me to come?'

'It's up to you. I think it'll be good. It's your research area in any case.'

'Really?'

'Yes, about Medieval travelogues. He's covering Ibn Fadlan, Ibn Battuta, Ibn Jubayr and Ibn Fudayl?'

'Ibn Fudayl?'

'Yes.'

'Who is the lecturer?'

'Professor George R. Sole from Bu Baqara university, Oman. He's on tour trying to recruit junior fellows for The Humanities and Arts Research Association Markaz.'

'Odd name, don't you think? The centre's acronym is HARAM – illicit.'

'Why should I? The Middle East is progressing so fast, that those terms are now meaningless. I hear the emir is walking around in white dresses.'

'That's a Jalabiya or thobe, it's traditional dress.'

She glared at me.

'I may be wrong of course,' drawing back my correction, 'so do you want me to attend?'

'Honestly,' she said, 'totally down to you.'

'Do you want to grab some food afterwards?'

Bethany paused for a moment.

'It's on me,' I quickly interjected.

'Okay, but you always pay. I don't like it. It's so patronising.'

'So?'

'Fine, but next time I will pay.'

'For sure.'

Sole gave a scholarly and erudite lecture that evening. There can be no doubt about it. The audience were smitten. That was hardly unexpected – this is how I had imagined him. He walked as he talked, as if he had watched those TED Talks that I tried to emulate, but could not do. He came to the lectern, checked an odd footnote and continued, added a witticism here and there which drew laughter from those who understood the joke and so considered themselves part of the elect, and those who did not get the cryptic reference but pretended to get it. He then turned his fire on some of the Marxists who had turned up to the lecture hall to 'hold him to account'. His riposte too seemed to have gone down very well. He was not flustered one bit and they were escorted out by the former Gurkhas who now worked as the university's security detail.

But this time I was not going to let him pass off my work as his. I stood up, and to the great embarrassment of Bethany, asked him directly where this manuscript of Ibn Fudayl was.

'Oh, it's you again!' he said, 'The man who thinks he wrote my book! This man believes I am impersonating him and so he confronts me here. Very well, I didn't wish to embarrass this fellow in front of his peers. But since he is trying to do so to me, I am obliged to clarify how I came about this manuscript. I discovered this folio in 2007 whilst rummaging around in the Assad Library in Damascus. It slipped out of the pages of one of the biographies I was reading. I immediately spotted its import, and realising that nothing goes unnoticed in the country, had but two options. I could follow the practice I learnt at the SOAS library: when one did not have credit for photocopies then one ripped the relevant pages out and transported them home like a philistine. Or I could pop the book in my jacket. I opted for the latter.'

There was laughter at his story.

'That is a lie!' I shouted, 'Where is it? Where is the folio?'

'Here it is.' He nodded at Bethany, who promptly showed the manuscript in its full glory to the audience on the projected screen behind the lectern. And there it was, fully authenticated and catalogued by the Bodleian Library.

I was astounded by that. What could I say? Was my mind so powerful that it could also conjure up objects too?

Bethany did not go to dinner with me that evening, I sent her 56 messages and various emojis to apologise for embarrassing her, but she did not respond. In fact, she did not respond to me the day after nor the day after. I even went and knocked at her flat in Hampstead but she didn't open and I left leaving a letter explaining my actions to her.

Several days later, I received a letter from my publisher, Evan, explaining that he was intending to sue me. That the publisher of 'the real author, George R. Sole' had shown him incontrovertible evidence that I had impersonated him all along. That Evan had to withdraw 'the first edition immediately from the shelves and pulp them'. I had to reimburse him for the expense his publishing house had undergone to produce the book. I was ruined. I tried to call him. I tried to send him emails from friends who made comments on the story when I first wrote it to demonstrate that it was not I but my character that had done so. And yet, I could not but marvel at my act of creation – this is exactly how my character would behave! Why was I so exasperated? If you know your child to be selfish and spoilt then why be surprised when he acts thus?

Yes, but it was inconvenient. I sent Evan text messages that were dated, showing undeniable proof how my friends had laughed at the story as it was shared amongst us. How could it be that I was being sued? When Evan did not reply to my messages, I wrote back saying that it was I who would be suing him and also Amazon for copyright breaches amongst other things.

I even marched to the Police and filed a report saying that someone called George Richard Sole was impersonating me and my book. They wouldn't give me a crime reference number but suggested that I should call Central and North West London NHS Foundation Trust on 0800 023 4650. 'They will be able to help, sir.'

When I called them, I realised it was the NHS mental health help line. How was I to debunk these absurd claims? I needed to go back to basics and as I walked about Russell Square pondering my strange predicament, who did I see sitting in the open pavilion of the coffee shop in the park?

Bethany was wearing a French beret and gloves, sitting with Professor Emeritus George R. Sole, whose hand I noticed rested on her knee. They were having a coffee and cake and I found the sight unacceptable and incestuous. He had crossed the line. He spotted me, she spotted me. They did not acknowledge me but I noticed a knowing smile on the former, as if he knew what he was doing and what territory he was crossing. I pondered as I walked towards them. This creation of mine had become an open enemy, a nemesis. Was he not worthy of punishment? This ingrate? Would I his author be guilty of murder if I destroyed him? Would I be unjust? Surely I can do whatever I wished with him and no one could judge me?

Yes, said a voice within, but what about consciousness? You have given him consciousness. Your creation is no longer yours. It has a life of its own. It's murder. Look at the child and the father. The child comes from the father and yet, should the father kill him, he would do something wrong – for the child is a separate entity. Would Moses be wrong for killing his son if God ordered him thus? And so, I debated with myself about all such things and I remembered the story of Khidr, the ever-wandering mortal who killed a child because he knew that the child would grow up to be disobedient to his parents. Khidr also knew that God would replace that child with a good child and so he proceeded to murder the innocent child. There were no sanctions on the murderer. In fact, Moses, who had accompanied him, did not intervene in such a seemingly unjust act. I could not solve the question in my head and so I resorted to what I felt: this George Richard Sole was my creation. The creator cannot be held accountable by the created; a writer can do away with his character by crunching up his paper and throwing it in the bin, and he is not wrong. And so, taking a leap of faith, I approached them, seized the butter knife on their table and shouted, 'Allahu Akbar!' or 'God is Most Great' in the English language and plunged the knife into Sole's neck.

Bethany screamed, people around me screamed. The clients rushed away from me. I tried to explain to them as they brought out their phones filming me that I was not committing murder but simply putting an end to my character's life. That they were quite safe, that I was not a violent man. No one tried to overpower me as they filmed me live on Facebook explaining my actions whilst I kept an eye on my creation, watching his life energy ebb away. I heard him mutter things as he bled out. I thought I heard him call out for 'Hanzala' or perhaps it was 'Hannah'. As I was soon surrounded by armed police, whom I later discovered were anti-terror police, I expected the body to vanish in front of me as you might see in the movies, but the body was still there even as paramedics came to give him first aid. Whilst Sole was taken to St Mary's, I was taken to Paddington high security police station where I was interrogated by Special Branch officers.

Instead of asking me about the relationship between me and Sole, they asked me question about ISIS and Syria and other such things I knew little about. The short of it – I was not granted bail and I was remanded in custody. The prime minister held a COBRA meeting on my account. My solicitor, Mr Williams, advised that I plead guilty and we could point to mental health issues and show that there was an 'absolute alienation of reason'.

But that to me seemed contrary to truth and I was determined that I should walk out of court a free man. I was not guilty. That George Richard Sole should be no more and yet he was. I read the press reports as I awaited my trial. They were fantastic, focusing on the words I had used and my apparent religiosity, which mosque I prayed at, which company I kept. They trawled up my connections to an extremist Bosnian calligrapher from Croydon who had been fired for trying to make a weapon that would zap Serbians from space. They even trawled through my book to show what an extremist I was.

The Home Secretary answered questions and ordered an immediate review as to my appointment at SOAS and wondered out loud if I could be deported somewhere. Why weren't the signs of my radicalism not spotted? Meanwhile, there were others who agitated against me. Piers Morgan could not quite figure out why no one had read the book I had authored. Note here that Sole was no longer mentioned. All the signs were that I (only I) was the author of the

book. It was replete with extremism, he said. Sales of the first edition
of the book went up enormously, and I was recognised as its author.
Sole had perished, symbolically at least, and I was content. I did not
feel guilty, for just like God cannot be held accountable for what He
does with His creation, how shall I be questioned about the character
I had given flesh too?

But still, there was the question of the body. Why did it not vanish? I
could not understand this until one day it came to me as I woke up to the
sound of my cell mate in prison coughing.

What an epiphany! In order for the body to vanish I must write him out.
And so, I got some paper and wrote an epilogue to *The Travels* and wrote
Sole out of existence. I then asked my solicitor to send it to Evan, who
gladly complied with my request, reissuing an e-book with the extract
included in the hope of increasing sales. After a few days, I got a visit from
my solicitor. I had expected him to come. He looked puzzled and
perturbed.

'I just wanted to let you know that the Crown Prosecution Service are
no longer pressing charges against you.'

'Why?' I asked knowingly.

'Well,' he paused, not knowing how to say it. 'Sole is alive.'

'Was he not in the morgue, Mr Williams?'

'Yes,' he said uncomfortably.

'Was the cause of death not established in the autopsy?'

'Yes.'

'So?'

'Well, he turned up at my office, pleading for your release.'

'Really?' I said, unsurprised.

'So the Crown Prosecution Service were quite puzzled by this strange
phenomena, and have dropped all charges against you since no murder was
committed.'

'Splendid,' I said, mimicking Sole's voice.

And so, I walked out of Belmarsh a free man, only to find you here in my
flat – oblivious to me and my existence, and quite puzzled as to how there
is someone who appears to be a clone of you standing on your doorstep. I
suspect that Sole, before he drove off the cliff at Seven Sisters as I had

written, had decided on a swan song to spite me. He decided to write you as his legacy and gift for me to wrestle with. And so there are two of us here, and I am writing this to make you understand that I am the original, the father, and you are only a creation of Sole's imagination which is tied to mine. And we must now figure out how to proceed.

SWAN LAKE QASIDA

Steve Noyes

NASIIB

After years of hard wandering, Samiira and I returned to the lake where we fell in love.
We were no longer as we were, but we fancied that the marsh-grass retained a double hollow
where we once lay together, cloud-spotting, fascinated by our laziness and laughing
at passers-by who said, 'The wildlife here is day by day getting larger and stranger!'
Parts of the lake-trail were now overgrown, the bridge-pontoons sagging, their boards wet.
There were ruddy gouges filled with water and narrow dry ridges at path-edges to negotiate.
The winter grass was still yellow, and half the lake's surface a chartreuse scum of algae.
Ducks as they paddled pushed it into soft folded piles like a rucked-up coverlet.
We stepped carefully down the muddy slope past slow-mo turtles, their shells
shiny tic-tac-toes of agate and hellodor, sunning with side-eyed reptile heads.
We were sensitive as heliotropes to all His signs, as to our moods and fancies,
Samiira's eyes reflective colouramas. Hard green blackberry vines,
Puffy chocolate rushes, red-headed finches fluttering the bushes,
and out in the lake, the oily brown loop of an otter's pelt gone sploosh.
We came to the rock-garden, where there were tiny pink anemones once
but now just thistles and dandelions spearing the cracked mud.
As the sky absorbs the lake, so now and then commingled in us.
Samiira's beauty compels me to reject extravagant comparisons,
because her inner bint still shimmies, no need of adornment,
her smile often shifting from eager to shy, as before a kiss.
With damp held hands, we came to the pavilion where we were wed
but the cedar beams of the roof were no longer fragrant and had darkened.
A large crack split the cement pad on which we made our vows
in front of our old boon-companions, yet we still heard their wild huzzahs
as we faced them, *zawj wa zawja*, joined in His holy name.
Hands around our eyes for goggles, we peered in the Nature House's windows.

The exhibits of birds' nests, beehives and ant colonies remained behind glass
as did the table where we signed the marriage-deed, a jaunty stuffed raccoon
rearing on hind legs for a witness, but much had changed. The sign
NATURE HOUSE now read NATURE SUCKS sprayed with a lewd graffito.
An injudicious fire in a garbage can had blackened the front door, and there was trash
blowing across the path into the parking lot, where someone had abandoned a shopping cart
full of sodden bundles; something had given way, some supported commonweal,
and yet, though its sanctity was compromised, the Nature House was not ransacked,
its windows whole, perhaps because no one thought it contained anything valuable.
We huddled as though audience to our younger selves, unaware of where we'd end.

RAHIIL

'I am disheartened, sore of mind, to find the haunts of our young love so spoiled.
It makes you wonder.' Samiira snorted and fixed her resolute eye upon me,
saying, 'Ya *'ayni*, do not repine. It is common for we water-skins to pass through time
and suffer change and leakage. Face it determined, as one of our tribe might fix his gaze
on the horizon, though his camel be slack-skinned and blade-ribbed after days of riding.'
We remained in the pavilion until twilight had set invisible finches singing
their last *taghrids* against the glimmering west-lands and pricks of the first stars
began to pattern the sky like glitter on a dark cloak of Egyptian cotton.

'Remember thou,' she said, 'when we lay at the open window at the family ranch
and smelled the smoke of forest fires, drifting, dissipating above the valley
and returning sage-spice wafted from the surrounding ring of hills,
while far above us, the milk of heaven spilled, to whorl and fill
our vision with the mansions and dimensions of His pleasure.
We were so effortlessly slap-happy, small and whole.'
'I doubt we shall ever go back; such are the springing traps of fate.
But since I lack a *kahin's* prescience, I'll trade disappointment for amazement,
like the far-roaming jinn, who, whereupon reaching the zone
where once they were wont to see a flaming star, were twice delighted
to hear the generous Qur'an, streaming through space in elevated tone.'
'High hope,' I said, 'to go where only those of smokeless fire may venture.'
'Let us ride on, then, and tamp that amazement into new amusements.'

HAKIIM

We stayed all night in that pavilion, sleeping shoulder to shoulder,
amid the splishes and splashes of river-rats in rustling reeds,
until the eastern sky promised and infused a paler azure.
'Ya Samiira, the Prophet, peace and prayers be upon him,
said, "Seek knowledge, though it be in China." We have travelled
to marvel at wisps of grass-calligraphy, to glimpse pagodas,
half-hid in pines on conical hills. We saw fireworks brighten
the mandarin-trees of Hainan Island; at Chichen Itza, we peered
into deep *cenotes,* and handclaps echoed *squawk* above a pyramid.
We've gawked at lively eyes in Raphaels; at profusely human Breughels…'
'Funny,' she said, 'in that Viennese gallery I remember only how
the parquet floor squelched under all those visitors.'
'Or in Istanbul blind Sinan's domes on fire with Iznik tile…
the Creator expands our human hearts towards his inimitable art.'
'Tourism!' she said, 'How romantic, yet we never went four hours
without coffee and a meal, while ancestors, far hardier, are buried
under sand with their sworn swords and the pillars of Iram.
While you're at it, soft adventurer, don't forget the outskirt factories.
The E-Z-Tread Carpet, The Tru-Foam Sofa, The U-Fill Storage-Cube.
All part of the crescive panoply of scaled invention.
We sought the vanity of ways to talk on paper,
certainly not strategies of being staid or richer.'
'Wallah!' I said. 'When I see our friends now, those madcap youths
who'd smoke hashish and dance like dervishes to burn off the buzz,
who hopped across continents with all they owned on their backs,
now groaning under mortgages, clocks ticking towards pensions,
I have no apprehension about whatever winding sand-tracts
are ahead, restlessness our homestead, and Allah the great Unsettler.'
'I just remembered. I didn't see any swans. Did you?' 'None.'
We gathered our belongings, as the gulls grew raucous in the dawn,
and made our way beneath coal-bellied clouds that gathered, threatening,
but did not burst in ragged wands until we were far from Christmas Hill.

TWO POEMS

Miran Gulzar

Seasons of Grief

As winter ends,
in Kashmir.
God envelopes grief
to overpower the deceitful spring.

And spring eventually
is cut short into summer.

Summer melts
overflowing into Autumn.
And Autumn slows
the coming of another winter.

Human time flows
to and fro in seasons of grief.
But how much of time
is too much of grief?

It rains madly
in every season.
And our boundaries become blurred
as we carry maps of each other.

We cross and sometimes infiltrate
only to see and hide
what is present and yet absent.

With a heart
of remembering and forgetting,
all too many seasons is too much grief.

Unwritten Words

On my shore,
the tides of you
water the absence.

The ripples
storm the moonlight
in-between,

Only to disappear
and appear back
with a fresh breeze.

The musical silence
drowns me like
a resting shipwreck-

before the waves
of the thousand
unwritten words
anchor on a safe surface.

REVIEWS

TWEETER FEEDS

Hussein Kesvani

Earlier this month, I received a notification from Twitter congratulating me on my ten-year anniversary as a member. The email featured an image depicting balloons, party hats, a cake and virtual exploding fireworks. The email – from 'The Twitter Team' – thanked me for a decade's worth of 'valuable' contributions to the platform (none of which were named), all while reassuring me of my status as a valued member of the so-called 'Twitter Community'.

By all measures, this was a routine, auto-generated email that I would have otherwise sent to my trash folder. But receiving the email caught me off guard, and for weeks, I felt a sense of unease and disorientation. Perhaps it was because the following month, I would turn 31, and so the email forced me to reckon with the stark reality. Rather than a twenties filled with adventures, risks and romance, the vast majority of these formative years – the last decade of my 'youth' – were spent in solitude, in front of screens, endlessly posting into cyberspace, hoping that people would notice and listen. To an extent, they did. While I initially signed up to Twitter in the hopes of landing a graduate job after university, the platform became essential to my eventual career path in journalism. My first (unpaid) internships were offered after editors read my Wordpress blog. As I grew my following, I was able to connect with senior editors and highly respected columnists, landed staff writer positions at leading digital media brands and even got offered a book deal. At the end of my twenties, I was no longer someone looking for attention and praise, but had received enough of it to become a minor internet celebrity in my own right, complete with a verified checkmark, invites onto radio and TV panels, and every so often, dubious offers to go on 'influencer' holidays to Dubai, funded by shady marketing agencies.

Yet, as I reflected on my decade being an active Twitter user, far from feeling accomplished or triumphant in my career goals, I'd found myself burnt out and exhausted. Moreover, I had grown disillusioned by the promises of the internet and digital publishing that had afforded me a degree of prominence. Rather than seeing social media and self-publishing sites as democratic tools that facilitated free speech and allowed people to speak truth to power, I'd found myself feeling weary when confronted with the ever-expanding abundance of online content, in the form of Tweet threads, YouTube videos, Substack blogs and TikTok trends. As more content was generated – all produced under the premise that such content creation was 'empowering', particularly if created by a minority – I wondered how much of the digital content I'd spent the past decade producing, had positively contributed to my own faith group, communities or broader society, and whether the majority of it had served only to amplify my own digital presence and 'personal brand', before dissipating into the digital ether. If, as technology companies and digital publishers kept insisting, content was truly empowering and democratic, why was I feeling more powerless and lacking in hope than at any other point in my life? Why, in spite of having a platform and public power, did I feel disengaged from politics, and unable to imagine a future worth looking forward to, or *wanting* to participate in?

Ayisha Malik, *The Movement*, Headline Review, London, 2022

Over the past few years, there has been an influx of books published that posit highly critical perspectives of social media platforms and the tech conglomerates who run them, reflecting a broader cynicism over the emancipatory possibilities of hyperconnectedness. Some of these criticisms originate in Silicon Valley itself. Former technologists such as Jaron Lanier, in *Ten Arguments For Deleting Your Social Media Accounts Right Now* (2019), argue that the social technologies that are prescient at almost every level of the human experience are deliberately avoided by their creators, who are well aware of the harms of addictive, exploitative technologies. Meanwhile, novelists including Patricia Lockwood and Hari Kunzru have explored the materiality of social media platforms within the contexts of late capitalism, observing its horrors and absurdities, the contours of social alienation in both digital space and the real world, to reach similar conclusions: that human beings lack the power to meaningfully challenge these technologies. That in the end, one has little choice but to succumb to its domination – or, in other words, to become 'extremely online'. Indeed, political events such as Brexit and the election of Donald Trump in the West, as well as violent nationalist movements spurred by digitally mediated conspiracy theories, make it easy to understand why such narratives are endearing, not least when, as exemplified by India's ruling Bharatiya Janata Party (BJP), reactionary, nationalistic political forces can leverage the affordances of social media platforms to entrench divisive, exclusionary politics. Moreover, as the internet becomes further monopolised by a handful of tech giants and, in turn, limiting the scope of our creative expression, it's no wonder why two in five internet users stopped using at least one platform entirely in 2021. Faced with hostile political environments online, alongside increasing participatory demands – namely, to keep on posting commercially friendly content- it makes sense that for many, abandoning social media entirely, feels a more authentic form of liberation, than the supposedly freer forms of communicative expression offered by open source publishing tools and individually tailored media networks.

At its heart, Ayisha Malik's latest novel, *The Movement,* asks whether individual liberation is truly possible in the era of advanced social media, and, by extension, whether one really has control over their self-image and right to self-expression, in an online environment that features increasing levels of surveillance, not just from governments or national institutions, but from other users. Set in the latter half of the 2010s and the early 2020s, the novel centres around Sara Javed, a well-known and successful author who, after having had a public statement made at a literary festival misconstrued and heavily distorted, publicly declares that she will stop speaking. While Javed's declaration had been intended only for herself - spurred by her own frustrations with the publishing industry and its fixations on rigid notions of racial and gender identity, as well as her specific, unresolved familial histories – the decision unexpectedly evolves into a global phenomenon far beyond her control, known as the 'Silent Movement'. From there, the novel follows an array of characters caught up in the evolving movement, as it spreads worldwide. Some, such as Sara's former friend and mentee, Roxy, feel betrayed by the decision to maintain silence rather than using one's voice to advocate for greater representation and diversity in the public sphere. Other characters, such as Grace – a lawyer and activist who finds herself at the centre of a public scandal involving her mute son, and Zainab, a Pakistani refugee fleeing an abusive marriage involving a husband who has joined The Silent Movement- do not have a direct relationship, but nevertheless are affected by Sara's decision in such a profound way that they themselves eventually become celebrities, and later, figureheads in the movement.

Sara's decision to keep silent is initially shown to generate public discourse, in the form of bemused and later, scolding blog posts and tweets, questioning her intentions, accusing her of performativity, and berating her for making choices that subsequently undermined - if not forcibly silenced – women, people of colour and other minority groups. Yet, as the novel progresses, The Silent Movement grows far beyond Sara's scope or control. It is appropriated by online celebrities and influencers, news websites and multimedia channels emerge from it, and later, world governments seize on the movement to win elections and excise power, holding elections in a world divided between those who are 'Verbal' and 'Non-Verbal', and where for the latter group, the Silent Movement offers a unique chance to re-shape the global system, after decades of unsuccessful organising and protesting. Eventually, as global politics is reshaped by her public declaration, Sara finds herself cast as a reluctant radical - uncertain of her new found roles and responsibilities, while simultaneously questioning whether her ardent commitment to silence is just an act of political process, or a convenient means of escaping conflicts and confrontations under the guise of a higher moral sanctity.

Readers of this novel may be tempted to consider it a reflection of the contentious political battles that have defined the past few years, perhaps drawing obvious parallels between the 'Verbals' and 'Non-Verbals' to binaries such as Trump and Clinton voters, or 'Leavers' and 'Remainers'. Others may view the novel as a critique of contemporary systems of communication - namely, of social media platforms in which unfair demands are placed on individuals to perform a 'correct' morality - to say the right words, in the right way, for an online audience with clear and specific expectations. Indeed, it is this understanding of social media platforms, and the insistence writers must participate within it, that underpins Sara's reasonings for silence: 'If she didn't speak, then others would speak for her. That had its own sense of liberation; learning to detach herself from the opinions of those closest to her. If she could master that, surely, she'd master life?'

At the core of *The Movement*, are questions about the value of words themselves. Nearly every character finds themselves questioning whether their words truly have power. In Sara's case, while words have provided fame, money and literary influence, the demands of a publishing industry heavily dependent on social media alongside a literary world keener on navel gazing and public takedowns, means that she finds only some of her words considered valuable and worth listening to. Meanwhile, the up-and-coming writer, Roxy, whose ascension emerges out of a culture of digital publishing in which trauma stories – particularly those from People of Colour and other marginalised communities – are extracted for commercial value, must also come to terms with her inability to verbally communicate with her former mentor. In the latter half of the novel, the stories of Zainab and Grace are intertwined. Unlike the other characters, who have public platforms and secured places in British high culture, both women find themselves having to navigate and survive in a new world even more hostile to them that has evolved out of Sara's viral campaign. Their journeys, as well as the friendship that blossoms between them as they seek to physically vanish from the auspices of the state, serves to illustrate, succinctly, that the choice to speak or remain silent is negligible when one finds themselves at the receiving end of state sanctioned violence. Indeed, it is this observation that, in my view, allows Malik's novel to stand apart from other contemporary novels that address the dominance and excesses of social technologies. Tempting as it may be to blame social media for the degradation of democratic politics and social relationships, the stark reality is that such a statement only holds when one has power and ownership over one's own words, and subsequently, the liberty to withdraw them. Though the Silent Movement may not have been what Sara had intended, it is her class position that allows her to decide the level of her involvement, eventually going so far as to seemingly disappear entirely as the world descends into further political chaos. Sara's decision to vanish and reject political participation entirely, stands in stark contrast to Zainab and Grace, both of whom are rendered as political fodder, components of a culture war that neither initiated, nor consented to being participants in.

There is a certain irony in writing about relatability in relation to *The Movement,* not least because Malik — whose previous novels were met with praise for representation and diversity in the literary space — uses this novel to explore its limitations and restrictions, as well as where industry discourse around representation can serve to further marginalise under-represented writers. Indeed, embedded in *The Movement* is a harsh critique of the past decade of the publishing industry itself, and the way that, while presenting as being more open and embracing of writers from minority communities, instead functions to further exploit and extract financial value from them. Moreover, moments in the novel, such as Sara's frustrations with endless questions about her ethnic and familial identity, her faith and whether she was doing 'enough' to fix the publishing industry, mirrored many of my own experiences in the aftermath of publishing my first book in 2019. At a time when writers — especially those at the beginning of their careers, are also under pressure to be influencers and activists, with ready-made Instagram infographic friendly answers to any question thrown at them — I found myself deeply sympathetic to Sara's decision to withdraw from public life entirely. This is not to say that one should feel sympathy for the attention well-known writers receive, but rather, that *The Movement* is astute in observing the limits placed on words, and those who form them, when they are understood through multiple processes of digital mediation. In the words of Sara Javed: 'Eventually, your words would be taken out of your own hands.'

What's left then, as the novel nears its end in the aftermath of a general election that serves as a referendum between 'verbal' and 'non-verbal' ways of living, is a sober reminder that, in spite of the technology that surrounds us, and the abundance of words that it can produce, we still exist in a material world where our existence is dependent on human relationships. This is exemplified by Roxy, who having fulfilled her dream of becoming a highly regarded public figure, finds more comfort in reconnecting with an estranged family member. She writes in a notebook: 'a single action meant more than any words could capture'. Again, it is tempting to interpret this through the maxim of 'Twitter is not real life'.

But, in my view, this would be a disservice to Malik – not least because, in the aftermath of the Silent Movement, social media platforms have not disappeared or waned in popularity, but have successfully co-opted the Silent Movement as a progressive rebranding. Instead, Malik asks the reader to interrogate how they understand choice, and the extent to which it is afforded. In *The Movement*, silence begins as a personal choice, before evolving into a commercially and economically friendly lifestyle, and later, with the choice of silence being forcibly revoked, an act of political defiance. Fundamentally, then, Malik's conceptualisation of silence also serves to pose a deeper question about how free we truly are in society, and whether access to words is enough to truly *be* emancipated.

Such questions are essential. As the contemporary configuration of capitalism continues to decay, and world governments turn increasingly to authoritarian tendencies, debates around 'free speech' and censorship, often leveraged by reactionaries with the least at stake, often purport that 'more speech' is needed to sustain a so-called 'healthy' democracy. *The Movement* correctly challenges this broadly unquestioned political notion, to show that an endless supply of verbiage, digital content, across more open-source publishing platforms, can often be even more stifling and restrictive, serving to further disempower us from meaningful political participation. But crucially, Malik reminds us that it needn't be this way: that we can exist with technology, and still remember our obligations and responsibilities to other human beings; and that it is the forging of these relationships, that ultimately lays the foundations of real political liberation.

REFORMING CONVERSATIONS

Samia Rahman

The email dropped innocuously into the Muslim Institute's info account. Hopeful for an exciting event invitation or notification of a fascinating new publication just out, I opened it. But quickly realised this was not some generic semi-spam, but an incendiary provocation by a right-wing journalist with Islamophobic form. If mishandled, it could really blow up in our faces: 'We are aware that a journalist has said that she interviewed Ghayasuddin Siddiqui and Kalim Siddiqui many years ago and says that she discovered that they went to Tehran and asked Ayatollah Khomeini to pass the fatwa. She believes that, if Ghayasuddin Siddiqui and Kalim Siddiqui had not made that trip, the fatwa would not have been issued.'

It was 2019 and media outlets were trawling over events 30 years ago exactly, that culminated in the Rushdie Affair; the outcry over the publication of *The Satanic Verses* that would impact the British Muslim community for many years to come. A couple of weeks before the email materialised, *Independent* columnist Yasmin Alibhai Brown, a long-standing friend of Ghayasuddin Siddiqui, had made the astonishing claim in a Radio 4 interview that was referenced by the author of the email. It shouldn't have been much of a surprise therefore that a vulture would swoop down and fly off with such intoxicating prey.

Ziba Mir-Hosseini, *Journeys Toward Gender Equality in Islam*, Oneworld Academic, London, 2022

If I remember correctly, it's true to say that the day after the Radio 4 interview, there had been low-level disquiet in the Muslim Institute camp. After all, this was a serious allegation being made against the founders of what had been the original incarnation of the Muslim Institute, even though it bears little resemblance to the Fellowship society we run today.

There was some fleeting talk of issuing a clarification, but we all agreed that any engagement with hearsay would only fuel the non-story and prove counter-productive, particularly as the Muslim Institute had not actually been referenced. So upon receiving the email, and after some renewed consultation, I avoided any 'unknown number' phone calls, which is fairly healthy practice anyway in my opinion, and prepared a two-sentence shutdown that I wrote on a piece of paper and carried around in my coat pocket for the next few weeks, glancing at it every time I thought I might forget what I needed to say in case I should be door-stepped like the Z-list celebrity I always dreamed I would grow up to one day be.

The thing is, we knew how the more sensationalist fringes of the media operate, just as Kalim Siddiqui understood how to garner headlines and build his political capital and profile in his heyday. This wasn't the first time this claim had emerged, although it had been dormant for many years, and the late Siddiqui had cultivated the ambiguity of the actual circumstances to his advantage. By playing the media at their game he was able to situate himself at the centre of seismic historic events regardless of the actual role he had played. In the biography of his life, written by Critical Muslim deputy editor C Scott Jordan, Ghayasuddin Siddiqui spoke at length about the mythology surrounding his and Kalim Siddiqui's role in the Rushdie affair. The Siddiquis (no relation to each other incidentally) had initially been inspired by the Islamic revolution in Iran, fervently supporting the postcolonial nation's severing of exploitative Western ties. Keen to establish an Islamic resistance to Western hegemony, they became frequent guests of Iranian intellectuals at conferences in Iran; reciprocating by hosting Iranian dignitaries in the UK. But by 1989 this enthusiasm had faded to disillusionment, and it was a chance encounter with Mohammad Khatami at Tehran's Mehrabad International airport, a mere few hours before the fatwa against Rushdie was announced, that spawned the tale of alleged influence. Whatever conversation had passed between Kalim Siddiqui and Khatami (Ghayasuddin Siddiqui remembers standing a short distance away from the men while they talked briefly so was not privy to the entire exchange), to suggest that these two British-Indian activists could abruptly influence the carefully strategised political machinations of the Islamic Republic of Iran, would be quite a stretch of the imagination.

The Siddiquis saw themselves as reformers, which in light of the stories swirling around about their influence in Iran may seem incongruous. But for them the revolution was a victory for Muslim intellectuals and thinkers who would dismantle the corrupt and stagnant remnants of the Shah's regime with reformist Islamic rule. Of course, this did not happen. But the fact that this was the reform they idealised, is poignant.

In *Journeys Towards Gender Equality in Islam,* the Iranian-born academic Ziba Mir-Hosseini revives such poignancy. Her description of her anthropological research, and specifically her life's work on Islamic law and gender, reflects a deep disillusionment not unlike the one Ghayasuddin Siddiqui speaks of during that period's latter sunset. Mir-Hosseini writes: 'In the early 1980s, when I first started attending the Tehran branches of the post-revolutionary family courts, presided over by Islamic judges, women who came to court ... used every occasion ... to remind the judge of his role as custodian of the Shari'a, and of the injustice of a system that could not protect them.' Despite the imploring of the women, desperate for restorative justice in the face of cruelty, hardship and mistreatment by men, the judges repeatedly upheld unfair decisions they declared were Qur'anic deliverance. Women were horrified to find that their husbands were being given free rein to take a second wife without seeking their permission, and were allowed to divorce without impunity, often leaving them and their children abandoned and destitute. The injustice that had been meted out to Iranians by the tyrannical rule of the Shah, considered a puppet of Western interests, was merely replaced by a brutal theological dogma that seemed to show no mercy, declaring that it was carrying out God's work. Mir-Hosseini's response was to become a reformer.

Reformists are a diverse group, and the fight for reform is routinely exploited by anti-Islam actors seeking to frame the debate around their vision of diametrically opposing Western values. The journalist seeking to write a 'gotcha' story about the founders of the Muslim Institute no doubt has firm ideas of what constitutes reform of Islam, particularly where women's bodies are the contested sites upon which the male gaze settles in its assessment. Ghayasuddin Siddiqui went on in later life to pursue reform through activism, and became a firm ally in the movement to advance feminist causes, leaving behind his one-time alignment with the Ayatollah of Iran. This plurality of thought within the reformist movement is what Mir-Hosseini's book articulates as it offers a fly-on-the-wall glimpse into conversations between and among some of the great Muslim intellectual thinkers of our times.

Mir-Hosseini graduated from Tehran University in 1974 and was in the final year of completing her PhD in Social Anthropology from the University of Cambridge, when the Islamic Revolution occurred. After returning to Iran, less enamoured by the revitalisation of political Islam than Kalim Siddiqui had been, she faced patriarchal oppression in her personal and private life before returning to Cambridge and the UK in 1984 to embark upon a career in academia. The notion of political Islam as a civilisational and intellectual reformist project failed miserably to liberate Iranian women such as Mir-Hosseini whose lived experience under the theocratic regime was one of stark gender inequality.

It was this lived reality, and the claim by Mullahs in Iran that they were establishing the first Islamic state in the modern world, that prompted Mir-Hosseini to begin her quest to understanding what gender equality meant in faith: 'my research in these family courts was the beginning of my search to make sense of the gap between the ideals of Islam and legal practices in countries such as post-revolutionary Iran, where the government and the judiciary claim to be implementing Shar'ia.' Mir-Hosseini did this by studying the foundations upon which this movement was built – not solely through political activism. She was one of the founders of the global movement for justice and equality in the Muslim family, Musawah, and was involved in the Kuala Lumpur-based Sisters in Islam. She also co-directed in 1998 the brilliant documentary *Divorce Iranian Style*, which depicted tenacious Iranian women navigating the patriarchal legal system to secure divorce. She did all this while continuing to question the assumptions about gender equality located in the interpretations of scriptures.

Journeys Towards Gender Equality in Islam is Mir-Hosseini's attempt to carve a space in which feminism can reside in Islamic thought. It is also the journey of her fellow travellers and how they have influenced each other's thinking and the discussions that have shaped their varied perspectives. The book devotes itself to conversations she has had over the decades, with six fellow reformers, many of whom she counts as friends. She foregrounds this at the beginning of the book, by first looking at three thinkers who she describes as representing 'the transition from Neo-traditionalist to Reformist approaches to gender'. These are the early twentieth century journalist and Tunisian independence activist Tahir Haddad, the renowned Pakistan-American scholar Fazlur Rahman, and the more contemporary Egyptian Islamic studies scholar Nasr Hamid Abu Zayd who died in 2010. Mir-Hosseini acknowledges the work of these luminaries and teases out the nuances of their writings. In particular, she lays out their contribution to the discussion around gender equality against a backdrop of increasing interest in political Islam as a means to challenge Western hegemony, as characterised by the efforts of Kalim and Ghayasuddin Siddiqui and their vision for the original Muslim Institute.

Early in the book, Mir-Hosseini introduces the reader to a distinction that runs throughout the publication – the definition of *fiqh* and Shari'a, terms used almost interchangeably in so much Islamic studies discourse. The variation in understanding of these concepts even among the thinkers interviewed for the book, is fascinating to note. When Musawah was launched in 2009, which is when the idea for the book was also first mooted, the concepts were clearly defined in their mission pamphlet, *Framework for Action*. Sharia (the way) is defined as 'Muslim belief in God's will, as revealed to the Prophet Muhammad'; and '*fiqh* ('understanding') is Islamic jurisprudence, the process and the methodology for discerning and extracting legal rulings (*ahkam*) from the sacred sources of Islam: the Qur'an and the Sunna (the practice of the Prophet, as contained in Hadith, Traditions). Like any other system of jurisprudence, *fiqh* is human, temporal and local.'

The spirited dissection of these concepts by the three male and three female subjects whose interviews form the bulk of Mir-Hosseini's book, is an illustration of the intellectual duelling and development of thought that the founders of the Muslim Institute probably had in mind, and would no doubt have enjoyed participating in. The six contributors to the book are Abdullahi An-Na'im, amina wadud, Asma Lamrabet, Khaled Abou El Fadl, Mohsen Kadivar and Sedigheh Vasmaghi. Mostly these were names with which I was already familiar so the opportunity to be privy to their inner-most thoughts and mode of reasoning was one I devoured greedily.

Biographical information humanises the words of these scholars, and concluding each focused chapter on each individual with a compelling reflection on the interview, even feedback from the interviewee on how they felt she had captured the exchanges that may have taken place over the entire past decade, enhances the books accessibility. It is a digestible way to understand subtly diverse positions and how the subjects navigate their thought-processes. Mir-Hosseini's interviews with Abdullahi An-Na'im, a knowledgeable man with humanistic values who delivered a talk for the Muslim Institute in 2012, interrogating the notion of a secular Islamic state, belie a tension between the two thinkers that illustrates the constructiveness of disagreement. An-Naim is very much influenced by the work of Sudanese scholar Ustadh Mahmoud Mohammed Taha, while Mir-Hosseini leans to Haddad, Rahman and Zayd, but it is their difference in opinion when it comes to defining fiqh and Shari'a, that provides some of the more fiery engagements contained in the book.

The other journeys towards gender equality in Islam she catalogues are equally enriching, with nuggets of information interspersed with flashes of unique personalities that compel the reader to seek out more about these brilliant minds. The warmth of the friendship between amina wadud, and Mir-Hosseini is a joy to witness. The two women reminisce about their shared history and meaningfully support each other's intentions and struggles. The chapter of interviews with Moroccan essayist and medical doctor Asma Lamrabet, looks at how she combines universal ethics with the humanitarian ideals of Islam, in what has come to be known in Morocco as 'third-way' feminism. Lamrabet was greatly influenced by the eminent Moroccan sociologist Fatima Mernissi, who she collaborated with, founding the Fatima Mernissi Chair at the Mohammed V University in Rabat, in 2017, two years after Mernissi's death. Both wadud and Lamrabet, alongside Mir-Hosseini of course, have pushed boundaries in the debate on hijab, mixed congregational prayers and the exclusionary nature of secularism when it comes to Islamic feminism, all while undertaking a personal journey toward finding their own place in feminist discourse.

While the women interviewed by Mir-Hosseini often draw on personal experience to inform their pursuit of gender justice, An-Naim, Khaled Abou El Fadl and Mohsen Kadivar remain resolute allies in the journey toward gender equality in Islam. Khaled Abou El Fadl, Professor of Law at UCLA and Chair of the Islamic Studies Interdepartmental Program, is an Egyptian public intellectual, trained in Islamic jurisprudence. A vehement critic of puritanical Islam and advocate of women's rights, specifically in his pushbacks against Wahhabi teachings, is driven by his ability, as Mir-Hosseini explains, to employ methodology that equips readers of his work with the tools 'to distinguish between that which is "authoritative" in Islam and that which is "authoritarian"'. Again and again in her interviews with fellow reformers, Mir-Hosseini acknowledges the debt she owes their research and scholarship and how collaborative efforts have contributed to the development of her ideas. On El Fadl's 2001 publication, *Speaking in God's Name*, she describes how it 'came at a critical juncture in my own journey; Abou El Fadl demystified the whole process of juridical construction, and enabled me to see how what is claimed to be a religious law (*hukm shar'i*) is constructed as such, and how to approach textual sources from an ethical perspective in line with contemporary notions of justice'.

The intersections of reformist thinking are on full display in Mir-Hosseini's book. Interviewees relate the ways in which they have negotiated methodology, jurisprudence, historical events such as 9/11, personal oppression whether that be gender injustice or political persecution, and have expanded their thinking, often in relation to each other. Mohsen Kadivar trained in a traditional seminary in Qom, and was a student at the time of the revolution. In his chapter, we learn of the state oppression he faced while a professor in Islamic philosophy, theology and political thought at Tarbiat Modares University in Tehran. His call for democratic and liberal reforms resulted in his imprisonment in 1999, after which he re-located to the US and continued his work there. Mir-Hosseini explains that 'I have found two of Kadivar's reformist ideas of particular importance ... The first is his notion of a human rights-based understanding of fiqh ... The second ... is what Kadivar calls "ijtihad in principles and foundations"'. Once more, *Journeys Towards Gender Equality* permits the reader to follow the trajectory of reformist thinking and the wealth of expansive scholarship that can be accessed by reading beyond the book itself.

The uniquely structured chapters of the book encompass memoir, biography, anthropological and sociological analysis as well as theological exposition. A thirst that can only be quenched by wider reading is inspired by its remit of thought-provoking and stimulating conversations. Well-known figures in the reform movement I thought I knew a considerable amount about already, are given a depth and dimension by the articulation of their work and life in their own words of informality. And the book also introduces fresh ideas and unknown names in the reform movement that I was not previously aware of. This is the case with the final interviewee, Sedigheh Vasmaghi, whose chapter left me despairing at the inhumanity of those wilfully placing obstacles along the path of reformers seeking gender equality in Islam; and motivated me to renew my own commitment to activism and research in the fight for gender equality, simply in awe at the courage and indefatigability of this woman, and so many unsung (s)heroes like her.

Vasmaghi was born and educated in Iran. A published poet, she completed a PhD in *fiqh* and principles of Islamic law in 1998. By the time Iran's Green Movement ignited in 2009, which Kadivar reflects on more closely in his chapter, Vasmaghi was critically engaging with fiqh, and became a prominent figure in the movement, writing vociferously to draw attention to the human rights abuses perpetuated by the regime and the injustices of the legal system's treatment of women and families. In 2011, she fled to Europe and continued her scholarship and activism there, also meeting Mir-Hosseini. In 2017 she and her husband decided to return to Iran, despite facing a court conviction and an almost inevitable custodial sentence. Upon her return she was imprisoned and eventually released, and although currently working on another book, is banned from leaving the country and awaits another court appearance. Mir-Hosseini doesn't hide her anxiety and fear for her fellow reformer's precarious situation, yet the calm with which Vasmaghi explains her need to reside in Iran and continue the reformist fight in the country of her birth is humbling. The two women discuss their body of scholarship, their distinct approaches to gender reform, what led them to focus on *fiqh* and their views on how to rethink Shari'a; issues explored by all of the interviewees with unique precision of mind and motivation.

The series of dialogues in Mir-Hosseini's book are an illuminating, enjoyable and easy-to-read window into the minds of some of our most innovative reformist thinkers and the variables that led them to embark upon a journey toward gender equality in Islam. As the imagined role of the reformer continues to be interrogated and subverted, it is also championed in spaces where open discussion and debate are sanctioned, such as the Muslim Institute, or on the pages of *Critical Muslim*. The fact that these spaces exist, including this book and its valuable contribution to the conversation, gives hope that the journeys toward gender equality in Islam may one day transcend the planes of ignorance and find their eventual destinations.

THERE'S SOMETHING ABOUT MARY

Giles Goddard

For over a hundred and thirty years the house of Mary in Ephesus (modern day Selcuk in Turkey) has been a place of pilgrimage for Christians and Muslims. It is believed to have been the last resting place for her and John the beloved disciple of Jesus and was declared a place of pilgrimage by Pope Leo XIII in 1896. Thousands of Muslims visit the house of Mary every year, especially when they have great worries, leaving many prayers and intercessions on a long wall adjacent to the house. In 2006, after Pope Benedict XVI caused much dismay to Muslims in his Regensburg lecture, part of his attempt to mend fences involved visiting the shrine later that year. He acknowledged that it is a place of prayer for Christians and Muslims alike, and in so doing underlined the significance of Mary as a person who offers rich opportunities for reflection on gender, patriarchy and faithfulness across both traditions.

Indeed, this tiny house on top of a hill in Western Turkey is one of many places where Mary is a focus of faith for Islam and Christianity. In Egypt, Muslim witnesses are repeatedly cited by the Coptic church when they are seeking to prove the veracity of appearances of Mary. Similarly in Lebanon, Iraq and Pakistan, Marian sites are joint places of pilgrimage, and although growing Wahhabi influence has undermined these acts of collective witness, they remain important.

Mary is mentioned more in the Qur'an than she is in the Bible. A surah (chapter) is named after her (Maryam), and the miraculous birth of Jesus is narrated twice, in Surah Al 'Imrān and Surah Maryam, as well as her own birth and childhood in Surah Al 'Imrān. She is the only woman named in the Qur'an, and her significance as a parallel and forerunner for Muhammad in Qur'anic typology as the bearer of the divinely revealed Word can hardly be underestimated.

But there have been few comparative studies of Mary's significance for Christians and Muslims. This is surprising, given the increasing amount of good interfaith scholarship, some of which I have reviewed in recent issues of *Critical Muslim*, most recently 'Bonding in Abrahamic Faiths' in CM41: Bodies.

Riding to the rescue are Muna Tatari and Klaus von Stosch, both professors of systematic theology at German universities. *Mary in the Qur'an* is, according to the authors, the first systematic study of Mary written jointly by a Christian and a Muslim. This study is very timely – not least because it shows how the figure of Mary, as a boundary breaker, a liminal figure, challenges the dominant patriarchal narrative in both Christianity and Islam.

It covers much ground, offering detailed diachronic analysis of the accounts in the Qur'an and delving below the surface of the differing Gospel representations. The book considers the evolution of Mariology in early Christian thought, and also in the Byzantine Empire dominant at the time the Qur'an was revealed – identifying in a variety of ways how the significance of the figure of Mary can be understood in both Islam and Christianity, in the sixth and early seventh century and now. The authors serve a rich meal. All except the final chapters were written jointly, and the sense of discovering new and shared ground is palpable.

There is no unanimity between the depictions of Mary in the New Testament. Only the Gospels of Matthew and Luke include narratives of Jesus' birth, and in Matthew's Gospel Mary is subordinated to Joseph. Luke's account of Jesus' birth, on the other hand, gives Mary great prominence – the angel Gabriel appears to her rather than to Joseph. It is Luke who gives the text of the Magnificat to Mary – her revolutionary shout of joy after she has accepted the invitation from Gabriel to bear the Son of God:

> He has shown strength with his arm;
> he has scattered the proud in the thoughts of their hearts.
> [52] He has brought down the powerful from their thrones,
> and lifted up the lowly;
> [53] he has filled the hungry with good things,
> and sent the rich away empty. (Luke 1: 51-53)

In the Gospels of John and Mark, Mary as the mother of Christ has an ambiguous relationship with her son. The first miracle Jesus performed, in John's Gospel, is the changing of water into wine at the wedding at Cana, but when Jesus is asked by his mother to take action as the wine is running out, his response is, 'Woman, what has this to do with me? My hour is not yet come.' And in Mark's Gospel the first encounter we hear about is when Jesus' mother and brothers come to take him away because he is believed to be out of his mind. So, although Mary is an important presence in the Gospel narratives, her significance is multi-layered: she is, in Luke, clearly a pivotal figure with parallels in Jewish tradition (her shout of triumph is modelled on Hannah's song of delight in I Samuel in the Hebrew Scriptures when she is told that she will give birth to a son), while in the other Gospels her significance is more as part of Jesus' entourage, one of several Marys who each in their own way have close relationships with him.

Muna Tatari and Klaus von Stosch, *Mary in the Qur'an*, Gingko, London, 2021

Even Mary's virginity is a feature only of the Lucan and Matthean accounts – and in Matthew, only glancingly: Mary is found to be pregnant 'by the Holy Spirit,' and Joseph's response to the news of his fiancée's pregnancy is given much more prominence. Luke, however, in the account of the appearance of Gabriel to Mary, emphasises Mary's virginity: 'How can this be, since I am a virgin?' and it is this which resonates down the centuries.

What is not in doubt is that in all the accounts, Mary is (contrary to stereotypes) a strong and reflective woman who comes from a tradition of strong and active women in the Hebrew Scriptures. The genealogy of Jesus in the Gospel of Matthew includes four women, all of whom are outsiders in one way or another – Rahab is a prostitute, Ruth is from Moab – and all of whom are pivotal in Israel's history. Far from being meek and mild, as so much Christian art has portrayed her, Mary's gesture of obedience, her *fiat* – let it be unto me according to your word – comes from a position of strength: she gives active assent to her role as the bearer of God's son, and it is this which is picked up and embroidered over subsequent centuries.

Tatari and von Stosch focus on how Mariology developed in Syria and the Byzantine Empire in the first to fourth centuries, recognising that the

Qur'an is responding and reacting to the typology of Mary which may have been prevalent in and around Mecca and Medina at the time of Muhammad. They cite the apocryphal gospel, the Protevangelium of James, and the work of Ephrem the Syrian and Jacob of Sereugh. Recent research has demonstrated that the Qur'an was in dialogue with those elements of the Christian tradition.

The Protevangelium of James seems to have offered some of the source material for the account of Mary in the Surah Al'Imrān. It goes into detail about Mary's childhood, practically telling us how she did at school. Jacob exalts Mary, naming her as the new Eve and identifying her as an archetype of the Church. Ephrem and Jacob are both part of the miaphysite tradition, which denied the dual nature of Christ and was condemned as heretical at the Council of Chalcedon in 451CE. Consequently, miaphysite Christians were forced out of the imperial centres towards the margins, and would have had a significant presence in the Arabian Peninsula. Mary was formally given the title Theotokos – the God-bearer – at the Council of Ephesus in 431CE. She became part of imperialist propaganda and subsequently the Byzantine emperors were responsible for exalting her as the miraculous warrior who delivered a series of military victories for the emperors, including saving Constantinople.

The ambiguity of the New Testament portrayal of Mary is amplified in the Qur'an. Here, we meet a woman who is mysterious and yet earthy. The Qur'an clearly gives emphasis to a figure who is prominent in the Christian theology of the time and has roots firmly in the Jewish scriptures, a person who gave miraculous birth to the Word of God and whose response to Allah was both exemplary and unique.

The great Surah Maryam, Surah 19, is the earliest revelation which refers to her, in the mid-Meccan period (around 610 – 622 CE). The account of her encounter with 'Our Spirit' follows hard on the heels of the miraculous birth of John to Zechariah, but Mary is given greater prominence, both in her own right and as the mother of Jesus the servant of God. She is someone who speaks to God with confidence and wisdom; her silence is not the silence of passivity but silence as a symbol of hope; and she is of course not depicted as the mother of God but as the mother of the word of God, Jesus. Both Jesus and Mary have particular significance in the Qur'an as signs, manifestations of God's word; but even more important in this context is that this Surah seems to be an attempt to build bridges between Jews and Christians in Mecca. Thus Surah 19:30: 'I am the servant of God. He brought me the Book (*kitab*) and made me a prophet, and made me blessed wherever I may be.'

The Qur'an seems, through the citing of Mary and Zechariah, to be 'systematically embracing all three scriptures', and the book's intention 'is quite openly to honour the Jewish and Christian traditions in equal measure'. The significance of Mary's virginity is different in the Qur'an to the Gospel of Luke:

> How can I have a Son when no man has ever touched me, nor am I an adulteress? Thus did our Lord speak: 'It is a matter easy for Me. We shall make him a wonder to mankind and a mercy from Us – a decree ordained.' (Qur'an 19.20)

Here, the conception of Jesus by God's Spirit is meant to symbolise not the purity of the Christ child, unsullied by the sin of the world, but rather the power of God to overcome all physical limitations. Mary's virginity underlines God's creative power in bringing the Word into the world.

In Surah Al 'Imrān, Mary's childhood is given more detailed treatment. It seems likely that this surah, from the later Medinan period (around 622 – 630 CE), is drawing on the legends about Mary which are also reported in the work of Ephrem the Syrian and the Protevangelium of James. The blessed child granted to the wife of 'Imrān – a girl rather than the expected boy – is dedicated to God's service in the temple, ministered to by angels, chosen above all the women of the world, prostrating herself to God and, again, being given her child by the power of God: 'He merely says it to "Be!" and it is' (3:47).

There are other hints of richness in the portrayal of Mary. In Surah Maryam she goes into the east, into an unknown place, and there sets up a screen to veil her from others. She leaves, in other words, the known world and travels towards a place where God can speak with her – perhaps picking up the story of the flight into Egypt in the Gospel of Matthew but giving it a different focus. In summary, according to Tatari and von Stosch:

> Mary as a prophetic figure ... is touched inwardly by the word of God. The person who on numerous occasions is acknowledged as a human corporeal

manifestation of God's benevolent word is given birth to by Mary ... and in so doing she opens herself up to other words and scriptures of God.

But was she a prophet, according to traditional Islamic criteria? This controversial question is considered by Tatari and von Stosch. Their conclusion stops short of declaring her a prophet but, they say:

> It could at least be established that she had the most intimate contact with God and his angels and in the process was touched by holiness and taken into God's service. She was the recipient of a heavenly message and was, like the prophets, singled out and honoured.

There is more. The authors suggest that Mary's prostration to God is a deliberate response to the portrayal of her as a warrior queen by the Byzantine empire: her humility is a sign of her purity, and this in turn reflects the radical nature of her relationship with God. And the importance granted to her as a woman, consecrated to God's service in the Temple, has major implications: 'Mary is the decisive counterargument to the position that women can't be consecrated to the service of God. Women too are worthy.'

The authors summarise:

> Above all Mary is the first person who calls upon God as a compassionate deity. In other words, she is looking for a quite particular intensity in her relationship with God and is exemplary in the way in which she conducts a dialogue with him. For all her humility, Mary comes across as shrewd and theologically innovative ... engaged in an intensive relationship with God based on dialogue. ... Mary appears as a linking figure who connects the three monotheistic religions. She is a perfectly ordinary woman who through her trust in God's power comes to focus entirely on God in the figure of her son: together with Jesus, this orientation towards God makes her a symbol for humanity.

Mary and Muhammad are messengers, who both receive the word of God, are bound to it mystically, implement it in an exemplary fashion, and are prepared in a special way for their extraordinary roles, Mary through her virginity and Muhammad through being unlettered. Both evade simple definition:

Mary is both active and passive. She does not stay silent out of a lack of eloquence, but to accentuate the word of God as conveyed through Jesus Christ … she is the patron saint of liberation struggles – Mary and Muhammad thus combine female and male roles in a way that confounds customary expectations of gender roles … boundary breakers as regards the traditional demarcation of transcendence and immanence.

It is this which leads Tatari and von Stosch to foreground her as a bridge builder and as someone whose ambiguity reflects the ambiguity at the heart of faith.

There is a well-known Christmas carol recounting the Annunciation – when Gabriel came to Mary in Luke's Gospel. The first verse is:

The angel Gabriel from heaven came
His wings as drifted snow his eyes as flame
'All hail' said he 'thou lowly maiden Mary,
Most highly favoured lady,'

Gloria!

Schoolboys for centuries have changed the words. Most highly *flavoured* lady, they sing – as though Mary was an ice cream or a milkshake. I remember passing the choir's rehearsal room a few years ago at St John's Church in Waterloo, London, as they were preparing for the carol service; I heard them singing the revised words and giggling.

But there is something about Mary which lends itself to irreverence, for it is not absolutely clear quite where she fits – and in this, she becomes especially a figure for our time. She is a liminal figure both in the New Testament and in the Qur'an. To the point where, according to Tatari and von Stosch, she may be described not as Queen of Heaven (one of her traditional Christian titles), but Queer of Heaven. The Qur'an, they note, speaks almost exclusively to men. But in their reading of the story of Mary, time and again God confounds our restrictive perceptions and practices and the injustices that arise from them. They refer to the work of Muslim scholar Kecia Ali, paraphrasing her argument as follows:

Even the differences between the two accounts of Mary given in Q3 and Q19 confirm that a queer route is the best way to appropriate the legacy of Mary, since the depictions of Mary are neither totally at variance nor is there any way in which they can be reconciled with one another and combined into one ... Ali argues the case for cherishing the 'messiness' of the Qur'an and so proclaiming the virtues of its vagueness, transgressive nature and capacity to confuse as just a different route to God.

The depiction of Mary demonstrates that the Qur'an cannot be seen exclusively as a patriarchal text. This sense of Mary as an ambiguous and boundary-breaking figure is also reflected in contemporary Christian queer and feminist theology. However, this parallel treatment of Mary as queer, as someone outside the norms of gender and sexuality, may be a step too far for some. But it is interesting that contemporary scholarship in both traditions has lighted upon this as a way of understanding the Mary of the Qur'an and the Mary of the Bible. It is certainly true in both traditions that she is a person who challenges preconceptions of gender stereotypes. In other words, she can be seen as subversive in both Christianity and Islam – in Christianity, through her revolutionary shout of praise, the Magnificat, and in Islam through her embrace of her confident relationship with Allah.

Mary in the Qur'an is a fascinating and challenging investigation of the multiple ways in which Mary the bridgebuilder can contribute to Christian and Muslim relations. This positive but enigmatic model of female faithfulness is perhaps a reflection of Muhammad's own relationships, and it has inspired generations of Muslim women. I warm to this story of Caliph Umar's complaint to the Prophet in which Mary's enigmatic presence can be felt even though she is not explicitly mentioned:

> One day, I was angry with my wife ... I scolded her for contradicting me. Her response was this: 'Why are you criticising me for contradicting you? I swear by God, the wives of the Prophet contradicted him and one of them even ostracised him for an entire day.' I replied: 'If any of you do such a thing, it'll be the end of you for sure. How can you be sure that God won't be prompted by the Prophet's anger to direct his ire at you and ruin you?' At this, the Prophet just smiled.

ET CETERA

}

ON SADHGURU'S SPIRITUALITY

Saad Mohammed Ismail

Jagadish Vasudev, better known as Sadhguru, is an Indian spiritual guru of international renown. If you listen to him enough times – as I have – you come away with the impression that *spirituality* is the only sensible alternative to the regressive and old-fashioned belief in *religion*. Religions, and in Sadhguru's view, Abrahamic religions in particular – with all their notions of a traditional creator-god, scriptural morality, and heaven and hell – are well on their way to extinction, or at least should be. In this sense Sadhguru is only echoing the view of the New Atheists such as Richard Dawkins, who have long prophesised and hoped for 'the end of religion' and the triumph of science. Sadhguru unthinkingly hops on this bandwagon, since according to him spirituality is closer to science than to religion.

Sadhguru's Isha Foundation claims that it 'does not promote any particular ideology, religion, or race, but transmits inner sciences of universal appeal'. The turn of phrase is telling. Spirituality as 'universal inner science' is supposed to be the panacea to the particularity of religion, which is itself coterminous with ideology and ethnicity. We will see presently why such posturing can be deeply problematic. Blind to its own particularity, it promises a false sense of universalism that it cannot deliver. It is only a small step from there to associating with oneself the objectivity and indisputability of science, and with the Other the emotionality and dogmatism of belief.

More broadly, Sadhguru's pronouncements on 'religion' lie on the same level of intellectual sophistry as that of Dawkins – which, if I must spell it out, is not a flattering remark at all. But, by rehashing Dawkins-esque views on religion, Sadhguru secures for himself a double victory. Firstly, he can marshal the New Atheist polemics against Abrahamic religions in his favour, and so he has his work cut out for him. Secondly, he garners fans who in their fits of teenage rebellion might have acquired a scepticism of traditional authority, but who – perhaps due to their teenage impatience – might have stalled at that stage, and could hardly sustain a long-term and thorough-going period of critical enquiry and exploration. Sadhguru, very much like Dawkins, panders to the lazy sceptic – one who takes an ahistorical view of his or her own scepticism, considers all religious traditions to be patently false while ironically admitting his or her ignorance of them, and holds a triumphant belief in 'Western Enlightenment' values. Although when pressed on this last point, such a person would be at a loss to enumerate what these values actually were, let alone defend them intellectually. In fact, behind this veneer of the rationalist-sceptic, there seldom lies any deep engagement whatsoever with philosophy, religion, or history.

Yet, there is no denying that both Sadhguru and Dawkins hold much appeal. The average follower of either of these figures may also outshine a regular believer when it comes to critical thinking. And, it is perhaps this failure of religious traditions and institutions to empower their masses with independent thinking that serves as the cause of much self-embarrassment for them. At this level, Sadhguru/Dawkins may be seen to perform an important salutary function: to awaken the masses from their uncomprehending slumber. But to be awake is not a one-time action, it requires constantly being awake and vigilant. The waking jolt of scepticism can itself come to sound like a lullaby when one starts becoming complacent and comfortable within the new-found belief-system of 'scepticism'. The only authentic way to stay awake, therefore, is to be sceptical of one's own scepticism, and sceptical of that scepticism, and so on, ad infinitum.

I will leave Sadhguru's more overt politics aside. Much deserved ink has already been spilled along those lines. Instead, I seek to lay bare the political posturing of what is generally accepted to be a benign and 'apolitical' spirituality.

In one sense, Sadhguru defines spirituality in opposition to religion, but in another sense, spirituality in his view is the very kernel of religion itself.

Now, if religion is merely a husk, one can easily come to the conclusion that this husk is disposable and essentially useless if one retains the kernel. One has to wonder what this shapeless kernel of spirituality looks like when stripped of the 'form' of religion. Is there such a thing as a formless spirituality? The answer to this question hinges on an important conceit of all neo-spirituality: the presumption that spirituality is essentially neutral.

Sadhguru is hardly the first to capitalise on this common confusion. For one, Sadhguru is very clearly an heir to Osho (formerly known as Rajneesh) and Krishnamurti – both twentieth century spiritual mavericks who also share the New Atheistic contempt for religion and God. Secondly, Sadhguru comes as the latest popular instalment in a long line of English speaking neo-spiritual gurus – a lineage arguably inaugurated by Swami Vivekananda's 1893 speech at the World Parliament of Religions at Chicago. One can indeed situate Sadhguru in the context of a tradition of 'American Veda', to use the author and spiritual counsellor Philip Goldberg's term.

But what if the fundamental presumption of neo-spirituality is itself false? What if there is no such thing as a neutral spirituality? This is my core argument: there is no such thing as a formless, neutral, unprejudiced, objective spirituality that is immediately and universally accessible to anyone who pursues it from any place and at any time. Those who talk of universal spirituality or 'Spirituality' (with an uppercase 'S'), make the same mistake as the Enlightenment philosophers who speak of universal reason or 'Reason' (with an uppercase 'R'). Such a naïve view of 'reason' has become increasingly untenable to hold in our times with increasing acknowledgment of colonialism's intellectual racism, as well as the increasing appreciation of understanding non-European cultures and traditions on their own terms. According to the contemporary philosopher Alasdair MacIntyre, it is an:

> illusion to suppose that there is some neutral standing ground, some locus of rationality as such, which can afford rational resources sufficient for enquiry independent of all traditions. Those who have maintained otherwise either have covertly been adopting a tradition and deceiving themselves and perhaps others into supposing that theirs was just such a neutral ground or else have simply been in error.

Thus, rationality requires the framework of a tradition to operate from and within, even as it may critique some elements of that tradition. A blank slate *(tabula rasa)* cannot produce philosophy. To reason, one needs to build on a series of assumptions, about logic and the rules of reasoning, about language, grammar and the structure of propositions. Similarly, spirituality cannot exist except within a tradition, bearing a certain language, and having a certain form – even as it seeks to expand itself beyond the confines of a single framework. Going beyond itself first requires being within.

So when neo-spiritual gurus speak of spirituality in neutral terms – either when pitting it against the 'parochialism' of religious traditions, or by celebrating it as Reason's conjoined twin – they are actually peddling a particular kind of spirituality (as opposed to other kinds) under the guise of Universal Spirituality.

More specifically, Sadhguru's spirituality seems to be 'Indian/Indic' in its broad contours – in the sense that it utilises images and metaphors from traditions that originated in India (the fact that the indigenous Muslim and Christian traditions are excluded from Sadhguru's sense of the Indic/ Indian is another telling tangent). Surely, there is nothing wrong in privileging certain religions over others as sources for your philosophy. What is problematic in Sadhguru's approach, however, is that values such as spirituality or inclusivity are seen to be the sole preserve of Indic traditions. Abrahamic traditions are especially disparaged as being the very antithesis of these values (the disparagement no doubt comes easy when these traditions are classed as 'foreign'). To say that Hindu traditions are more spiritual than Abrahamic traditions presumes a prior definition of spirituality based on which the comparison is made – a prior notion of spirituality, based on which one form of spirituality is seen as being more or less spiritual than the other. Thus, the measuring-scale is pre-fixed and biased towards one object over another even prior to the actual act of measurement or comparison.

This is the problem when one speaks of 'spirituality' – which is always a loaded term and, not unlike the category of 'religion', is a modern western invention defined largely as a shadow or negative space of the secular, as the cultural anthropologist Talal Asad points out. Instead of speaking of distinct entities such as Islam or Christianity or Hinduism (which themselves contain much internal diversity), when we speak of 'religion' in the abstract, the term will have to be defined either in terms of a particular belief or ritual or practice or any other arbitrary parameter – but which will always be an arbitrary parameter, especially when looked at from the point of view of an external religious tradition to which the parameter in question is not central.

Sadhguru quite clearly fails to register the polemical misgivings and misrepresentations of Abrahamic religions in New Atheist literature or popular culture in general. Thus, one finds him uncritically adopting these tropes in his otherwise considered pronouncements. Whatever the cause for this blind spot – perhaps being 'foreign' traditions, he does not feel the need to be intellectually responsible about them – he is nevertheless unable to recognise these traditions as so many 'spiritualities'. Of course, he does acknowledge them as spiritualities in one sense, but at the same time he views them as too encumbered by the weight of dogma and doctrine to be able to offer unimpeded spiritual edification. By contrast, 'Indic' traditions are seen to be doctrinally 'thin', if not without doctrine altogether – and entirely supported by 'pure experience' alone. Thus, the assumption that Indic spiritual practices are essentially empirical and scientific in nature and that Abrahamic spiritual practices are only partially so, if at all, and are dogmatic and unthinking for the most part. If one's own belief is seen not as a belief but as simply common sense or the way things naturally are, it is so only because it is too close to view to be noticed, like a pair of saffron tinted spectacles giving the illusion that the world itself were saffron.

It will be illustrative to examine this rhetoric of spirituality-as-empiricism in the parallel case of modern Buddhism. The philosopher and scholar of Buddhism Evan Thompson terms this phenomenon 'Buddhist exceptionalism': 'the belief that Buddhism is superior to other religions in being inherently rational and empirical, or that Buddhism isn't really a religion but rather is a kind of "mind science," therapy, philosophy, or way of life based on meditation.'

Apart from the highly problematic assumptions about science that this type of Buddhist Modernists make, Thompson argues that:

From a philosophical perspective, the problem with Buddhist exceptionalism is that it presents Buddhist theories of the mind as if they're value-neutral descriptions, when they're based on value judgments about how to cultivate or shape the mind to realize the supreme Buddhist goal of nirvana. In philosophical terms, the theories are normative—they're based on ethical value judgments—and soteriological—they're concerned with salvation or liberation. Buddhist theories of the mind lose their point if they're extracted from the Buddhist normative and soteriological frameworks.

Now, it is from a similar empiricist conceit and from a Hindu exceptionalism (for want of a better prefix), that the classical Greco-Roman inspired theological and philosophical traditions of Islam, Christianity, and Judaism are summarily dismissed as irrelevant to any philosophy or psychology in the modern day. A distinguished psychology professor and acquaintance of mine who is known for his pioneering work in 'Indian psychology' once remarked in my presence that he does not understand all the fuss about debating 'the existence of God' or 'the problem of evil', saying that they are really not problems for us, but for 'them' – that is, for Abrahamic religions. Now, there may be a valid argument here about the limitations of contemporary philosophising about God in Abrahamic apologetics – but it is a criticism too casually made to mean all that. Sadhguru certainly dismisses Abrahamic intellectual traditions as unworthy of recognition. Let me remind you that his grasp of Abrahamic religions is restricted for the most part to that of Richard Dawkins. And there is something to be said about the rebranding of Hinduism or Buddhism as 'secular' ways of life as opposed to the 'religious' lifestyles of the Abrahamic faiths. Whereas, in fact, a traditional believer of the Abrahamic faiths and a traditional Hindu or Buddhist would have much more in common with each other than with a secular atheist. It is only when one uncritically surrenders to atheistic common-sense that it seems more natural to seek for a link, however tenuous, between Hinduism and the disenchanted world of atheism, as opposed to recognising that all traditional religions have shared an enchanted cosmos as their natural home.

Admittedly, Sadhguru's brand of a 'godless spirituality' also has its reciprocals in the New Atheist camp. Sam Harris, who appears to have taken up the mantle of a spiritual guru quite gracefully, in his book *Waking Up: A Guide to Spirituality Without Religion*, presents a case for cultivating a kind of Buddhist Vipassana Meditation – or rather a secular watered down version of it that is stripped of its religious trappings and simply rebranded as 'mindfulness'. Harris seems to have successfully experienced, and is subsequently teaching, this elusive practice of 'watching one's thoughts'. 'You are not your thoughts. You are the space in which your thoughts occur,' as another modern guru Eckhart Tolle writes in his *The Power of Now: A Guide to Spiritual Enlightenment*. This is indeed a deeper way of identifying oneself not with the fleeting contents of consciousness but with consciousness itself within which these states occur.

Harris, Sadhguru, Tolle, and indeed Osho, all offer you a way of 'being spiritual without being religious' – where spirituality is synonymous with mindfulness and apparently little more. This kind of spirituality that has no moorings in a broader intellectual or religious tradition may be good for individual satisfaction and self-gratification but is far from a practical social model, and more importantly, is dangerously devoid of ethics. The philosopher Slavoj Žižek observes that such 'modern mindfulness' is the most suitable spirituality under capitalism. Where a person engaged in fuelling an exploitative, demeaning, or simply mindless corporate system may take a few moments out in the 9-5 for 'mindful meditation', attain inner peace, and get back to oppression and exploitation.

What is also problematic here is the idea that the term 'spirituality' should be practically reduced to the practice of mindfulness/presence, and should have nothing to do with other religious practices of devotion to God or character cultivation through the performance of good works and service to others. However, the latter practices/actions are all equally important to the cultivation of not just an individual sense of inner peace, but a broader state of being at peace with others, the cosmos, and God, through fulfilling the rights of each. It is not enough to merely vacuously 'think' oneself at peace with no moral action whatsoever.

Now, to be fair, what these spiritual movements highlight is a part of traditional religion which many religious believers mired in mechanistic piety have lost sight of. Mindfulness is an essential practice in my view – although far from sufficient on its own. When divorced from the larger religious and ethical tradition within which such mindfulness practices were traditionally rooted, they can serve anarchic purposes and even serve the ego. Thus, to dispense with devotional/theistic spirituality, as Sadhguru seeks to do, is not only a hasty move, but a positively reckless one. The good news however, is that Sadhguru's spirituality isn't nearly as unhinged from its ethico-religious traditions as he would like to claim.

Sadhguru does appropriate tradition in his own way. But he isn't forthcoming about the fact that his own unique blend of a godless spirituality belies the historically predominant tendencies for the *bhakti* (devotional) path in India. It is true that the Sankhya and Mimamsa philosophical systems in orthodox Hinduism are indeed non-theistic, and that Shankara's Advaita too conceived of Absolute reality as *Nirguna Brahman* or The God-beyond-qualification. However, this is far from the full story. Theism has a long and distinguished pedigree in Hinduism. One need only think of the two most widely read epics, the *Mahabharata* and the *Ramayana*. The *Bhagavad Gita* in the *Mahabharata* introduces God through the *avatar* of Sri Krishna. In fact, both Krishna and Ram are regarded as avatars of Vishnu, and the cult of Vishnu (or Vaishnavism) itself is a pre-eminently bhaktic or devotional path. Indeed, the pure non-dualist Shankara himself is known to have composed devotional poems to a personal God. Shankara would also probably reprimand Sadhguru were he to learn of the latter's utter disregard for scriptural studies. In Shankara's epistemology, the Vedas are absolutely indispensable to knowledge of both *dharma* (religious obligations) and *brahman* (absolute reality). A purely autonomous quest unaided by scriptures or by a traditional teacher will not lead to much success in leading a virtuous life, let alone usher in the self-realisation of Brahman. The great sage of the nineteenth century Sri Ramakrishna Paramahamsa, warns that the *jnana* (intellectual) *yoga* path may be misappropriated and misapplied if it were to be embarked upon without the unfoldment of certain virtues within the aspirant. It is for this reason that he recommended *dharma* and *bhakti* (devotional) *yoga* for most spiritual aspirants. Practising 'right conduct of life' is likened by Sri Ramakrishna to 'using soap on a dirty cloth' and the act of 'meditation' to 'washing the cloth clean'. 'Both are essential', he says, 'and not until through these means the evils of ignorance and misconception are washed away can spiritual peace be attained.'

It is clear that Sadhguru-style modern appropriations of certain traditions and insouciant dismissals of others can only be sustained through a thoroughgoing a-historicism and an inability to read contextually. Echoing

Dawkins again, Sadhguru maintains that he need not read about other traditions in order to dismiss them. 'All I need is right here (gesturing to the brain) ... All I need is within me,' as he often says. In a clearly unflattering moment, he even extends his self-sufficiency to the point of saying 'I don't need to read other books'. Now, on one level this final remark speaks of a high spiritual station of self-sufficiency, which Sadhguru may genuinely experience. It is important to recognise that the spiritual skill in question, call it mindfulness/presence, is, like any skill, a product of regular training. However, one must bear in mind that to be accomplished in one skill does not necessarily make the person a master of all skills in life. Even a skill as fundamental as mindfulness/presence, while certainly giving you a lot, nevertheless leaves you lacking in mastery over so many other facets of life. For instance, it teaches you nothing of history, or even about public reason or ethics – which need to be socially navigated and learnt through instruction, social engagement, and cumulatively over time.

My criticism towards Sadhguru is not therefore to question the value of his genuine insights, but to take the guru to task for not being intellectually humble enough to recognise his own limitations. I will be the first to admit that I have much to learn from him in certain matters, but will he admit that he too has a thing or two to learn about philosophy, history, and other traditions? Will he have the decency to admit that spiritual insight isn't the monopoly of select traditions to the exclusion of all other religious traditions of the world? Finally, can Sadhguru indeed give up the conceit of a tradition-less and apolitical spirituality?

TEN TOP POLITICAL FIBS

Politicians say the darndest things. Perhaps sometimes it's unfair to fixate on whether it was right or proper for certain things to be said, especially when an individual is caught off guard. Remember when US President Barack Obama called the rapper Kanye West a 'jackass' for interrupting Taylor Swift's acceptance speech at the MTV Video Music Awards in 2009? That was when Obama thought the interview was off-the-record – yet he stands by this quote even today. George W Bush was also widely pilloried for his 'Yo, Blair!' greeting to UK Prime Minister Tony Blair at a G8 meeting in 2006, again when he probably assumed this was off the record – Bush's defenders insist it was the slightly less undignified-sounding 'Yeah, Blair.'

Such quotes can become positive spin during a period of popularity (as with Obama) or as negative publicity to underscore a leader's unpopularity (as with Bush). But in the grander scheme of things, they can be considered benign. The stakes get raised when the things politicians say carry grave consequences in relation to ethics, governance, and lives and livelihoods. Consider the palimpsest of untruths, denials and obfuscations by outgoing British prime minister Boris Johnson over a succession of scandals during his brief and controversial tenure. Did he and his staffers knowingly break lockdown rules by partying while the rest of the country was traumatised by the ravages of the Covid-19 pandemic? Was he already aware of the allegations of sexual conduct before appointing Chris Pincher as his Deputy Chief Whip? The lies over Partygate might have caused distress to the many people who lost loved ones to the pandemic, but it was the Pincher debacle that was the clincher in Boris's political downfall.

Boris Johnson is not the first politician to have lied – colossally and brazenly, too – and neither will he be the last. As the veteran American journalist Jeff Greenfield once said, 'well, politics is war, and in war, truth is the first casualty.'

This issue of *Critical Muslim* focuses on ignorance, which makes a consideration of such manipulations of truth and lies especially apposite. What is the line that separates truth from untruth and the stupid from the sublime? What is the boundary between ignorance and enlightenment? We present a list of verbatim quotes from politicians that we can pore and argue over as though they were lines of poetry or verses of scripture. In no particular order, here are some of the quotes from the more recent past that have caught our imagination.

1. Donald Rumsfeld, 2002

Reports that say that something hasn't happened are always interesting to me, because as we know, there are known knowns; there are things we know we know. We also know there are known unknowns; that is to say we know there are some things we do not know. But there are also unknown unknowns—the ones we don't know we don't know. And if one looks throughout the history of our country and other free countries, it is the latter category that tends to be the difficult ones.

The late Donald Rumsfeld was Secretary of Defense during George W Bush's administration, from 2001 to 2006, and was one of the architects of the US-led invasion of Afghanistan in 2001 and Iraq in 2003. It was found later that the pretext for the US-led invasion of Iraq – the allegation that Iraqi dictator Saddam Hussein was still actively stockpiling weapons of mass destruction – was unsubstantiated. It is within this context that Rumsfeld's 'there are known knowns' quip gained legendary status.

Taken on its own, this quote is uncontroversial. It's a basic analytical framework, based on much research at the Pentagon – the Johari window – which was already used in NASA and other project management circles. But it is Rumsfeld's use of it in a 2002 press briefing to justify yet another imperialist military project by the US government that has earned its enduring position as a classic example of Orwellian obfuscation.

2. George W Bush, 2007

'This government does not torture people. We stick to US law and our international obligations.'

Speaking of the consequences of lying, this late 2007 quote by Bush when he was nearing the end of his second term is particularly chilling. Bush uttered these words *after* the *New York Times* reported in 2005 that the US Justice Department secretly authorised harsh interrogation techniques for terror suspects. Even after President Obama admitted that the CIA tortured terror suspects, Bush's vice-president, Dick Cheney, continued to deny that waterboarding qualified as torture. In fact, Cheney maintained that he would 'do it all over again' if he had to because it was effective. There is lying, as exemplified by Bush, and then there is the manipulation of concepts and definitions to avoid being called a liar, as exemplified by Cheney. In the case of Obama, there's making excuses even after telling the supposed truth about torture:

A lot of those folks were working hard under enormous pressure and are real patriots....It is important, when we look back, to recall how afraid people were after the twin towers fell, and the Pentagon had been hit, and the plane in Pennsylvania had fallen and people did not know whether more attacks were imminent.

3. Bill Clinton, 1998

'I did not have sexual relations with that woman, Miss Lewinsky.'

There is a fine line between telling an outright lie and manipulating concepts and definitions, albeit beyond recognition. President Clinton's infamous denial about his relationship with former White House intern Monica Lewinsky was, of course, a lie. But the phrasing of it suggests cognitive contortions that might have made it somewhat more palatable for his own personal conscience. Perchance he didn't regard the definition of 'sexual relations' as extending to fellatio?

4. Mahmoud Ahmadinejad, 2007

'In Iran, we don't have homosexuals like in your country. In Iran, we do not have this phenomenon. I don't know who has told you we have that.'

Western liberals collectively gasped in outrage and disbelief when Iranian president Mahmoud Ahmadinejad uttered these words to an audience at Columbia University in 2007. It appeared to be a lie of staggering dimensions. Of *course* there are 'homosexuals' in Iran, as in every nation on earth, and they have been there since the beginning of time. Beyond Ahmadinejad's strange phrasing, however, his claim was actually not that different from the rejoinders made by many postcolonial activists from the Global South. 'Homosexuality', after all, is a relatively modern term of Eurocentric coinage, and global lesbian, gay, bisexual, trans, queer and intersex (LGBTQI) activism has long been accused - even by queer and trans people in the majority world - as overwhelmingly white, European and middle-class. In Iran, in particular, there were historical and culturally specific terms to identify a young man - *amrad* - who was the object of an older man's romantic and erotic desires. But neither party would have expressed their desires or identities as 'homosexual'. This qualifier is definitely not a defense of Ahmadinejad - the difference between him and postcolonial queer activists from the Global South, including queer Muslims, is that he was justifying existing homophobia in Iran, including the sentencing of minors to death. Progressive activists in Muslim contexts are challenging Eurocentric and secularist definitions of gender and sexuality to *expand* basic rights and freedoms. It is not just the context of a claim that is important, but its intent.

5. Donald Trump, 2010

'With the coldest winter ever recorded, with snow setting record levels up and down the coast, the Nobel committee should take the Nobel Prize back from Al Gore.'

It is not at all difficult to find a quote from former US President Donald Trump in which he denies the reality of human-made climate change. But this one is special not only because of how it is structured but because he said it in 2010, six years before he was elected president. In it, Trump invokes verifiable, empirical evidence – the 'coldest winter ever recorded' – to challenge a prevailing misunderstanding of climate change as being solely about linear global 'warming'. This quote also conveniently confuses short-term weather patterns with long-term climate change. Trump then uses this commonsense, plain-talking 'wisdom' to turn the scientific evidence for climate change into ideological warfare. It's ignorant but, as continues to be clear amongst vast swathes of the US population, it's effective.

6. Jair Bolsonaro, 2022

'The indications are that something wicked was done to them.'

As with the other items on our list, the ramblings of climate deniers such as Trump would not be so frightening if they did not also have chilling reverberations in so many other parts of the world. Brazilian President Jair Bolsonaro, for example, continues to borrow shamelessly from Trump's playbook, not only to justify the continuing destruction of the Amazon, but to wash his hands off the persecution and murder of environmental and human rights activists. As with Trump's quote on climate change, this one is not an outright lie. Of course 'something wicked' (some outlets translate Bolsonaro's phrase as 'some malice') was done to the environmental journalist Dom Phillips and the indigenous rights advocate Bruno Pereira. They were murdered, simply for defending people and planet. But notice the passive construction of Bolsonaro's statement - it allows the actual perpetrator(s) of that 'something wicked' to disappear, and for the authorities to shift the blame back onto Phillips and Pereira for venturing into 'dangerous' and 'complicated' territory.

7. Mike Pence, 2016

'…the truth is that this culture of political correctness has tied the hands of law enforcement around this country.'

These were Mike Pence's words when he was Governor of Indiana, before he became vice-president in the Donald's presidency. Famous for his anti-abortion and anti-Black Lives Matter stances, this quote could have been referring to either of these issues. But Pence was speaking to the late Rush Limbaugh, the conservative radio show host, about that *other* so-called threat so beloved of the Far Right - Islam. Not treating every Muslim as a potential terrorist was, in Pence's estimation, a manifestation of 'political correctness' gone mad.

8. Sarah Palin, 2008

'I can see Russia from my house.'

Sometimes a statement's idiocy is so clear that it needs no explanation, right? Wrong! Former governor of Alaska and Republican vice-presidential nominee Sarah Palin has often been lampooned for this surreal quote. In reality, this was a line from Tina Fey's impersonation of Palin during a *Saturday Night Live* sketch. The actual quote from Palin is, in fact, a fact. Her exact words were: 'They're our next-door neighbors, and you can actually see Russia from land here in Alaska, from an island in Alaska.' But this is far from a defence of Palin. Using the empirically verifiable visibility of Russian soil from Alaska in response to a question about one's expertise in international relations is, frankly, a little bit eccentric. It brings to mind a quote by Christina Ricci's character Lucia from *The Opposite of Sex*: 'I went to a bar mitzvah once. That doesn't make me Jewish.'

9. The pundits vs the voters, 1960

This list might appear heavily skewed against individual politicians, and mostly American ones at that. There's a reason for this – political spin seems to have been honed into an art-form and a mainstay in American cultural life. Often, the joke is not just on the politicians – it's also on the voters and the so-called pundits. Here's an excerpt from a piece in *Time* magazine, in relation to the 1960 US presidential election:

In Washington, so the story goes, Republican top strategists huddled, and all were glum indeed – except one. 'I'm sure we'll win, there's no doubt about that,' he enthused. Everyone wanted to know the reason for his confidence. Answer: 'I have a deep and abiding faith in the fundamental bigotry of the American people.'

The Republican presidential candidate that year was the infamous Richard Nixon, the incumbent vice-president at the time. Nixon was defeated by John F Kennedy, but later won the presidency in 1969.

10. FBI Director Ben Harp from Point Break, 1991

We're giving the last word on ignorance and enlightenment to yet another American, albeit a fictional one. Fans will be able to quote this infamous exchange by heart:

Ben Harp (played by John C McGinley): You know nothing. In fact, you know less than nothing. If you knew that you knew nothing, then that would be something, but you don't. You're a real blue flame special, aren't you, son? Young, dumb and full of cum, I know. What I don't know is how you got assigned out here in Los Angeles with us. Guess we must just have ourselves an asshole shortage, huh?

Johnny Utah (played by Keanu Reeves): [quietly] Not so far.

CITATIONS

Introduction: Ignorant Things by Ziauddin Sardar

Lucy Ellmann's collection of essays, *Things Are Against Us*, is published by Galley Begger Press, Norwich, 2021. Irfan Ahmad Khan's massive tome, *Reflections on the Qur'an: Al-Fatihah and al-Baqarah*, is published by Islamic Foundation, Leicester, 2005.

Robert Proctor quote is from *Agnotology: The Making and Unmaking of Ignorance*, edited by Robert Proctor and Londa Schiebinger, Standford University Press, 2008, p2; Daniel DeNicola quote is from his book, *Understanding Ignorance*, The MIT Press, 2017, p154; Linda Martin Alcoff quote is from her article, 'Epistemologies of Ignorance: Three Types' in *Race and Epistemologies of Ignorance*, edited by Shannon Sullivan and Nancy Tuana, State University of New Yor Press, 2007, p48, 47; Andrew Bennett quotes are from *Ignorance: Literature and Agnoiology*, Manchester University Press, 2009, p15, 16. James Baldwin's work is discussed in 'Managing Ignorance', the chapter by Elizabeth V Spelman, in *Race and Epistemologies of Ignorance*.

Franz Rosenthall's *Knowledge Triumphant: The Concept of Knowledge in Medieval Islam* is published by E J Brill, Leiden, 1970; and Al-Ghazzali's *The Book of Knowledge* (a segment of *Ihya Ulum al-Din*), translated by Nabih Amin Faris, is published by Asharaf, Lahore, 1962; and James Baldwinis *The Fire Next Time* is published by St Martin's Press, New York, 1993.

The *Routledge International Handbook of Ignorance Studies*, edited by Matthias Gross and Linsey McGoey, 2015, is essential reading to understand the dimensions of ignorance that need our attention. There is excellent discussion of agnotology and its limitation, as well as 'undone science' and the emerging discipline of political sociology of science in the special issue, entitled 'Ignorance: Widening the Focus' and edited by Laura Barbier,

Soraya Boudia, Maël Goumri and Justyna Moizard-Lanvin, of *Revue D'Anthroplogie des Connaissances* 15 (4) 2021.

On postnormal perspective on ignorance and zombie disciplines, see Ziauddin Sardar, 'The Smog of Ignorance: Knowledge and Wisdom in Postnormal Times' *Futures* 120 102554 2020; and Liam Mayo and Shamim Miah, 'Zombie Disciplines, Anticipatory Imagination and Mutually Assured Diversity in Postnormal Times' in *Emerging Epistemologies: The Changing Fabric of Knowledge in Postnormal Times*, edited by Ziauddin Sardar, International Institute of Islamic Thought, London, 2022.

See also: Nicholas Cusanus, *Learned Ignorance*, translated by Germain Heron, Yale University Press, 1954; Daniel R DeNicola, *Understanding Ignorance*, MIT Press, 2017; Matthias Gross, *Ignorance and Surprise: Science, Society and Ecological Design*, MIT Press, 2010; Nicholas Rescher, *Ignorance*, University of Pittsburgh Press, 2009; Stuart Firestein, *Ignorance: How it Drives Science*, Oxford University Press, 2012; and Renata Salecl, *A Passion for Ignorance: How We Choose Not to Know and Why*, Princeton University Press, 2020.

'The Undeclared War', written by Peter Kosminsky, was broadcast on Channel 4 during June and July 2022.

Know That You Do Not Know by Bruce B Lawrence

The majority of citations are taken from Franz Rosenthal, *Knowledge Triumphant: The Concept of Knowledge in Medieval Islam* (E.J.Brill, Leiden, 1970, reprinted in 2007, with introduction by Dimitri Gutas). Included was a reference to Rosenthal's major translation of Ibn Khaldun, *The Muqaddimah: An Introduction to History* 1970, reprinted in abridged version by NJ Dawood and with new introduction by Bruce B. Lawrence, Princeton University Press, Princeton, NJ, 2005.

Also cited is Khairudin Aljunied, *Hamka and Islam: Cosmopolitan Reform in the Malay World* (Cornell University Press, Ithaca, 2018), and further discussion of *barzakh* logic can be found in Bruce B. Lawrence, *Islamicate Cosmopolitan Spirit* (Wiley Blackwell Manifestos, Hoboken, NJ: 2021).

The Enlightenment of Ignorance by Linsey McGoey

The James Madison quote can be found in Ilya Somin, 2013, *Democracy and Political Ignorance*, Stanford, CA: Stanford University Press.

Tony Blair's interference in the BAE investigation was reported by David Leigh and Rob Evans in 'How Blair put pressure on Goldsmith to end BAE investigation', *The Guardian*, 21 December 2007, available at https://www.theguardian.com/world/2007/dec/21/bae.tonyblair

On 'white ignorance', see these works by Charles Mills: 1997's *The Racial Contract,* Ithaca: Cornell University Press, and his 2007 contribution, 'White Ignorance', in *Race and Epistemologies of Ignorance*, edited by Shannon Sullivan and Nancy Tuana, New York: SUNY Press.

The sexual harassment and discrimination in Ford plants was reported by Susan Chira and Catrin Einhorn in 'How tough is it to change a culture of harassment? Ask women at Ford', *New York Times*, 20 December 2017, paywalled at https://www.nytimes.com/interactive/2017/12/19/us/ford-chicago-sexual-harassment.html.

The elite denialism of Liz Truss and Rishi Sunak was analysed by Nesrine Malik in 'What the absurd class cosplay of Rishi Sunak and Liz Truss tells us about Britain', *The Guardian*, 25 July 2022, available at https://www.theguardian.com/commentisfree/2022/jul/25/rishi-sunak-liz-truss-britain-class-tory-leadership

My own works that I drew upon for this article include the 2012 article, 'The Logic of Strategic Ignorance', in the *British Journal of Sociology* 63 (3), pp. 533-576, the 2019 book, *The Unknowers*, London: Zed Books, and the 2020 article, 'Micro-ignorance and macro-ignorance in the social sciences', in *Social Research*, 87 (1), pp. 197-217.

There is also the *Routledge International Handbook of Ignorance Studies*, which I co-edited with Matthias Gross, now in its second edition.

Ilm, ignorance and Climate Change by Shanon Shah

Ebrahim Moosa's essay, 'The Debts and Burdens of Critical Islam', appears in *Progressive Muslims: On Gender, Justice and Pluralism*, edited by Omid Safi (Oxford: Oneworld, 2003), pp. 111–127.

For my overview of existing paradigms of *ilm* in Islam, I consulted Mudassir Ahmad Dass, 2015, 'Epistemological Paradigms of Islamic Knowledge: An Overview', *Hazara Islamicus* 4(2), pp. 37–50; Ali Raza Mir, 1999, 'Multiplicity of Knowledge Forms: Lessons from Islamic Epistemology', *American Journal of Islamic Social Sciences* 16(3), pp. 99–106; Ziauddin Sardar, 2006, 'Rescuing Islam's Universities', pp. 43-54, in *How Do You Know? Reading Ziauddin Sardar on Islam, Science and Cultural Relations*, edited by Ehsan Masood (London: Pluto Press); and Kate Zebiri, 1997, *Muslims and Christians Face to Face* (Oxford: Oneworld).

Ziauddin Sardar's typology of ignorance can be found in his 2020 article, 'The Smog of Ignorance: Knowledge and Wisdom in Postnormal Times', *Futures* 120, pp. 1–12. For more on ignorance, see Daniel DeNicola, 2017, *Understanding Ignorance: The Surprising Impact of What We Don't Know* (Cambridge, Massachusetts: MIT Press). On denial, there is the classic text by Stanley Cohen, *States of Denial: Knowing about Atrocities and Suffering* (2013, Malden: Polity Press). It's also worth exploring the classic, first published in 1990, by Ziauddin Sardar and Merryl Wyn Davies, *Distorted Imagination: Lessons from the Rushdie Affair* (London: Grey Seal Books). For insights on Black feminist thought, I consulted Patricia Hill Collins, 2009, *Black Feminist Thought* (New York: Routledge Classics). On critical pedagogy, a foundational text is Paulo Freire's *Pedagogy of the Oppressed* (1996, London: Penguin).

A good, albeit slightly dated, introduction to the complexity of the climate crisis and how to communicate it, is George Marshall's *Don't Even Think*

About It: Why Our Brains Are Wired to Ignore Climate Change (2015, London: Bloomsbury).

For my discussion on Egypt, I relied mostly on a 2013 peer-reviewed article by Andreas Malm and Shora Esmailian, 'Ways In and Out of Vulnerability to Climate Change: Abandoning the Mubarak Project in the Northern Nile Delta, Egypt', *Antipode* 45(2), pp. 474–492.

On Malaysia's environmental track record, I used the following: Mustafa K. Anuar, 2012, 'Reporting the Environment: Human Rights, Development and Journalism in Malaysia', *Asia Pacific Media Educator* 22(2), pp. 253–62; Jarni Blakkarly, 2015, 'Malaysia's Indigenous Hit Hard by Deforestation', *Al Jazeera*, available at https://www.aljazeera.com/features/2015/4/2/malaysias-indigenous-hit-hard-by-deforestation; Faris Hadad-Zervos, 2017, 'Malaysia Launches the World's First Green Islamic Bond', *World Bank Blog*, available at https://blogs.worldbank.org/eastasiapacific/malaysia-launches-the-worlds-first-green-islamic-bond; Fraziali Ismail, 2020, 'Climate Action in the Malaysian Financial Sector', *Bank for International Settlements*, available at https://www.bis.org/review/r201020f.htm; Ethel Khoo, 2019, 'Malaysia Continues Efforts to Reduce Carbon Footprint', *The Edge Markets*, available at http://www.theedgemarkets.com/article/malaysia-continues-efforts-reduce-carbon-footprint; Mourad Mekhail, 2018, 'Green Sukuk Will Be Vital to Achieving COP21 Goals', *World Finance*, available at https://www.worldfinance.com/banking/green-sukuk-will-be-vital-to-achieving-cop21-goals. There is also the excellent resource on independent environmental journalism, Macaranga: https://www.macaranga.org/.

On the different dimensions of Saudi Arabia that I covered – human rights, religious politics, climate change policies and international negotiations, fossil fuels and geopolitics, and some perspectives of the Kingdom's defenders and critics – I consulted: Saleem H. Ali, 2017, 'Reconciling Islamic Ethics, Fossil Fuel Dependence, and Climate Change in the Middle East', *Review of Middle East Studies* 50(2), pp. 172–78; Madawi Al-Rasheed, 2005, 'Saudi Religious Transnationalism in London', pp. 149–68 in *Transnational Connections and the Arab Gulf*, a volume which she also edited

(Oxon: Routledge); Madawi Al-Rasheed, 2007, *Contesting the Saudi State: Islamic Voices from a New Generation* (Cambridge: Cambridge University Press); Madawi Al-Rasheed, 2020, 'A Vision for a Democratic Saudi Arabia Free from the House of Saud', *Middle East Eye*, available at http://www.middleeasteye.net/opinion/future-saudi-arabia-should-not-be-left-hands-house-saud; Climate Action Network International, 2009, 'Saudi Arabia Awarded Fossil of the Day for Oct. 5th', available at http://www.climatenetwork.org/blog/saudi-arabia-awarded-fossil-day-oct-5th); Climate Action Network International, 2015, 'Saudi Arabia Wins Big in Fossil Awards', *CAN News*, available at https://eco.climatenetwork.org/cop21-eco6-5/; Daniel Nilsson DeHanas, 2013, 'Of Hajj and Home: Roots Visits to Mecca and Bangladesh in Everyday Belonging', *Ethnicities* 13(4), pp. 457–474; Binoy Kampmark, 2015, 'Fossils of the Day: Saudi Arabia, Australia and "The Spoilers" at the COP21 Paris Climate Summit', *Global Research*, available at https://www.globalresearch.ca/fossils-of-the-day-saudi-arabia-australia-and-the-spoilers-at-the-cop21-paris-climate-summit/5494935; Jim Krane, 2019, *Energy Kingdoms: Oil and Political Survival in the Persian Gulf* (New York: Columbia University Press); Bruce Lawrence, 2017, *The Koran in English* (Princeton: Princeton University Press); Pew Research Center, 2013, 'Saudi Arabia's Image Falters among Middle East Neighbors', *Pew Research Center's Global Attitudes Project*, available at https://www.pewresearch.org/global/2013/10/17/saudi-arabias-image-falters-among-middle-east-neighbors/; Brenda Shaffer, 2011, *Energy Politics* (Philadelphia: University of Pennsylvania); Norman K. Swazo, 2010, 'Negotiating the Climate Change Regime: The Case of Saudi Arabia', *Middle East Review of International Affairs* 14(4), pp. 11–25.
The hadith on seeking a fatwa of the heart can be found in full at https://hadithanswers.com/seek-a-ruling-from-your-heart/. The Wisdom in Nature (WiN) website is https://www.wisdominnature.org/.

Ziauddin Sardar has also written extensively on *ilm* and Islamic environmental ethics. See his edited works: *The Touch of Midas: Science, Values and Environment in Islam and the West* (Manchester University Press, 1984); *An Early Crescent: The Future of Knowledge and the Environment in Islam* (Mansell, London, 1989); and his essay, 'Guardians of the Planet: Muslims and the Environment', pp. 91–107 in the 2006 volume, *How Do*

You Know? Reading Ziauddin Sardar on Islam, Science and Cultural Relations, edited by Ehsan Masood (London: Pluto Press).

Muslim Traditions of Learned Ignorance
by William Franke

This essay is based on my books *On What Cannot Be Said: Apophatic Discourses in Philosophy, Religion, Literature, and the Arts* (Notre Dame, Indiana: University of Notre Dame Press, 2007), and *Dante's Paradiso and the Theological Origins of Modern Thought: Toward a Speculative Philosophy of Self-Reflection* (New York: Routledge, 2021). My book, *On the Universality of What is Not: The Apophatic Turn in Critical Thinking* (Notre Dame: University of Notre Dame Press, 2020), focusses on the issue of universality and takes up a cross-cultural approach especially in chapter 7: 'Liberal Arts Education Worldwide Unlimited Inc.: The Unspeakable Basis of Comparative Humanities.' I develop this argument further in *Apophatic Paths from Europe to China: Regions Without Borders* (Albany: State University of New York Press, 2018).

On Ibn Arabi, see Salman H. Bashier, *Ibn al-'Arabi's Barzakh: The Concept of the Limit and the Relationship Between God and the World* (Albany: SUNY Press, 2004); Henry Corbin, *L'imagination créatrice dans le soufisme d'Ibn 'Arabi* (Paris: Flammarion, 1958).

The parallel between Ibn Arabi and Dante is suggested by R.W.J. Austin in his introduction to *The Bezels of Wisdom*, p. 7. See further Peter Dronke, *Dante's Second Love: The Originality and Contexts of the Convivio* (London: Routledge, 1996). The *Treatise on Unity* is actually ascribed by other scholars to a disciple of Ibn al-'Arabi named al-Balyani (d. 1288). See Alexander D. Knysh, *Ibn Arabi in the Later Islamic Tradition: The Making of a Polemical Image in Medieval Islam* (Albany: SUNY Press, 1999), p. 316. On the tension between pantheism and monotheism in Ibn al-'Arabi, see Saiyid Abdul Qadir Husaini, *The Pantheistic Monism of Ibn al-'Arabi* (Lahore: Sh Muhammad Ashraf, 1970).

On Rumi, see Annemarie Schimmel, *I Am Wind,You are Fire:The Life and Work of Rumi* (Boston: Schambhalo [Random House], 1992), which provides an authoritative introduction;

J. Christoph Bürgel, "Speech is a ship and meaning the sea': some formal aspects in the ghzal poetry of Rumi,' *Poetry and Mysticism in Islam: The Heritage of Rumi*, edited by Amin Banani, Richard Hovannisian and Georges Sabagh (Cambridge: Cambridge University Press, 1994); 'The Wisdom of Exaltation in the Word of Noah' in *The Bezels of Wisdom*, trans. by R.W.J. Austin (New York: Paulist Press, 1980), pp. 73-77; and 'The Exaltation of Light in the Word of Joseph,' in *The Bezels of Wisdom*, trans. R.W. J. Austin, 124-27.

'The Reed Flute's Song' is translated by Fatemeh Keshavarz online at: The Reed Flute's Song | The On Being Project; 'This is how it always is' is from *The Essential Rumi*, trans. Coleman Barks (San Francisco: Harper, 1995). The Ibn Tufayl quote is from *Hayy Ibn Yaqzan*, edited by Lenn Evan Goodman (Los Angelos: gee tee bee, 1991), pp. 149; and the A J Arberry quote is from *Mystical Poems of Rumi*, First Selection, Poems I-200, trans. by A. J. Arberry (Boulder, Colorado: Westview Press, 1979), pp. 5-6.

See also: Toshihiko Izutsu, *Sufism and Taoism: A Comparative Study of Key Philosophical Concepts* (Berkeley: University of California Press, 1984), Majid Fakhry, *A History of Islamic Philosophy*, 2nd ed. (New York: Columbia University Press, 1983); Robert Javelet, 'Saint Bonaventure et Richard de Saint-Victor,' in *Bonaventuriana. Miscellanea in onore di Guy Bougerol*, eds. Chavero Blanco and Francisco de Asís (Rome: Antonianum, 1988), pt. 1, 63-96; Dale M. Coulter, 'Contemplation as 'Speculation': A Comparison of Boethius, Hugh of St Victor and Richard of St Victor,' in *From Knowledge to Beatitude: St Victor, Twelfth-Century Scholars and Beyond. Essays in Honour of Grover A. Zimm Jr.*, edited by. E. Ann Matter and Lesley Smith (Notre Dame: Notre Dame University Press 2013); Gregory B. Stone, *Dante's Pluralism and the Islamic Philosophy of Religion* (New York: Palgrave Macmillan, 2006); Alexander Treiger, *Inspired Knowledge in Islamic Thought: Al-Ghazālī's Theory of Mystical Cognition and its Avicennian Foundation* (New York: Routledge, 2012); William C. Chittick, *Science of the Cosmos, Science of the Soul: The Pertinence of Islamic Cosmology in the Modern World* (Oxford: Oneworld, 2007); and Seyyed Hossein Nasr, *Knowledge and the Sacred* (Albany: SUNY Press, 1989).

Sensing Jinn by Alireza Doostdar

I am grateful to Nick Lorenz for research assistance and comments on this essay.

For more on the prayer-writer I mention in this essay, see my other writings, including *The Iranian Metaphysicals: Explorations in Science, Islam, and the Uncanny*, 2018, Princeton, NJ: Princeton University Press.

On the 'ethnographic X-files', see Andrew Apter, 2017, 'Ethnographic X-Files and Holbraad's double-bind: Reflections on an ontological turn of events', *Hau: Journal of Ethnographic Theory* 7(1), pp. 287–302.

A recent overview of jinn in the Islamic tradition is Amira El-Zein, 2017, *Islam, Arabs, and the Intelligent World of the Jinn*. Syracuse, NY: Syracuse University Press.

On confusions and ambiguities in occult ontology (and anthropological understandings of it), see my book, and also David Graeber, 2015, 'Radical alterity is just another way of saying "reality": A reply to Eduardo Viveiros de Castro', *Hau: Journal of Ethnographic Theory* 5(2): pp. 1–41.

On the 'uncanny', see Sigmund Freud, 1955, 'The "Uncanny"', in *The Standard Edition of the Complete Psychological Works of Sigmund Freud,* edited and translated by James Strachey, pp. 217-52, Vol. 17, London: The Hogarth Press and the Institute of Psycho-analysis. On the 'numinous', see Rudolf Otto, 1958, *The Idea of the Holy*, translated by John W. Harvey, Oxford: Oxford University Press. And on the 'difficulty of reality', see Cora Diamond, 2003. 'The difficulty of reality and the difficulty of philosophy', *Partial Answers: Journal of Literature and the History of Ideas* 1(2), pp. 1–26.

On the befuddling ambiguity of jinn, see also Vincent Crapanzano, 1980, *Tuhami: Portrait of a Moroccan*, Chicago: University of Chicago Press; Stefania Pandolfo, 2018, *Knot of the Soul: Madness, Psychoanalysis, Islam*, Chicago: University of Chicago Press; and Christian Suhr, 2019, *Descending with Angels: Islamic Exorcism and Psychiatry*, Manchester: Manchester University Press.

Other works cited were Eugene Thacker, 2011, *In the Dust of this Planet: Horror of Philosophy*, Winchester, UK: Zero Books and Muhammad ibn Mahmud Tusi, 1966, *'Ajayeb al-Makhluqat*, edited by Manuchehr Sotudeh, Tehran: Nashr-e Ketab.

Who is Afraid of CRT? by Gordon Blaine Steffey

References in order of appearance: Nikole Hannah-Jones, 'The Idea of America,' *The New York Times Magazine*, 18 August 2019, 16-26; Jeffery Hayward, 'Knocking Down Barriers,' Perspectives Blog, Fannie Mae, 8 June 2022, https://www.fanniemae.com/research-and-insights/perspectives/knocking-down-barriers; Jamilah Pitts, 'Teaching as Activism, Teaching as Care,' Learning for Justice, May 15, 2020, https://www.learningforjustice.org/magazine/teaching-as-activism-teaching-as-care
Parents Defending Education, https://defendinged.org/about/

Gary Peller, 'I've Been a Critical Race Theorist for 30 Years. Our Opponents Are Just Proving Our Point For Us,' The Big Idea: Opinion, Politico, 30 June 2021, https://www.politico.com/news/magazine/2021/06/30/critical-race-theory-lightning-rod-opinion-497046; Richard Rothstein, 'A 'Forgotten History' Of How The U.S. Government Segregated America,' Fresh Air, NPR, 3 May 2017, https://www.npr.org/2017/05/03/526655831/a-forgotten-history-of-how-the-u-s-government-segregated-america; Richard Rothstein, *The Color of Law: A Forgotten History of How Our Government Segregated America* (New York: Liveright Publishing, 2017); and Gregory Smithsimon, 'How to See Race,'

Aeon, 26 March 2018, https://aeon.co/essays/race-is-not-real-what-you-see-is-a-power-relationship-made-flesh

The President's Advisory 1776 Commission, *The 1776 Report*, January 2021, can be downloaded from: https://trumpwhitehouse.archives.gov/wp-content/uploads/2021/01/The-Presidents-Advisory-1776-Commission-Final-Report.pdf; The White House, *Executive Order on Combating Race and Sex Stereotyping*, 22 September 2020, https://trumpwhitehouse.archives.gov/presidential-actions/executive-order-combating-race-sex-stereotyping/ and the White House, *Executive Order On Advancing Racial Equity and Support for Underserved Communities Through the Federal Government*, 20 January 2021, https://www.whitehouse.gov/briefing-room/presidential-actions/2021/01/20/executive-order-advancing-racial-equity-and-support-for-underserved-communities-through-the-federal-government/

The Parameters of Science by Colin Tudge

Reference, in order of appearance in the text, are as follows.
Colin Tudge, In Mendel's Footnotes: Genes and Genetics from the 19th century to the 22nd. Jonathan Cape, 2000. Jane Goodall has written at least half a dozen books about her beloved chimpanzees. The first was *In the Shadow of Man*. HarperCollins, 1971. See in particular Frans de Waal's *The Age if Empathy* (New York, Harmony Books, 2009. All of de Waal's books are worth reading.

In *Behavioural Enrichment at the Zoo* (Van Nostrand Reinhold Company New York) Hal Markowitz describes attempt to make the lives of captive animals more interesting by setting them tasks – and speaks for example of ostriches showing (and presumably feeling) pride when they succeed. Yet ostriches are not normally noted for their sensibility!

Richard Dawkins, *The Selfish Gene*. 1976. Oxford University Press, Oxford; Denis Noble, *The Music of Life*. Oxford University Press, USA, 2006. Nessa Carey, *The Epigenetics Revolution: How Modern Biology Is Rewriting Our Understanding of Genetics, Disease, and Inheritance*. Columbia

University Press. 2017; Tim Spector, *The Diet Myth*. Orion Books, London, 2015.

Karl Popper, 'The Problem of Induction' in *A Pocket Popper,* edited by David Miller, Fontana Press, 1987; Thomas Kuhn, *The Structure of Scientific Revolutions*. University of Chicago Press 1962; Isaac Newton is quoted in Peter Medawar, *The Limits of Science*, Oxford, 1985. Albert Einstein, *Living Philosophies*, Ams Press Inc. New York. 1931; and Fyodor Dostoyevsky, *Crime and Punishment*, 1866.

I discuss the order of magnitude of different species in my book, *The Variety of Life*, Oxford University Press, Oxford, 2000. See also: Colin Tudge, *The Secret Life of Trees*. Allen Lane, London, 2005, and *The Great Re-Think*, Par Publishing, Tuscany, 2021.

The Can of Ham by James Brooks

Video of dead Arkansas cattle can be viewed at https://bit.ly/3c8KEbq. Estimate of 2021 East African child mortality from 'East Africa: Quarter of a million children may have died of starvation this year', Save The Children statement, 9 December 2021, available at https://bit.ly/3uCSoZv.

Quote on belief in capitalist ideology from Mark Fisher 'Capitalist Realism: Is There No Alternative?' (Zero Books, 2009). Statistics on microwork from Phil Jones 'Work Without The Worker: Labour In The Age Of Platform Capitalism' (Verso, 2021). Screen time statistic from 'UK screen use in 2022: a need for guidance', University of Leeds policy brief, 10 March 2022, published as a PDF at https://bit.ly/3ADR8Jm. António Guterres quotes from speech published on United Nations website as 'Secretary-General warns of climate emergency, calling Intergovernmental Panel's report "a file of shame", while saying leaders "are lying", fuelling flames' at https://bit.ly/3NVsdDZ. Video of Prince William's Platinum Jubilee speech available at https://bit.ly/3c3cl5c. The screenplay for 'Last King Of Scotland' (2006) was written by Peter Brock and Jeremy Morgan, after the novel by Giles Foden.

A Key to All Conspiracies by Robin Yassin-Kassab

The parent of the child who stopped praying is quoted in 'It's scary work but I'm determined. We will make Pakistan polio-free.' *The Guardian* 4 May 2022.

A reflexologist's surgery is not at all an unlikely place to hear a conspiracy theory. A long-running podcast called 'Conspirituality' (see www.conspirituality.net) investigates the prevalence of right-wing stories in the New Age and 'wellness' movements.
'53% of Republicans view Trump as true US president.' Reuters. 24th May 2021.

For my commentary on the white supremacists marching at Charlottesville, see 'A Syrianized World'. www.qunfuz.com. 12th August 2017.

For the proportions of Republican voters or French citizens who believe the Great Replacement theory, see 'A deadly ideology: how the 'great replacement theory' went mainstream'. *The Guardian*. 8 June 2022. For the connections between Serb fascism and the Great Replacement theory, see The Balkans in Rightwing Mythology, by Adnan Delalic and Patricia Zhubi. www.antidotezine.com. 10 June 2019.

Anti-Semitism has famously been called 'the socialism of fools'. In the same vein, Leila al-Shami has written of 'the anti-imperialism of idiots'. www.leilashami.wordpress.com 14th April 2018. Similarly, see my 'Is Corbynism anti-Semitic?' www.qunfuz.com 4th August 2018 and 'Genocide Denial' www.qunfuz.com 22nd April 2018.

Kémi Séba is quoted in 'The Congolese student fighting with pro-Russia separatists in Ukraine.' *The Guardian*. 8 June 2022

Bloodlands: Europe between Hitler and Stalin by Timothy Snyder (Basic Books, New York, 2010) recounts the organized slaughter of 14 million people between 1933 and 1945 in the lands between Germany and Russia. In a different way, Vasily Grossman's great novel 'Life and Fate' also explores the practical similarities between fascism and Communism.

The God that Failed (Hamish Hamilton, London, 1050) is collection of essays by disillusioned Communists, including Arthur Koestler and Richard Wright.

See also: Peter Pomerantsev, *Nothing is True and Everything is Possible: Adventures in Modern Russia* (Faber and Faber, London, 2017) and *This is Not Propaganda: Adventures in the War Against Reality* (Faber and Faber, London, 2020).

A History of Forgetting and Ignorance by Alev Adil

For Cicero's notion of memory palace, see Marcus Tullius Cicero, *The Loeb De Oratore Cicero, De Oratore, De Fato, Paradoxa Stoicorum, Partitiones Oratoriae*. Translation by E. W. Sutton and H. Rackham. Loeb Classical Library. Heinemann, London, 1942.

On the history of Cypriot Muslims, see: Peter Mackridge, *Greek-Speaking Muslims of North-East Turkey: Prolegomena to a study of the Ophitic sub-dialect of Pontic*, Byzantine and Modern Greek Studies, Oxford University Press, 1987; Bruce Clark, *Twice a Stranger: The Mass Expulsions that Forged Modern Greece and Turkey*. Harvard University Press, Cambridge, Massachusetts, 2006; Ahmet An, *Kıbrıs'ın yetiştirdiği değerler: 1900-1920/ Values Cultivated in Cyprus:1900-1922* Akçağ, Girne 2005; and Anne Cavendish, editor, *Cyprus 1878 The Journal of Sir Garnet Wolseley* Bank of Cyprus Cultural Foundation, Nicosia, Cyprus, 1995.

On the history of Imam Mustafa Nuri, see Ahmad Sami, 1914-1918 Cihan Savaşı Kıbrıs İngiliz Esir Kamplarında Ölen Ve Mağusa'da Toprağa Verilen Şehitlerimiz/ Our Martyrs who Died in the British Prisoner of War Camps in Cyprus and were Buried in Famagusta During the 1914-1918 World War' *Kıbrıs Araştırmaları ve İncelemeleri Dergisi/ Cyprus Research and Analysis*

Journal , 1 (1) , 95-103 2017; Fadıl Niyazi Korkut, *Hatıralar/Memories* Edited by Harid Fedai and Mustafa H. Al- tan, with a foreword by Harid Fedai, Eastern Mediterranean University Press, Famagusta 2000; *Özcan Karaca, Dövüştüler, Götürüldüler, Dönemediler: Esarette Kalanlari/ Those Who Fought, Who Were Taken, Who Failed to Return: Those Who Remained in Captivity* MSN Yayincilik, Istanbul, 2017; and Ulvi Keser, Ulvi (2007) 'Genç Türkiye Devleti'nin Cumhuriyet Kazanımları ve Bunların Kıbrıs Türk Toplumuna Yansımaları/ The Achievements of the Republic of Young Turks and Their Effects on the Turkish Cypriot Community' Çağdaş Türkiye Tarihi Araştırmaları Dergisi/ *Journal of Modern Turkish History Studies*, 6 (14), 41-83 2007 (https://dergipark.org.tr/en/pub/cttad); Metin Akar and Oguz Karakartal, '1. Dünya Savaşı'nda Kıbrıs'taki Esir Türk Askerleri ve Gazi Magosa Çanakkale Şehitliği/ First World War Prisoners of War in Cyprus and the Gallipoli Martyrs of Famagusta'. *TÜDEV Denge*. 2020/9: 19-28; Ali Nesim, 'Mustafa Nuri Efendi', *Yeni Kıbrıs*, Nisan/April 1990, Lefkoşa; and *Newsweek*, Volume 84, 1974 p.46.

See also: Metin Heper and Bilge Criss, Bilge (2009), *Historical Dictionary of Turkey*, Scarecrow Press, Lanham, Maryland, 2009; Tolgay Ahmet, 'Şiirin hüzünlü kadını Feride Hikmet'/Feride Hikmet, poetry's melancholic woman' *Kibris Gazetesi 24.03.2019*. Lefkoşa, 2019.

I used the resources of PRIO (Peace Research Institute Oslo). http://www.prio-cyprus-displacement.net/default_print.asp?id=339 accessed 2.06.2022; and interviewed historian Tuncer Bağışkan on 31.05.2022.

Reforming Conversations by Samia Rahman

To find out more about the history of the Muslim Institute visit https://www.musliminstitute.org/about/overview and see C Scott Jordan, *A Very British Muslim Activist: The life of Ghayasuddin Siddiqui*, (Beacon Books, Manchester, 2019). See also: Stuart Schaar, 'Last Word on Fatima Mernissi' in *Critical Muslim 18: Cities*, Hurst, London, 2016.

On Sadhguru's Spirituality by Saad Mohammed Ismail

For Sadhguru's more overt politics, see Rajshree Chandra, 'An (Un) Enlightened Sadhguru in King Modi's Court.' (*TheWire*, 01/01/20) https://thewire.in/politics/an-unenlightened-sadhguru-in-king-modis-court. A journalistic survey of the Western reception of Hinduism can be glimpsed in Philip Goldberg's *American Veda: From Emerson and the Beatles to Yoga and Meditation How Indian Spirituality Changed the West* (New York: Harmony Books, 2010). For the quote from Alasdair MacIntyre see his *Whose Justice? Which Rationality* (University of Notre Dame Press,1988), p. 367.

For an account of the modern invention of the category of 'religion', see Talal Asad, *Genealogies of Religion: Discipline and Reasons of Power in Christianity and Islam* (Baltimore and London: Johns Hopkins University Press, 1993). See also Sophia Rose Arjana, *Buying Buddha, Selling Rumi: Orientalism and the Mystical Marketplace* (Oneworld Academic, 2020); and the first half of Irfan Ahmad's *Religion as Critique: Islamic Critical Thinking from Mecca to the Marketplace* (Oxford University Press India, 2018). On the modern (re)definition of Hinduism, see Richard King, *Orientalism and the Modern Myth of 'Hinduism'* (Numen 46, no. 2, 1999), 146-185.

For a rigorous critique of the 'scientific' posturing of spirituality in the case of modern Buddhism and of 'Buddhist exceptionalism' in general, see Evan Thompson, *Why I Am Not a Buddhist* (Yale University Press, 2020). For Slavoj Žižek's remarks on modern mindfulness, see his talk *The Buddhist Ethic and the Spirit of Global Capitalism*. 2012 https://www.youtube.com/watch?v=qkTUQYxEUjs .

For the rich diversity and development of Hindu traditions see Gavin Flood, *An Introduction to Hinduism* (Cambridge University Press: 1996). Swami Prabhavananda's *The Spiritual Heritage of India* (London: George Allen & Unwin, 1962) is a very readable and compelling introduction to the spiritual dimensions of Hinduism in general and the Advaita (non-dualist) school in particular. A robust philosophical introduction to the Advaita tradition is Anantanand Rambachan's *The Advaita Worldview: God, World, and Humanity* (State University of New York, 2006). For Shankara's views on the indispensability of scripture, see Rambachan's *Accomplishing the Accomplished: The Vedas as a Source of Valid Knowledge in Śaṅkara* (University of Hawai'i Press; 1991).

For further reflections on politics of spirituality, see my essay *Why Shashi Tharoor Is a Hindu: The Politics of Inclusivism,* published on *Project Noon.* https://projectnoon.in/2022/01/21/why-shashi-tharoor-is-a-hindu-the-politics-of-inclusivism/

The List: Top Ten Political Fibs

The Donald Rumsfeld quote is legendary and his Wikipedia page has all the original citations you need. The George W Bush quote can be found at http://news.bbc.co.uk/1/hi/world/americas/7030383.stm and Barack Obama's 'admission' of the CIA's use of torture is at https://www.theguardian.com/world/2014/aug/01/obama-cia-torture-some-folks-brennan-spying. Bill Clinton's infamous quote can be found everywhere. Mahmoud Ahmadinejad's quote is also pretty ubiquitous, but here's an easy source: https://abcnews.go.com/US/story?id=3642673. The quote on climate change by Donald Trump can be found at https://www.thedailybeast.com/cheats/2010/02/15/trump-denies-global-warming. The version of Jair Bolsonaro's quote we have used was reported in *The Guardian*: https://www.theguardian.com/world/2022/jun/13/dom-phillips-bruno-pereira-bodies-found-brazil. The transcript of Rush Limbaugh's interview with Mike Pence can be found at https://www.rushlimbaugh.com/daily/2016/09/19/governor_mike_pence_calls_the_show/. The full context of Sarah Palin's quote and its appropriation by *Saturday Night Live* is at https://www.csmonitor.com/USA/Politics/2011/0603/Political-misquotes-The-10-most-famous-things-never-actually-said/I-can-see-Russia-from-my-house%21-Sarah-Palin. The *Time* magazine quote on the 1960 US presidential election is taken from the second edition of *The Penguin Dictionary of Modern Humorous Quotations*, 2002, p. 237.

Finally, to revise your knowledge of the best quotes from *Point Break* (yes, we're assuming you've watched the film or at least know of it), go to https://en.wikiquote.org/wiki/Point_Break.

CONTRIBUTORS

Alev Adil is a poet and performance artist and former Head of the Department of Communication and Creative Arts at the University of Greenwich ● **James Brooks** is a science and technology journalist ●**Alireza Doostdar** is Associate Professor of Islamic Studies and the Anthropology of Religion at the University of Chicago Divinity School ● **William Franke**, Professor of Comparative Literature at Vanderbilt University, Nashville, Tennessee, is the author of *On The Universality of What is Not: The Apophatic Turn in Critical Thinking* (2020), and *Dante's Paradiso and the Theological Origins of Modern Thought: Toward a Speculative Philosophy of Self-Reflection* (2021) ● **Giles Goddard** is Vicar of St John's Church, Waterloo, London ● **Miran Gulzar** is a poet based in Kashmir, India ● **Saad Mohammed Ismail** is a medical doctor based in Karnataka, India, and the founder and editor of www.projectnoon.in, an initiative that critically explores Hindu-Muslim dialogue ● **C Scott Jordan** is Executive Assistant Director of the Centre for Postnormal Policy and Futures Studies and Deputy Editor of *Critical Muslim* ● **Robin-Yassin Kassab** is a writer based in Scotland ● **Hussein Kesvani** is a journalist and author of *Follow Me, Akhi: The Online World of British Muslims* ● **Bruce B Lawrence** is Marcus Family Humanities Professor of Religion at Duke University ● **Linsey McGoey** is Professor of Sociology and Director of the Centre for Economic Sociology and Innovation at the University of Essex ● **Steve Noyes** is a British (and Canadian) Muslim writer and poet living in Sheffield ● **Samia Rahman** is the Director of the Muslim Institute ● **Gordon Blaine Steffey** teaches Comparative Philosophy and holds the Barbara Boyle Lemon '57 and William J. Lemon Chair of Religion and Philosophy at Randolph College in Lynchburg, Virginia ● **Shanon Shah** is Deputy Editor of *Critical Muslim* and Director of Faith for the Climate ● **Colin Tudge** is a science writer and author of many books, including *The Great Re-Think* (Pari 2021*),* now available online.